CW00921801

Michael Fer

Late 90's. purchased.

MY SENTIMENTS EXACTLY

KEITH BAXTER

MY SENTIMENTS EXACTLY

OBERON BOOKS
LONDON

First published in 1998 by Oberon Books (incorporating Absolute Classics)
521 Caledonian Rd, London N7 9RH

Tel: 0171 607 3637 / Fax: 0171 607 3629

e-mail: oberon.books@btinternet.com

Copyright © Keith Baxter 1998

Copyright photographs © the copyright holders

Credits: Versions of 'Goodbye Morgan', 'Graceful Living', 'Catching the Sudden Subway' and 'Private Lives and Laughter' were published in, respectively *The Times*, *The Sunday Telegraph*, *The London Magazine*, *The Daily Telegraph*.

Keith Baxter is hereby identified as the author of this book in accordance with Section 77 of the Copyright, Designs and Patents Act, 1988. The author has asserted his moral rights. All rights reserved.

This book is sold subject to the condition that it shall not by way of trade or otherwise be circulated without the publisher's prior consent in any form of binding or cover other than that in which it is published and without a similar condition including this condition being imposed on a subsequent purchaser. No part of this book may be broadcast or reproduced in printed form, photocopied, on microfiche, or in any electronic format (including the Internet) without the prior consent of the publishers and/or the copyright holders.

British Library Cataloguing-in-Publication Data
A catalogue record for this book is available from the British Library.

ISBN 1 84002 053 9

Cover photograph: Keith Baxter with Charley by Derek Aslett

Back cover photograph: Nigel Norrington

Cover design and typography: Richard Doust

Printed in Great Britain by MPG Books Ltd, Bodmin.

For my sister and brother, and Tisha;
for Richie, Tommy and Brian;
and not forgetting Charley

PHOTOGRAPHS

The publishers are grateful to the following for their kind assistance in providing photographs and for permission to reproduce them in this book: Bert Andrews, Anthony Buckley, Gianni Bozzachi, Nobby Clark, Michael Codron, Margaret Fehl, The Harvard Theatre Collection, The Houghton Library Harvard University, The Illustrated London News Picture Library, Douglas Jeffery, Jas. D. O'Callaghan, The Raymond Mander & Joe Mitchenson Theatre Collection, Richard Mangan, Stephen Morton-Pritchard, Nigel Norrington, Robert C. Ragsdale, John Swannell, Angela Thorne, Nicholas Tikhomiroff, John Timbers.

Copyright remains with the copyright holders. Every effort has been made to trace copyright holders, though in a few instances it has not been possible. The publishers undertake to pay the normal reproduction fee on identification.

CONTENTS

ACKNOWLEDGEMENTS

My first article ever to be published – *Goodbye Morgan* – was written for Mary Ann Madden in New York nineteen years ago while I was idling around waiting for my Green Card. She told me not to waste my days. "Write! Write anything! But write!" The story of my last visit to E. M. Forster was written to keep the peace. It was written as a private present to her, but she insisted I should offer it for publication and it was accepted by *The Times*. Other pieces followed, and three produced plays, but none of them would have seen the light of day if it had not been for Mary Ann. My gratitude to her is immense and my affection for her, as she knows very well, has no limit.

George Trescher gives me a home in New York and is imperturbable when I arrive without warning and interrupt his schedule, whether it is arranging Arnold Schwarzenegger's wedding, or some grand bash at the Metropolitan Museum. He is kind but not sentimental, and wise without being smug. He is also very funny and endlessly supportive. Some of these pieces were written at his dining room table and now is the proper time to thank him.

My publisher James Hogan is a ruthless editor and a relentless grammarian, but he has patience and tact and his authors are extremely well fed and cared for. I am grateful to him for the painstaking way he has handled this book.

PREFACE

On that November day in Newport, not so long ago it seems, though it is more than sixty years, at eleven o'clock in the morning the world stopped for two minutes. Cars pulled over to the kerb, men in the streets took off their hats, women shushed their babies.

I was on a tram with my mother going to the Top Shops. She checked her wristwatch. Already the tram was braking as she shut her eyes saying she was going to say her prayers. Everyone else did the same.

"What are you praying for?" I asked.

It was Armistice Day and they were praying for the dead.

"I don't know any dead."

My mother told me to be quiet, close my eyes "and just be grateful."

At that moment the tram stopped.

The future, as I grow older, seems ever more tantalising and exciting, but the past is a pleasant place for a sojourn, filled with experiences which shaped my life and friends who moulded my ideas. Although most of these friends are dead, in my mind they still live, fully-fleshed and as vital as they were in the days these chapters recall.

These chapters were written at different times, and occasionally they overlap a little. Yet for me they amount to a unified whole in one special sense – they are all linked by the echo of laughter. For if there is one special quality that my friends pictured here shared, it was a keen sense of the absurd and an irrepressible sense of humour.

The advice my mother gave me that November morning – to be grateful – is the impulse behind this book. I have never ceased to be grateful that life has led me along such happy paths, even if now and then I have tripped and twisted my ankle.

The pieces have been assembled from scratched notes made at the time, from letters which friends were kind enough to return, and from rudimentary diaries. Versions of some of the pieces have been published before as articles and I am grateful to *The Times*, the *Daily Telegraph*, the *Sunday Telegraph* and the *London Magazine* for their permission to include them in this memoir.

Keith Baxter
Bosham, 1998

One

WHEN THE TRAM STOPS

"Why do you want to be different from the
beasts? Beasts are delightful. If they
had a sense of humour and the gambling
instinct they would be perfect."

James Bridie *Daphne Laureola*

A Lithuanian tightrope-walker once told me that the question he was most often asked was whether he was terrified of heights. "Would I fly from trapeze in such case?" he said. The question actors are most often asked is how on earth they remember their lines. An aerialist afflicted with vertigo would no more set foot upon the highwire than an actor born without the knack of memory would set foot upon a stage. An incident in the life of the actor, Mícheál Mac Liammóir illustrates how one's memory busies itself with more than the elementary drudgery of learning words. He was filming in Morocco when he received a message in his hotel room that his partner had been killed in a car crash. He ran to the lobby. A mirror loomed before him on the staircase. He caught sight of his ashen face and the tears which streaked it, and as he dashed downstairs he registered the message being transmitted to his memory.

"This is how you looked when your heart was breaking; this is how you felt. Remember it."

All actors are both blessed and cursed with an inbuilt computer which chugs away from childhood memorising, observing, cataloguing and storing sensations and experiences to be reclaimed later and put to use. It would be nice to be able to shut down the computer but only mortality can operate the switch. Not every moment in our lives is recorded, but the particular and the peculiar are never forgotten. Some of my early recollections are so graphic in my mind that, looking back over forty working years, it is all too plain to see how, even as a child, an actor's memory was already at work.

One of my earliest memories is of a man my father called Monkey, who lived near our house in Llwynderi Road in Newport, then a very busy South Wales port. Monkey was barrel-chested, nut-brown with a wrinkled, friendly smile and a generous spirit. I knew nothing about nicknames, but I had been to Bristol Zoo. My child-size hand was not much smaller than his own, and when he reached down to slip me a coin on my birthday the thin wrists protruding from his shirt-cuffs were matted with curly brown hair. This did not surprise me, for I believed that under Monkey's blue suit was hidden a wiry furry body and a long curled tail.

A few doors away a teenage girl sometimes stood silent in her front garden. I never heard her speak. I was told she was "strange". Her parents had refused to send her to an Institution. On Sunday mornings after church we might meet Margaret with her parents. The men raised their hats, and when my mother said, "Hello Margaret" Margaret's mother plucked her daughter's sleeve. But Margaret stared ahead, focused on some conundrum of her own and was silent. One autumn afternoon, when I'd just spent my sweet ration on a small bag of toffees and was sitting on the garden wall, I saw Margaret watching me as I munched. I held out the bag. Carefully she selected a toffee. Delicately she unwrapped it, but instead of eating it she threw it in the hedge. While I scrabbled for it among the dead leaves Margaret laughed. It was a terrible laugh. That eldritch screech was the only sound I ever heard her make.

At the top of the street was an empty house which no one talked about except in whispers. One afternoon the woman who lived there went to the cinema while her little son came out for a walk with us. My brother wanted him to stay for tea but my mother had run out of cake and sent the boy home where his father was waiting for him with a hammer. When the boy's mother returned from seeing *Mrs Miniver* she found the house empty, the kitchen running with blood, the pipes wrenched from the wall, the car gone. Her husband had driven to Usk where he threw his dead son into the river and then killed himself.

Sometimes we went cycling and picked wild flowers for my mother; primroses from the woods at Henllys, and bunches of bluebells which festooned the handlebars but were almost dead before they could be put into a jug. One day I came home from school and presented my mother with scented tea-roses and delphiniums. She was distracted, preparing supper, and showed no surprise at the extravagant bouquet, but when I came to the table I was satisfied to see the flowers prominently displayed. Next day I returned to get some more. I was cutting roses with my penknife when a woman cried out "What are you doing, what are you doing!" I remember how nicely dressed she was, holding an odd assortment of books, a vase and a cushion. She had not been there yesterday. She was standing in the bombed-out ruins of her house and I was stealing flowers which bloomed so abundantly in the debris of her garden. "What are you doing?" she cried. "This is my house. This is my garden. Those are my flowers!" Tears streamed down her face as she pointed to the desolation. "Mine!"

In the back garden of our house my father built an air-raid shelter. A paraffin stove sputtered and traced strange patterns on the corrugated roof. Too young to realise the implications of War, I listened to the hiss of shrapnel falling through the laurel hedge. The guns boomed and the little shelter shook. Sometimes when my mother was asleep we crept to the door to watch the searchlights sweeping wildly across the sky until one of them caught an enemy plane in its powerful beam. As the doomed pilot tried desperately to manoeuvre his escape all the other searchlights immediately focused on the trapped aircraft until the ack-ack guns found their range and blew the invader into smithereens. Shameful to think now of the elation it gave us.

In the daytime the shelter was a children's playhouse, better than a wigwam, more secret than a tree. For the bribe of a square of chocolate one little boy was eager to pull down his pants and show off his bottom; after a while he didn't bother to wait for the chocolate. He is now a Judge in Chancery.

My mother's great-grandfather Thomas Henry Howell was born in 1822 in a village in Dyfed. He took off to be a sailor and at the age of twenty-five, with Welsh as his first language, he was a married man and master of the brigantine Active, sailing out of Liverpool. Three years later his career was in ruins. He was arrested and brought ashore at Newport where his cargo of gunpowder was impounded. It was 1839, the Chartist insurrections were at their height, and Captain Howell was accused of bringing explosives to the rioters. He was given a whacking fine and a criminal record. Reduced to penury, he took enthusiastically to religion and with equal zeal to drink until, sodden with alcohol, he abandoned his wife and children to the solace of the Welsh Ebenezer Chapel and went back to sea. He died in Cuba of yellow fever in 1858 and was buried at Matanzas.

Fortunately his teenage son was a boy of enterprise. The Victorian commercial age was cranking into top gear. Newport was a boom town and young Thomas Henry Howell's fortunes boomed with it. His father's regrettable history was quickly forgotten – in a boom town many prosperous citizens had noisy skeletons in their own cupboards. In due course Alderman Howell's career reached its dizzying apotheosis: he became Mayor of Newport and secretary of the Ebenezer Chapel. He died in 1926, a rich man, owner of an Iron and Steel business and left ten children. Welsh had been slowly eliminated in his household. After all, when Lloyd George came to discuss Welsh separatism at a Newport rally, it was a fellow Alderman who had shrieked, "We want none of your damn Welsh nonsense here!" and Alderman Howell would equally have recognised that it was the English side of his bread that would get the butter.

Alderman Howell's eldest son, the third Thomas Henry Howell, married an Englishwoman and gave his four children sturdily anglo-saxon names: Kenneth, Eric, Marian (my mother), and Marjorie. A framed photograph of Uncle Kenneth stood on my mother's dressing-table. He was dressed in a frock, looking rather prissy, but since he was playing Portia in the school play perhaps it was just the expression he'd adopted for the role. Uncle Kenneth died before I was born. As a child I sensed that there was some riddle about him for his name was rarely mentioned save in melancholy tones. It was not until I was in my late teens that the mystery was unravelled when I was swotting for the summer exams and overheard my mother talking to Olwen Williams in the garden below my bedroom window. On leaving school after the First War Uncle Kenneth had entered the family firm. It made no difference that he was not interested in Iron and Steel, and would never be capable of running the business when his father died: as the eldest son it was his only, inevitable destiny. However, he was homosexual.

Presumably, anxious to escape the claustrophobia of living in a small town, Uncle Kenneth persuaded his father to open a London office and settled in a flat in Gower Street where his instincts could find free licence. He soon took up with the Serbian violinist Bratza and he was even acquainted with the great soprano Tetrazzini. He ate in raffish bistros in Soho and collected some good furniture. He was not however happy. He made occasional trips back to Newport which he found impossibly bourgeois, reducing his gentle mother to tears by the coldness of his manner, criticising her table, her clothes and her style. In the summer of 1931 Uncle Kenneth went on holiday for several months to Gibraltar. He also spent some time in Tangier and fell ill. Perhaps it was the heat, or the scented atmosphere, or the unabashed sensuality of the Souk which made him feverous. He returned to his hotel in Gibraltar. His room was on an upper floor overlooking a terrace. In the early hours of the 8th September he threw himself from his window and his body was found lying on the terrace. The inquest found that he was dead before he fell. He had slashed himself in a frenzy with his razor.

I was born in Newport where my father was Piermaster at the docks. In 1944 he was promoted. This meant a move to Barry in Glamorgan and a change of school. Barry was a very different town from Newport, more robust, more fun and much more Welsh.

In Wales it has never been considered peculiar that a child should be fascinated by the arts. Schools all over Britain may have their Sports Day but nowhere else, except in Wales, do schools have an Arts Day as well. On 1st March at Eisteddfodau in schools all over Wales, the beefiest young rugby player and the jolliest hockey girl competed with their fellows in fierce appreciation of music and the spoken word. Outside school there were Choral Societies; in 1945 in Barry you could pick between three rival versions of *Elijah* at Christmas. And there were Amateur Dramatic Societies where the competition was deadly. At home my mother and father both played the piano and my sister was graced with a natural mezzo-soprano voice of great sweetness and purity. My brother and I sang in the church, and until my voice broke I belonged to The Romilly Boys' Choir whose founder was the father of the Welsh composer Grace Williams. Our repertoire of Welsh songs was augmented by Schubert and Brahms and we travelled by bus to sing in chapels in the valleys. Between the Wars the Romilly Boys had sung "all over America", but by the time I joined them the bus never got beyond Merthyr.

My mother would often use Welsh phrases. It was always "nos da" and never "goodnight" and we went to "gwely" not "bed". She was a woman of considerable spirit. Ill as a child with double pneumonia and whooping cough (a potentially lethal combination in those pre-antibiotic days) she had spent a year in bed, and until she was fourteen wore a calliper on her leg so that she would always walk with a limp. A doctor thought she should be sent to school in Sussex for a change of air. Clearly it did the trick for she was rarely ill again.

When I became an actor it was generally assumed that it was the Welsh in me that was expressing itself. Though it was indeed true that a childhood in Wales had bestowed on me a love for music and language, it was the wild temperament that I inherited from my father which drove me into the theatre and my father was an Englishman from Norfolk.

Stanley Baxter-Wright was the eldest of four children and grew up in a comfortable house in Norwich. In 1914 when War was declared he added two years to his age and ran away to join the Royal Navy. After the armistice he transferred to the merchant service, took his Master's ticket and sailed from Liverpool for South America on the El Paraguayo via South Wales. As chance would have it, one of the stewards on the El Paraguayo had been in the army with my uncle who had told him to telephone if ever the ship put into Newport. My grandmother duly invited the steward for lunch and he took Stanley with him. My mother was helping to prepare the meal. After a four-year engagement she married Stanley. Eventually, he came ashore for good and from then on we moved around South Wales until he became Dockmaster at Swansea where he died in 1960 and was buried at sea off the Mumbles.

My father was a man of violent emotion and in my early years I was very frightened of him. My sister was a girl of sunny temperament and my brother was a handsome boy of great character and charm. I was the youngest child and the only one my father ever attacked. There was nothing ritual about his violence. But there was something about me that clearly drove him into a rage and because I was a child I had no idea how to correct it. Perhaps it was something in his own nature that he recognised and feared. His name for me until the day I left for Korea was "woodenhead". His temper would explode and he would rush to attack me. The earliest memory I have of my sister is of her voice pleading with him, attempting to intercede, trying to stop his blows; and when my aunt Margaret, on a visit from Norwich, told him to watch his behaviour my father ordered her from the house.

Sometimes my father took to carrying me, yelling, upstairs into the bathroom and shoving me into a cupboard. Alone, as the tears subsided, afraid of the dark, I learned how to manipulate the cupboard door until the latch slipped and then emerge. I sat on the edge of the bath until I heard his footstep on the stairs. Then I would retreat into the cupboard till I was released. It was no use expecting my mother to intervene for she adored him, though she too was once the focus of a terrifying scene.

We had packed for a summer holiday in 1940. My brother and I were in the kitchen. We heard shouting. My father was trying to get out of the house and my mother, in tears, struggled with him as she pressed herself against the front door. His face contorted with fury, my father said he wanted to leave us. He would kill her, he said, repeating it again and again, grabbing at her, shouting at her as she implored him to stay. My brother and I cowered, watching from the kitchen. My sister, eleven-years-old but lion-hearted, pulled at him. Eventually he quietened down, went into the garden and sat on a kitchen chair for an hour until Mrs Jenkins from next door took him a cup of tea which he accepted wordlessly. Later we left for Ross-on-Wye for our holiday and no one ever referred to that dreadful afternoon again, though for many years I relived it in my nightmares. What was the reason for it all? I never knew. He must have been under constant stress. His job at the Docks was dangerous; he was on duty during the worst bombing and, after his death, when my brother and I were going through his desk, we found a letter from the military commander of the district praising my father's gallantry. A soldier on sentry duty had fallen into the dock and was drowning. Stanley plunged into the freezing water and held him until help came. He saved the boy's life but my father was in bed for six weeks with rheumatic fever.

I was seventeen when my father last struck me. We had returned from a holiday in Cornwall, an eight-hour journey on a heat wave day. The evening was airless, everyone was edgy. My brother and I were unpacking. He was at Birmingham University where his natural ability on the rugby field had earned him golden opinions, but it was at the expense of his studies and he had failed his exams. I had written a long letter of sympathy which I had never posted and had forgotten. My brother, unpacking, opening a drawer to put away socks, found the letter. I forbade him to open it. I knew the outpouring of love would embarrass us both. He claimed the letter was his; I said it was mine because I had not sent it. We struggled for possession. The idiotic squabble grew fiercer, our clothes were sticking to us and our voices grew louder. My father roared into the room. Ignoring my brother he seized me by the throat, landed a savage backhander across my face, so forceful that it knocked me against the bedroom wall. I thought if he ever touched me again I would take a knife to him.

For years I held a grudge against him: all gone now. Those experiences, good and bad, helped mould me into the man I have become and the rage I inherited from my father has served me well as an actor. Had he lived, I would gladly have made friends with him. But I wish he had not made me afraid of the dark.

Later, my father was angered again because I refused to become an officer when I did my National Service, for rank impressed him; but he was very quiet when I told him I had applied for a posting to Korea. When the Embarkation Order came I telephoned to say goodbye. My parents raced for a train to London. They found me clambering aboard the bus outside the transit quarters in Goodge Street. My kitbag was labelled "Korea", my rifle was slung over my shoulder. I was in battle-dress, my new sergeant's chevrons bright on my sleeve. I must have seemed like a twenty-year-old stranger to my father. His face was ashen as he grasped my hand. For the rest of his life he tried to demonstrate his affection, but ice had formed inside me. Two years later when the troopship bringing me home docked in Liverpool he was standing on the quayside, patiently waiting as the ship tied up. He wore a bowler hat. He looked diminished. He came aboard but I had no idea what to say.

Circumstances eventually imposed a measure of reconciliation upon us. It was in 1960 and I was in London rehearsing Prince Hal. My father suffered a massive heart attack and was bed-ridden. No one told him that he could not live long, nor would ever work again, but he must have known that he was very weak. I went home to Swansea, and one afternoon I was alone in the house with him, sitting by his bed. Conversation was stilted.

In despair I gave him my Shakespeare and asked him to hear my lines. With his spectacles half down his nose he corrected me on every small mistake, laughing happily at Falstaff's shenanigans. He was not a theatregoer and had never spoken a word of Shakespeare since he had been an eleven-year-old Tribune in *Julius Caesar* at school in Norwich. He read with intelligence and simplicity. "This is wonderful stuff!" But my own thoughts were in disarray. What demon had put it into my head that I should read these scenes with him? For though my father had no knowledge of the story, I knew we were moving inexorably towards the scene when Hal visits his father on his deathbed. I suggested we had done enough but dad held onto the script, reading steadily, still correcting my mistakes, until there was no going-back and we arrived at the lines where the King and his son bare their pain to each other and achieve reconciliation. My father closed the book and lay back against the pillows. He thanked me for letting him share something of my life.

A little before he died, my sister and I went to see him in hospital. By then he had been told he would not return to work. He fought to keep from breaking down. My sister sat beside him.

"Cry if you want to Daddy."

As she held him gently and he began to weep I prayed to be moved but I felt nothing. Nor did I feel anything when his coffin slipped into the sea.

After his death it came as some surprise to me when my aunt from Norwich described him as a teenager coming home in his first uniform: "He was in the garden, so handsome, thin and dark." It was not a description I could reconcile with my memory of him, for he had always seemed so heavily built, grim-faced and tired: "And there were girls in the lane outside mad to have a peep at him. You could see their heads appearing and disappearing as they jumped up and down behind the wall!" Then later amongst some old photographs I found a picture of him, sunburnt and lithe, about my own age, grinning happily as he danced a hornpipe on the deck of the El Paraguayo and I realised I had never known him.

Later, quite by chance, I did find out a little more about him. In Soho in the Fifties Kettner's Restaurant in Old Compton Street still had a certain réclame. There was a waiter, a large elderly man with dyed blond hair scraped across a broad forehead. His sly waspishness contrasted amusingly with his bulk and when he listed the specialities de la maison he made little attempt to disguise the Yorkshire accent which underlay his French. He had been at Kettner's for years and could be easily coaxed to tell outrageous stories of Soho life between the Wars. Shooting an arrow into the air I asked him if he had ever known my Uncle Kenneth. I gave what little information I knew, but it was the suicide in Gibraltar that brought his memory into focus. He remembered my uncle, and quite well, but not kindly; Uncle Kenneth had been stingy with his tips. Mostly he remembered the crowd that Uncle Kenneth brought in; the violinists and singers.

"He liked music and pretty things, pretty people, pretty boys. He had a sailor friend. Beautiful! Never forgot *him*! Sat there with their arms entwined."

I asked if he could remember the sailor's name but he could not. It was a quarter of a century ago after all, but then as we left he cried: "His name was Ollie! Like in Laurel and Hardy." Then I wondered if George's memory had led him into a muddle and, in fact, it was not Ollie Hardy but Stan Laurel that he was thinking. My father's name was Stanley. He too was a sailor and perhaps my father had sat in that same restaurant all those years before I was born with his arm round Uncle Kenneth, whose grave I sought one summer amongst the thistles of the English Cemetery in Gibraltar.

Barry Island was described by Ralph Higden (1300-64) as one of the wonders of Wales, but Barry town itself was only sixty-years-old when we moved there in 1944. Recognising the natural resources of the coastline, David Davies of Llanidlam had produced a plan for deep-water docks at Barry, served by a railhead (to spite the English Marquess of Bute's monopoly at Cardiff), and the first sod in the construction of Barry Docks was cut in 1884. The Welsh writer, Jan Morris, compares the boom that followed with the Klondike, although the town that bubbled up around the docks had considerably more decorum than the Yukon, no doubt on account of the multiplicity of chapels. Nevertheless it was a robust town, and often a windy one, sitting as it does on the curve where the Bristol Channel widens towards the sea. It was not popular with Aunt Marjorie. "Bugger breezy Barry" she said, clutching her hat when I met her off the train. But there were beaches and ancient fossils, and a dinosaur's footprints had been found under the cliffs. There were parks and wonderful views across open water to Somerset and Devon. All my memories of Barry turn sooner or later towards the sea. My father took his living from it, and from almost every hilly street in Barry you could turn and see the water, you could hear the roar of the surf against the pebbles, you could smell it in the wind, you could feel the salt-spray on your face and taste it on your lips. The bustling port is derelict now, a wasteland of twisted iron girders, rusting railway tracks, gaunt corroded derricks reflected in the vast empty waters where in 1944 immense freighters with foreign names jostled for a berth, whilst more were at anchor in the roads outside the harbour, waiting for the tide. On those hot summerdays of my childhood my mother had tea waiting for us on the beach after school and my father would come there straight from work. Every morning during the heatwave of 1949 I rose at six-thirty and cycled to Neville Thomas's house. Those were the years of Rodgers and Hammerstein; their songs were everywhere. Outside Neville's house I whistled *Oh What A Beautiful Morning* until his window opened, and the two of us cycled on to Mike Fowler's.

Many years later I did a play in New York which Richard Rodgers produced. Richard Rodgers was very kind to me, but I told him that whenever I hear his music it is not Broadway that I think of, nor the South Pacific, nor the cornfields of Oklahoma. I'm a boy on a bicycle racing for the sea on summer mornings in South Wales before school.

The Grammar School system was then at its best and offered a very fine state education. The year I arrived in Barry five boys had won State Scholarships to Oxford and we had a whole day's holiday. The

Headmaster was a pleasantly ineffectual character who seemed to come alive only once a week, on Wednesdays at Assembly, when the Hymn, the Reading and the Lord's Prayer were all in Welsh. If we were dreading the first class of a Wednesday morning it could easily be delayed by a half-hearted singing of the opening hymn. "Boys! Boys! Is that the best you can do? From the top again, thank you Mr Davies!" And once again Mr Davies at the piano would crash out the opening chords of 'Calon Lan'.

Since it was wartime many of the teaching staff had been called up and replacements were retrieved from retirement. Mr David Rees took mathematics. His hair was snow-white, his amiable face pink and unlined, his smile a veritable dazzle of porcelain: he could have stepped right out of a stained-glass window, Tablets in one hand and Mount Sinai in the distance. He put up with a lot of tomfoolery from us but one day we must have overtried his patience. Rising, he summoned the ringleader to the front of the class. "Potter!" We had never seen him angry; the room was stilled in surprise. "Potter," he shouted, "come here this instant! I've condoned and indulged your nonsense long enough!" Mr Rees opened his desk and took out a worn gym shoe. He seized the startled Potter by the scruff of his neck and pulled him over his knee. We all sat agape. But as old Dai Rees raised the shoe, he suddenly sneezed and the upper set of his false teeth flew out and bounced off Potter's head. Quick as a flash Potter caught them in his hand and reached backwards to place them on his bottom. The uproar in class was uncontrollable. There were cheers which Dai Rees acknowledged with a bow, pushing Potter off his lap, throwing the gym shoe back in the desk and refixing his grin. He never had any trouble with us again.

Corporal Punishment was permitted in those days but there was no real enthusiasm for it and no serious beaters on the staff. For the more serious offences a caning by the Headmaster was prescribed, but it was hardly painful. Mr E. T. Griffiths was of a benevolent disposition, and his aim was in any case so imprecise that he once knocked over a jamjar of daffodils while swiping at Viv Thomas. On the only occasion I visited him I must have entered too precipitately, for he hadn't time to close a box of chocolates he'd just opened.

"Who sent you?"

"Mr Evans, sir."

"What offence?"

"Forgot to learn 'Nant-y-Mynydd' sir."

"A very lovely poem indeed."

With a heavy sigh he swallowed the remains of his chocolate, gestured me to bend over a chair and tapped me six times with the cane.

"Push the chair back against the wall, there's a good boy."

I did so and my eye fell on the chocolates.

"Take one with you, the one with the mauve bits on the top, I don't care for them at all."

Percy Fisher who taught English also carried a length of old bamboo. Fisher had been gassed in the First World War which left him slightly bug-eyed and with a limp. He had a gentle, myopic wife to whom he was devoted, and a Bedlington terrier which accompanied him to rugby matches. The dog peed liberally against the goalposts and once against my leg as I sucked my Half-Time lemon. Percy Fisher was an extremely popular teacher, though he did nothing to court the boys' favour, and being so naturally laconic, he never appeared aware of their affection. Handing out examination papers he would growl "them as dies will be the lucky 'uns." When he entered a classroom full of new little boys on the first day of term he would draw a chalk line on the wooden floor. Pointing at it with his cane would murmur "execution dock". But I remember only one unruly boy being summoned forward and that was the luckless Potter. "I shall demonstrate the verb 'to strike'. Bend over Potter please. Present tense; the master 'strikes' (whack!) the boy. Past tense; (whack!) the master 'has struck' the boy. Future tense; the master 'will strike' (whack!) the boy!"

Three passions governed Percy Fisher's life: cricket, rugby, and the English language.

"We must be free or die, who speak the tongue that Shakespeare spake!"

I was never interested in cricket, and my rugby game was distinguished more by energy than skill; but in his English classes Fisher had in me a disciple whose devotion, even if it pleased him, was never acknowledged. His lessons were peppered with odd quotations. Stevenson, Wordsworth and Carroll were favourites. His influence spanned many years. I first encountered him when I was a small boy and he taught me until I was eighteen. I swallowed everything he told me and never suffered from dyspepsia. At eleven and a half I learned about parsing. Fisher drew a toy train on the blackboard.

"Here is the engine. Here is the tender carrying fuel. The noun is the engine but the fuel is the verb. All these other little additions – adjectives, adverbs, conjunctions – they're all pulled along by the noun and the verb.

'Man proposes; God disposes.' A perfectly good sentence."

At thirteen he moved us on to analysis with equal enthusiasm, and in the same year we tackled *As You Like It.*

"Today you will begin to study Shakespeare. You will do this because it is on 'the Syllabus'!"

He hissed the word venomously, giving every sibilant its due. Where Shakespeare was concerned he was an idolater, yet although he was highly qualified with a first-class Oxford degree, he still treated academic theorists with contempt. With a mirthless laugh he would ridicule the contradictory opinions from scholars in the margins. "The groves of Academe!" he would say derisively, his bug eyes popping and his face reddening, and he would chant as an incantation "Beware the man at Cambridge called Rylands and the worser at Oxford called Rowse! The Jabberwock and the Jubjub Bird, beware beware!"

An enlightened teacher in so many ways, Fisher was convinced that the forced drudgery of studying Shakespeare in a classroom for an examination, instead of seeing the plays live on stage, would set up barriers in the boys' appreciation that might never be overcome. When we were working on the first Ghost Scene in *Hamlet*, he hurled his book down onto his desk with a clatter.

"Imagine going to this play and not knowing how it will end!"

There was little opportunity to see any of the plays, for none of the great Shakespearean actors ever came to Wales except Wolfit. We were taken in procession down Jenner Road to see Olivier's film of *Henry V* at the Romilly Cinema. Fisher was equivocal on the subject of Olivier, whom he thought vulgar.

"John Gielgud is the greatest actor in the world!" he declared, defying contradiction. None of us had ever heard of Gielgud, nor had the least idea how to spell his name, and there was fat chance of his coming to Cardiff, but I took Percy Fisher at his word.

Another memorable teacher was D. J. P. Richards (known as 'Dippy' and not only on account of his initials) who had been a well-known athlete. His speciality was the Competition Walk, and an extraordinary walk it is. Most extraordinary and ungainly was Dippy Richards in his shorts and bony legs, lurching round the school field in the summer evenings. He taught Geography and Geology and sometimes took boys on field

23

trips down to the beach to search for fossils. Approached by a boy with a hopeful face and a piece of red stone: "paleolithic sir?", Dippy snorted and threw it to the ground, "housebrick!"

Gwyn Thomas taught Spanish. His heart was not really in teaching. An acclaimed writer, much admired in literary circles, his books were published by Victor Gollancz in wonderful bright yellow covers. Two of his plays, *The Keep* and *Jackie the Jumper* would be produced at the Royal Court Theatre and I would appear in another, *Sap*, at Cardiff in 1974. They earned him little money and he could support himself only by teaching. His writing was illumined by a savagely mordant sense of the ridiculous. He grew up, one of twelve, in an impoverished family in the Welsh valleys. He won a Scholarship to Oxford where he was unhappy, and studied in Madrid. There were whispers that he'd fought in the Spanish Civil War but these were untrue. In fact, he was the gentlest, most pacific of men, yet his nickname 'Killer' stuck.

Killer's face was dark and saturnine and, in repose, a cloak of ferocious misery seemed to engulf him, but his lessons were so lively that boys passing down the corridor looked enviously at each other as they heard the gales of laughter rattling the windows of his classroom. I have no idea how well he taught Spanish since I had opted for French and Welsh, but simply to be exposed to his obliquely anarchic character was wonderfully refreshing and, fortuitously, there were plenty of opportunities to savour his worth. A shortage of space in the school meant that senior boys could choose which rooms to infiltrate and sit at the back to write up their essays. Many of us sought out Killer's Spanish classes. He bored easily in front of a class, slumping into lethargy as the boys scribbled, but it was easy to divert him into some mad recollection or anecdote.

"Lope de Vega, sir. Would you say they named Las Vegas after him?"

"Don't be cretinous Potter! (pause) You might as well suggest Rhonda Fleming came from Merthyr."

"Rhondda Who sir?"

"Fleming! One of the most pulchritudinous creatures ever to grace the silver screen."

Before you knew it we were off on a description of the growth of the cinema in the Rhondda Valley when the children, too poor to buy chocolate, happily chewed half a swede, while a surly pianist eyed the enemy with loathing as they poured in screaming to grab their places. For a penny – Killer said – you faced the screen, seated on plush; for a half-penny you sat behind it on cement, with the captions backwards; for an extra half-penny you got a spray of Flit disinfectant.

The lights flickered out and the silent film began. The children who could read shouted out all the captions as they appeared, battling with the pianist.

"And what with the munching of the swedes and the shouting of the kids and the thumping of the pianist all I ever got was a chronic tintinnabulation in my head that didn't disappear until Neville Chamberlain went to Munich."

Once a month we had a free film-show in school. A projector was set up in the Assembly Hall after the last class of the day. One of the masters worked the projector. He was a noted groper. His notorious conduct among the pupils became a source of much gaiety. His most innocent request was treated with ribald laughter.

"Fetch me a book, boy. It's in the storeroom, I'll show you where."

"Don't go!" the class yelled, followed by whoops and raspberries. But one older boy was always perfectly happy to follow the master into the storeroom. Each of his re-entrances was greeted with catcalls and cheers which the red-faced boy accepted with a contented grin. My turn soon came. As I sat in the darkened Hall, engrossed in the Will Hay film, *Saunders of the River*, I suddenly felt a large hand creeping along my upper thigh towards the hem of my shorts. "Yeeeowww!!" I yelled. The groper staggered back against the projector, knocking the reel from its ratchet. When my brother and I got home, my mother had tea ready. "How was the film?" she asked, slicing the Spam. "Broke down, as per," grumbled my brother, but I never let on. Amazingly, for years no one ever let on. Even some of the teachers had once been boys in the groper's classes and must have known his secret, but they kept silent too. But one day his luck ran out, though he escaped prosecution. He simply left. Out of sympathy for his family he was allowed to creep into an ignominious oblivion.

How the seed had been planted in my mind, and where it had come from I could not guess, but I certainly wanted to be an actor for as long as I could remember. At the age of seven I had made a sort of theatre in a bird-cage. Later I made a better one, with scenery cut from the back of Kellogg's Cornflakes packets, complete with cardboard figures which my beloved sister drew and painted. Then at ten years old I read the Lesson in St. Mark's. The irascible tenor who sat behind me in the choir, viciously prodding me and his son for inattention during Matins, called at my home next evening. He wanted to tell my parents about my reading. Eavesdropping I caught the word "extraordinary", and when he had gone my parents gave me a funny look. Four years later my brother was cast in a Boy Scout show in which he sang, with three others, *We're Four Little Fellows Who're Doing Their Best To Fill Up A Gap In The Programme*. If I hadn't loved him so much I could have died of jealousy. Then he got a part in a play at the Youth Club, but had to withdraw to study for his examinations. Generously, he suggested me as his replacement. It was the first time I had stepped on a stage, and after that, I knew I would never do anything different with my life.

My parents had never taken much notice of my announced intention of going on the stage; believing, no doubt, that it was a passing caprice. When it became obvious that I was not going to be deterred, various heavyweights were martialled to dissuade me. Godfathers took me on one side, the Rector had his say. Seeing I was obdurate, words like 'precarious' began to enter the family conversation. At length, Teifion Phillips, who taught history and produced the school play, came to see my parents and said they should let me have my chance. He found out how one auditioned for the Royal Academy of Dramatic Art and in 1951 I travelled up to London.

It was not my first trip to London. Since my father worked for the Docks, and the Docks were affiliated with the Railways, our train journeys cost us only quarter the normal fare. This meant that I could get to London quite frequently and, of course, I went to the theatre.

The first London theatre I entered was the Aldwych. I was thirteen years old, on a shopping trip with my mother and her friend, Mrs Williams. I was hoping to see Olivier or Richardson or, best of all John Gielgud, whoever he was, but my mother had other plans. During her engagement she and my father had been to a show in London, and though she couldn't remember what they had seen, she had never forgotten that Gertrude Lawrence and Noël Coward, then at the peak of their celebrity, were also watching the show from a box. Now, twenty years later, here Gertrude Lawrence actually was, acting in a play at the Aldwych, and mother was determined that we should see her. I dragged my heels into the matinee. Of course, I had never heard of Gertrude Lawrence. She was not on my list, and I was sure the play would be a stinker. It was *September Tide* by Daphne du Maurier. The men dressed for dinner in black tie, giving the actresses a chance to flaunt their satin and silk at the envious women in the audience, whose own drab finery had to be concocted with clothing coupons from their wartime ration books. Since Miss Lawrence was the star, it was also one of those plays where a character says something like – just before the First Act curtain – "Oh mummy do sing for us."

"No! I couldn't possibly!"

"Oh, mummy *please!*"

"Darling imp, you know mummy's silly voice has quite, quite gone!"

General protestations from the family and the rest of the characters: "Oh, I say!" and, "Please do!"

I do not say those *were* the words, I say they're the sort of words I remember. Eventually Miss Lawrence edged upstage centre towards the piano – yes of course there was a piano, my mother had spotted it at curtain-up, nudging Olwen Williams happily – and sang a pretty song. And then the curtain came down for intermision, and tea was handed along the rows on trays. It was dreadful; even I, at thirteen knew it was dreadful. Nothing of interest happened. It had no dynamic, the writing was jejune, it lurched towards bathos and plunged right in. Oh! if only it had been that same matinee during which, according to theatre legend, a stagehand was trapped onstage just as the Second Act curtain rose and scrambled into a cupboard, not knowing that an unaware Miss Lawrence must open the cupboard later, and the stagehand in full view of a dumbfounded audience touched his cap and said "Good afternoon, Miss Lawrence!" I suffered miserably through the play, was grouchy all the way back to Barry, and complained bitterly to everyone that I'd seen the very Worst Play ever. And yet and yet and yet... If it was so dreadful why is it I can still see Gertrude Lawrence in a lime-green evening dress standing in the well of the piano singing a number from *The Maid of the Mountains,* and still hear that strange mocking soprano that echoes in my memory as clearly as if it were last Tuesday? Why did the play arouse nothing in that child but contempt, while just to think of it now catches at my heart? Is it that in Gertrude Lawrence was embodied the whole spirit of Romance, and in the bitter-sweet fragility of her voice was the warning that all Love is evanescent and the teasing reminder of the fleet-footedness of Passion; and at thirteen all the agonies of Love and Passion and Romance were still unknown to me? I played in the Aldwych Theatre in 1990 in Coward's *Private Lives,* the play in which Gertrude Lawrence had been the original incomparable Amanda. My dressing room at the Aldwych had been hers on that visit when I was thirteen to see *September Tide.*

I did finally get to see John Gielgud. He was appearing at The Globe Theatre, Shaftesbury Avenue (now The Gielgud Theatre), in

Christopher Fry's *The Lady's Not for Burning* which I'd been assured was top-notch. In late spring half a dozen of us took the overnight train to London. Wales was playing England at Twickenham the next day. We wore striped scarves, carried rattles and leeks, and my sister lent me a Portuguese fisherman's cap which, stuffed with newspaper, stood two feet high above my head. The excitement at Cardiff was infectious as crowds pushed and shoved their way onto the train but during the long journey what with the singing and the lack of sleep we exhausted ourselves, and at five in the morning it was a very deflated crew that emptied onto the platform at Paddington. Nothing was open. There was nowhere to wash, there was nothing to eat, not a coffee stall in sight. Bleary-eyed we staggered out into Praed Street and hoofed it towards Marble Arch where we mooched around until Lyons Corner House opened, and then mooched around the West End. I went to the Globe Theatre and bought my ticket for John Gielgud in the five p.m. matinee of *The Lady's Not for Burning.* As soon as the performance was over, if I ran like the wind to Wyndham's near Leicester Square I could catch the evening performance of *Daphne Laureola* with Edith Evans. I had been assured that Dame Edith was another cracker and I certainly hoped it would be true, for the only ticket left was in the front row of the dress circle and it cost me twelve and sixpence (62½ pence).

Climbing to the upper circle at the Globe I felt quite breathless, but not from the stairs. Wales had beaten England and I was going to see John Gielgud!

The curtain rose, Gielgud appeared. Whether it was the heat, or the euphoria of a Welsh victory, or the excitement of seeing him, or simply that I had been on the go for twenty hours non-stop, as soon as he opened his mouth I fell sound asleep. I was woken by the applause at the end of the Act. I rushed to a landing where there was a circular window and spent the Interval with my head stuck out over Shaftesbury Avenue, breathing in the cold air. The bells rang for the Second Act. The curtain rose. Once more, as if hit over the head, I fell into a profound slumber. I was roused by a lot of shouting. Esme Percy was onstage, bringing the house down, and I sat up eagerly; perhaps I had nodded off only for a moment. But the play was almost over. To my dismay the curtain came tumbling down and the actors were taking their calls. I ran for the exit. No time to think about the fiasco of the matinee. I hurtled down the steps and across to Wyndham's.

I did not fall asleep for Dame Edith. She transcended any idea I had ever had about the work of an actor. Was it her voice? Certainly it was the Voice Remarkable, swooping and gurgling. Was it her movement? Certainly her body language was amazing. Was it her utter control of the audience. Yes, all of those things and more. Useless to attempt analysis, it was a complete ravishing of the senses. In the interval the woman next to me, heading for the bar, kicked my rattle under the seat. I could not even rise to let her pass. I was glued to my seat, shell-shocked. I knew that I was seeing greatness. I recognised it instinctively but I could not define it.

We talk of the genius of Olivier and genius was certainly his; but in his work, even when the brilliance of his talent left the audience agape, one was often aware of a performer dazzling us with his craft. The line between reality and simulation in Edith Evans's work was seamless; a role possessed her as completely as a succubus. Audiences felt like eavesdroppers; she gave not the slightest acknowledgment of their presence, no pandering for laughs, no overt seduction, and at the end when she took her call it was as though the audience was thanking her for being allowed to intrude into her private world for an hour or two. These days the standing ovation is almost obligatory. There was never a standing ovation for Dame Edith; it would have been unthinkable. Theatregoers were far too moved, too awed by her talent to stir. Applause for Dame Edith always started quietly, as the spell was broken and the audience came out of its collective trance.

Some years later, when she appeared in *The Chalk Garden* by Enid Bagnold, I used to see her quite frequently at parties. Sidling alongside I eavesdropped shamelessly, but never plucked up the courage to initiate conversation. Once, helping herself to salmon at a supper in Lord North Street, she turned to me and said, "Boy! Do you see any hollandaise?" I offered the sauce boat to her like the Grail, and as she dolloped some onto her plate she became quite chatty.

"An extraordinary thing happened to me this afternoon at the theatre. A bee stung me during my work!"

I was struck not so much by the effrontery of the bee, nor by her surprise at its presumption, as by the fact that she did not say it had happened during the matinee, nor during the play, but during "my work".

At home everyone wanted to hear about *The Lady's Not for Burning*. My friends surrounded me.

"What's he like, your hero, John Gielgud?"

I looked them straight in the eyes. "Superb! Electrifying!"

"And *The Lady's Not for Burning*?"

"Top-notch, as promised."

❖

In the summer of 1951 there was a school outing to London for the Festival of Britain. We trudged through an afternoon of stultifying boredom, traipsing through the tawdry Pavilions. The senior boys and girls, chaperoned by Teifion Phillips, were allowed to stay and see a show and catch the last train home from Paddington. The popular vote was for a comedy. There was a ticket booth near the Skylon. We were in line when Teifion Phillips joined us.

"What are you booking for?"

"Richard Attenborough and Sheila Sweet in *To Dorothy a Son* sir."

"Keith won't want to see that! He'll want to see John Gielgud!"

But I did want to see the Attenboroughs, and I did *not* want to be put to sleep again.

"John Gielgud's not in anything, sir!" I hoped wildly.

"Yes he is! Look at this poster! John Gielgud in *The Winter's Tale* – what a stroke of luck!"

Before I knew it Teifion had got me a ticket in the upper circle at the Phoenix Theatre. Wearily I trudged up the stairs to my seat, resentful of John Gielgud, hearing in my mind's ear the gales of laughter down the road at The Garrick Theatre where my friends were, no doubt, enjoying themselves, while I faced the misery of a Shakespeare play, and a play I did not know. Percy Fisher was right: studying Shakespeare at school had given me no love for the Bard. I had been thrilled by Wolfit as King Lear, but it was the actor, not the playwright who had knocked my senses into the middle of next week. What soon became clear, however, was that if I wanted to be an actor in the theatre, Shakespeare would have to be part of my life. Until then, I had tucked that realisation into the dimmest recesses of my understanding, hoping that it would be a long time before I would have to come to terms with it.

Picture then the scowling boy who sat slumped over the rails of the balcony, pessimism writ on him as brazenly as the badge on his school blazer, waiting moodily for the curtain to rise. The lights dimmed and there he was: John Gielgud, on the very lip of the stage, down right, in darkest crimson, gnawing his fist, breathing: "Too hot! Too hot!" into his knuckle. The words themselves were like a furnace, blazing their way into my brain, burning out all the nonsense and weeds that scholars cultivate around an appreciation of Shakespeare, and I thought again of Mr Fisher, "Beware the Jabberwock and the Jubjub bird!" It was a definitive production of the play by Peter Brook, and the cast was peerless; Diana Wynyard, surely the loveliest of actresses, Flora Robson, Lewis Casson exiting "pursued by a bear", and George Rose who ten years later would become such a good friend. I lost all sense of time.

The Winter's Tale was much longer than *To Dorothy a Son,* and when I ran to our group rendezvous in Leicester Square the others had been waiting for over an hour. We took the Underground to Paddington where we had to wait another hour for our train. I was aware of Teifion Phillips sitting on a bench nearby.

"It was wonderful, wasn't it?"

I stared at him. "You haven't spoken," he said.

It was true. Nor did I speak on the way home to Wales, and nor did I sleep when the others slept. I watched the lights in the dark outside, fizzing past the train windows, my mind teeming with images and sounds of the evening. That night John Gielgud turned a key inside my mind. He was graced with an incomparable voice, and he used it with wit and simplicity, making an unfamiliar language utterly accessible, spreading in front of me a map of discovery to a world of wonders. Over the years Gielgud has given me the greatest pleasure in many extraordinary performances, but pleasure in the theatre is by nature ephemeral; the gift he gave that schoolboy crouching over the rail of the upper circle at the Phoenix Theatre in 1951 has proved imperishable.

I cannot pretend that I remember my years at the Royal Academy of Dramatic Art with any extraordinary pleasure. In those days young men were required to complete two years National Service. It was thought good to enter the Academy straight from school, while still in a learning mode, then go into the Forces, return to graduate from the Academy and thus go straight into the profession. So I was too young to question the plodding curriculum of my first year at RADA, and too grown-up after Korea, to be patient in my second.

At first, I joined the Preparatory Academy of RADA, based in a house in Highgate. I don't think I learned a single useful thing while I was there. I heard my voice for the first time, and was depressed by its thinness, but did not see how learning to belt out *Funiculi, Funicula!* or *London Pride* was going to help. I shared a room with two other students in a hostel nearby, where the rules were strict and the food institutional. Until then, I had imagined the life of an actor to be gay and bohemian; it was a shock to find my days so regulated and the training so uninspiring.

There were, however, some talented students there; and thank goodness there was James Villiers. James was a tall young man of startling sang-froid. His rather disdainful manner concealed a genuine kindliness, and he knew a great deal about wine. Thirty years later I was to encounter him again in Holborn. I was waiting to use a telephone kiosk. I had been to the gym and was wearing a track suit and a scruffy scarlet windcheater. It started to rain and my unkempt appearance grew even more dishevelled. The kiosk became free, but I found it would accept only 20p coins. Proceeding down Kingsway came James Villiers, superbly dressed and hatted, carrying an umbrella. He moved like a galleon. "James! Do you have 20p?" I cried. James stopped, showing no sign of surprise at my disordered appearance, and dug into his pocket.

"Keith. My dear, how very nice to see you."

He handed me a coin. I remarked how smart he looked.

"On the way to the cleaner's."

There was a Dry Cleaner's on the corner.

"Sketchley's?" I asked.

"The Divorce Courts," he said and sailed slowly down towards the Law Courts in the Strand.

The Royal Academy of Dramatic Art, Gower Street was an improvement on Highgate, but not much. I made friends with Alan Bates and Roy Kinnear but we all sensed that something was badly wrong with the training. Many of the staff were very old. One teacher had walked on as a camel-driver in *Chu Chin Chow*; Nell Carter who directed us in *The Merchant of Venice* had played Nerissa to Irene Vanbrugh's Portia in 1913. We were taught ballet by an elderly, fine-boned former prima-ballerina who dealt with our lead-footed efforts very kindly. Not many things impressed Rudolph Nureyev, but he could never get over the fact that I had held Tamara Karsavina in my arms, who had danced with Nijinsky.

The Principal of the Academy was Sir Kenneth Barnes, an entrenched bonehead in his seventies, out of touch with modern ideas and fearful of change. To be fair, he was very good at finding money, and the Academy desperately needed it. Her Majesty the Queen was Patron, and the Queen Mother and Princess Margaret were fairly frequent visitors. Prudently cultivating this social trump card, Sir Kenneth encouraged wealthy parents to use the Academy as a kind of finishing school for their daughters and their sons, thereby ensuring a steady flow of money into the Academy's coffers whilst propping up a bogus social structure that was fast disappearing elsewhere. Let the winds of change blow down Shaftesbury Avenue. It would be some years before the breeze would be felt in Gower Street; and while Sir Kenneth had his back against the door there would be not the least hint of a draught.

In my second term I was involved in an incident that I still remember with rage. The Academy gave us a half-term break; long enough to go home to Barry. There was a very pretty girl from West Ham in my class. She was always in high spirits, very larky, and her cockney accent was beautiful. Her boyfriend was doing his National Service. He had a weekend pass and was arriving at Paddington on Friday. Since the trains to Cardiff left from Paddington, Barbara and I cut the last class and shared a taxi to the station. She did a quick change in the Girls' locker room and came dashing out. A taxi passed. We grabbed it with not a care in the world, and certainly no hint of what was to come.

I loved being with Barbara. That afternoon she was at her happiest and we laughed all the way to Paddington. Her soldier was standing by W. H. Smith's, and as I went to my platform the last glimpse I had of Barbara was as she threw herself into her boyfriend's arms in a flurry of gingham and giggles. When I returned to the Academy after the weekend I was summoned to the Secretary's office. I caught sight of Barbara, weeping in a room across the way. A man was waiting for me. He was a detective. A girl had lost five pounds and claimed it had been stolen from her locker. Between them, the Secretary, the Registrar, and the Principal had worked out that Barbara had stolen it and that she and I had spent it on a weekend together. They knew she had been in the locker room; they knew we had cut a class; they had watched us get into a taxi.

"Students like you can't afford taxis," said the Secretary balefully.

I told them I had been to Wales. They demanded my telephone number there and the detective dialled the number while I stood by, speechless with rage. The detective spoke to my mother for a moment, put down the receiver, brusquely apologised and said I could go. Before I could leave, a girl knocked on the door. She had come to tell the Secretary that the money had turned up after all, tucked into the toe of her ballet slipper, and she was terribly sorry if she had caused any trouble. She was mildly reprimanded and thanked for confessing her mistake. The detective shook her hand. She was, after all, a girl who had been Presented at Court. As he left the room to tell Barbara that she was not going to be charged, I turned to the Secretary, furious. "Why did you think it must be Barbara?" The secretary lowered her voice. "Barbara's from a very low background."

I might have quit RADA altogether if I not met Mary Duff in my third term. Miss Duff was a woman of startling severity who demanded that I do something about my voice.

"You sound as though your mother digs for coal with her fingernails" she said. "It's a very thin and plangent voice."

She also told me that I had a spark. Her manner was as austere as her clothes, but she was not devoid of humour, and I saw at once that she was a gifted teacher and so I started to work on my voice.

We were putting up the set for a class production of *Hedda Gabler* in the RADA Theatre under the supervision of Mr Howard-Williams, the dapper Head of Productions at the Academy, and lecturer on furniture. Peter Bowles, Albert Finney and I lugged the sofas and tables and lamps into position. Mr Howard-Williams called out into the auditorium of the Vanbrugh Theatre for Mary Duff's approval.

"Very nice, Mr Howard-Williams. Very nice. Only it's a little bare upstage. What it's really crying out for is something big up the back." "Aren't we all Mary?" said Mr Howard-Williams. Miss Duff gave a snort of laughter. Peter and Albie and I looked at each other in amazement. It was our first encounter with camp.

When it was time to interrupt my training at the RADA, and I was posted to Korea, Mary Duff wrote to me once a month. They were short sharp letters, full of news, fired off in her spidery writing. It was the thought of Mary Duff that sustained in me the idea that the Academy might actually have something to teach me.

The winter cold in Korea was intense, but our tents were snug and we had warm clothes. At eighteen the life was exhilarating, although in my first days I lived in a state of fear. It had been a long overnight journey north by train from Pusan to the railhead, then three hours in an open truck to the camp. A grizzled staff Sergeant showed me to my tent which was pitched (as I would soon discover) over the rough graves of a Korean soldier and a boy from Gloucester who had fallen in battle together. The old Sergeant told me not to unpack, and never on any account to get into my sleeping bag. Lowering his voice, lest the Enemy might overhear, he growled a warning: "When the Chinese come, they sneak up and plunge a bayonet right through the bag and you're dead before you can get your arms out!"

I swallowed his story as unquestioningly as I accepted the hot rum he gave me, and for three nights I lay shivering on top of my sleeping bag, too frightened to take off my clothes or my boots until a passing Sergeant Major poked his head into the tent to see how I was doing. It was the standard joke to play on newcomers, and I had fallen for it so completely that I was treated with increased affection. Being the youngest Sergeant in the Mess meant that I was often spoilt. Coming from Wales of course I was nicknamed Taffy, but everyone seemed to have a nickname: Chalky White; Sparks in Signals; Muscles, the PT instructor. I knew I was meeting people I would never have otherwise met and I loved it.

"Where were you from before this?" my best friend asked me. "Barry," I said. "What about you?"

"Pentonville."

I was never in any real danger in Korea. The war had ended, and though the rumour was that the Chinese would come "when the Imjin freezes" they did not, and then the rumour was that they would come "when the Imjin thaws" but they didn't come then either. Gradually everyone realised they were not going to come at all, and by then it was the summer.

The days passed quickly. Reveille was at five in the morning and work was over by mid-day, so unless there was some Regimental duty the afternoons were spent lazing naked by the Imjin and playing water-polo with the Americans.

I was sunbathing one day when the Regimental Sergeant Major's clerk came to find me. Sam McGregor, the RSM, was a tall Irishman, who kept a paternal eye on me. He was ashen by the time I arrived at his tent.

"Oh Taffy." he said. "Whatever have you done? I have to march you into the CO."

The Commanding Officer was a small, peppery man with an unwilling moustache, like a rat looking over a broom. He gazed at me with suspicion and did not suggest that I should be Stood At Ease.

"I have a signal here to send you to Divisional HQ. You're to see the GOC." I could see the RSM's eyes bulge. The Colonel gave me a nasty look. "I haven't the foggiest idea what it's about. March him out Mr McGeever."

A Jeep was waiting with a driver. "Going to see the General!" whispered the RSM with awe, "Oh Taffy, what's up?"

It was a mystery to me too. The journey down the Mark Clark Highway took over an hour, and I was covered in dust as I was marched into a very large tent with comfortable furniture and a planked floor. There were three Brigadiers and two full Colonels already waiting for the General. A Brigadier advanced towards me as I saluted. He wore the ribbon of the Military Cross.

"Hello Sergeant, would you like a glass of iced tea. Fred ducky – " (this to one of the Colonels) "give the boy some tea."

The officers shook my hand and sat me down. No one knew what the meeting was about and this amused them all mightily. The General soon arrived with his Adjutant. Everyone stood up and saluted and then sat down again, and General Horatio Murray barked: "My wife teaches painting to juvenile delinquents at Wormwood Scrubs. What do you make of that?"

Nobody knew what to think of it, so we all looked at the senior Brigadier who nodded encouragingly. It became clear that the General believed the men were in danger of being bored by inactivity.

"There's no fighting. Nothing to do but lie in the sun. No entertainment but Tit-and-Bum shows from Australia. It won't do!" He developed his theme: just as the young lads in English prisons had profited by his wife's art classes, so the soldiers in Korea should be offered some wholesome activity to fill their spare time.

"Art classes, sir?" asked the Brigadier, with barely a nuance of scepticism.

"Shakespeare!"

The General thought each Infantry Battalion ought to produce a Shakespeare play to be performed in the open air. There was a soldier in the Division, a student who had trained at the Royal Academy of Dramatic Art, he explained – and his eye turned benignly on me – and he thought everyone involved should have the benefit of my professional opinion.

"What about the girls?" I said.

"Don't need girls! Haven't got girls! Use boys! Shakespeare did!"

I agreed to submit a report to him. The senior Brigadier took my arm and led me to my Jeep.

"Listen Sergeant dear, the old boy's batty. The troops would never bear it. Hop in." Patting my bottom as I swung into the jeep, he told the driver: "Drive carefully, we don't want to lose the Sergeant."

Duly, I submitted my report, recommending that it would not prove feasible to mount a Shakespeare production, but adding that I would be happy to put on a good alternative. No costumes were available, and in Korea we had no civilian clothes, so I thought a play about soldiers might be the answer and what about R. C. Sherriff's *Journey's End*? General Murray's response was immediate: yes to putting on a good play; no to *Journey's End* ("It puts officers in a very bad light"). So I wrote to Mary Duff at RADA asking for a list of all-male plays with a military theme. By return the list came and I chose Christopher Fry's *A Sleep of Prisoners*. The General was enthusiastic.

Six weeks later we gave our performance at the Ship Inn, a large iron Quonset erected at the junction of the Brigades. The play takes place in a ruined church and we had done our best to transform the corrugated curved walls into Chartres. No slouch, the General had ordered make-up to be sent from Japan. Boxes of bright yellow paste and white powder arrived from the Kabuki theatre in Tokyo. They remained unpacked.

By seven o'clock the Ship Inn was packed. With nothing else to do and nowhere else to go, the soldiers had turned out in force, but there was no guarantee that they would stay. In *A Sleep of Prisoners* four soldiers take shelter in a bombed church. Each soldier has a dream in which the soldiers enact their predicament in Biblical terms: Cain and Abel; Abraham and Isaac; David and Absalom; Shadrach, Meshach and Abednego. It is a beautiful play, written in verse, but it proved incomprehensible to our audience. After only five minutes the silence was broken by the sound of a muffled pair of army boots making quietly for the exit. Others followed. The first leavers tried to be polite, and slipped away in ones and twos, but after quarter of an hour the trickle became a flood. Boots hammered up the wooden aisle, all discretion abandoned. I had slipped outside the building to make an entrance through the main door, and was trying to elbow my way through. Being in uniform, as the whole audience was, no one realised I was an actor.

"Let me pass, please let me pass!" An Australian gunner caught me by the arm. "Don't go in there mate," he said kindly, "it's bloody horrible!"

At the end of the evening less than thirty were left in the audience, and most of those were from my Sergeant's Mess, sticking it out in baffled loyalty. General Murray had not honoured us with his presence.

I got only one more glimpse of him before I left Korea. In September, at the Farewell Parade before the Regiment moved to Hong Kong, the General took the salute. He stood on a distant podium in a football field, and the words he weakly quoted from *King John* struggled against the wind.

"Nought shall make us rue, if England to itself do rest but true."

As we marched past his diminutive figure I expected never to see him again, but many years later, as I arrived for a dinner party in South Kensington, an elderly gentleman was dithering on the doorstep of a block of flats, wrestling with two overladen Sainbury's shopping bags.

"I wonder if you would press the bell for me. My hands, you see, are full."

I pressed his bell. Above it a label read: "General Horatio Murray."

There would be one further performance of *A Sleep of Prisoners* when we arrived in Hong Kong, and it was an altogether different experience. We were invited to play in the cathedral. We were allowed to remove the choirstalls, and spread straw and debris on the flagstones. During the occupation of the Colony, the Japanese had used the cathedral as an Officers Mess, and now we were being helped by clergymen who had been familiar with the building in those days. For our audience, and indeed for us, that performance of *A Sleep of Prisoners* was a profoundly moving experience.

When I returned to the Academy for my second year things were very different. The new Principal, John Fernald, had swept away a lot of old nonsense. There were some good actors among the students; Siân Phillips had arrived, and so had her husband-to-be Peter O'Toole. Richard Briers joined my class. I also met Alan Bates again and Roy Kinnear. They were living in a large flat in Battersea and there was space for me. The flat was a kind of crash-pad; if you could not get home at night you slept at The Mansions.

London was not too lively in those days. There were very few late night buses and the Tube closed down before midnight, and as poor students we could not afford to go to drinking clubs in Soho. The 44 Bus home to Battersea stopped at the Air Terminal by Waterloo Bridge. Sometimes Albert and I forked out for an overpriced coffee.

"Where are you off today Mr Finney?"

"Katmandu I think, Mr Baxter. How about you?"

"Caracas for me, non-stop."

My two years in the army had been virtually celibate. On R and R leave in Tokyo I had gone to the opera – *La Bohème* at the Hibiya Hall – and met a Japanese girl who worked as a secretary for BOAC (British Overseas Airways). I told myself I was in love, but...

In the Battersea flat there was another RADA student who was in his Finals Year. He had large, dreamy eyes and flaxen hair that tumbled in a Caravaggio mess across his brow. He often sat on the window-sill strumming a guitar, singing *Summer and Sunshine and Falling In Love,* the hit number from *Salad Days.* His slight lisp was enchanting beyond words. His pure white cotton shirt, disarmingly unbuttoned, offered a tantalising glimpse of half a nipple and a silken-smooth suntanned body. He wore khaki cotton pants casually crumpled around his long legs, and always went barefoot. Wherever he sat the sunshine always seemed to light him perfectly, and it never occurred to me that he was shifting with it to ensure the maximum effect. To me, straight from the rough-hewn masculinity of a Sergeants Mess, he was the quintessence of charm and style: Adonis, Narcissus, Rupert Brooke, Percy Bysshe Shelley, and everything I knew that I could never be. I was in thrall to him. I clumped around like a carthorse, bringing him toast, slopping the tea in the saucer, but he was barely civil. My voice was too loud, I did not know how to lisp, my dark hair was shaggy, my clothes inelegant, and I tended to knock things over. He had a girlfriend.

This paragon graduated from RADA, and twenty years passed before I saw him again in a modern-dress production of *Pericles,* playing a transvestite in a middle-eastern brothel, wearing a jock-strap and a lot of lipstick. He still looked adorable. He had married and had children, but some time later I saw him in the Food Hall at Harrods, picking over the Kiwi fruit, wearing a floral print frock, high heels, and a very pretty hat. Later he had surgery and told his friends that he was now a woman. He committed suicide two years ago.

At RADA, graduating students went through their paces in their last term in a Public Show at Her Majesty's Theatre. I was in O'Neill's *The Long Voyage Home* playing a Swedish sailor, described by the author as fat, blond, and balding. I was whippet-thin and raven-haired but no matter. One of my lines was, "You know, Miss Freda, I have not been home for ten years." Since I had been to Sweden as a boy, and had picked up a little of the language, I decided to augment the line by counting up to ten in Swedish. The Judges that afternoon were Margaret Leighton, Edith Evans and Eric Portman and they gave me the Bronze Medal.

Just before I left the Academy, shooting began on a remake of *The Barretts of Wimpole Street,* and I was cast as one of the nine Barrett children, with Jennifer Jones playing Elizabeth. The film was made at the MGM Studios in Borehamwood, hell to get to by 7.30 a.m. from Battersea, taking two buses and the Tube. The particular rewards were that one of my sisters was the magical Virginia McKenna and another was Maxine Audley. What a warm-hearted loving woman Maxine Audley was, utterly feminine, stylish and elegant, witty but never malicious, bawdy but never vulgar, wise but never judgmental, and such fun! The best reward of all, however, was that John Gielgud was to play my father (in the role created in the earlier film by Charles Laughton). We were all very shy of Gielgud. I was much in awe of him, of course, but he quickly put everyone at ease. Both Maxine and Virginia had acted in his companies so they were old friends. *The Barretts of Wimpole Street* was a poor film, but I had never made a film before and it was my first job. I enjoyed every second. Our lunches in the commissary were hilarious and instructive. Maxine asked Gielgud what he would be doing after the film.

"Oh I don't know, I'm terribly out of work!"

I thought, "My God, I've only just started and here's one of the greatest actors in the world with no job ahead of him."

"Is this what it's going to be like?" I asked Maxine.

"Yes" she said, "yes, get used to it!"

On the next sound stage they were shooting *Anastasia*, and one lunchtime Virginia spotted Yul Brynner coming towards us with Ingrid Bergman.

"Oh, he's so handsome!" sighed Maxine.

"The most handsome man in the whole world," agreed Gielgud.

"You know him, John?"

"Not really" said Gielgud.

"Now's your chance," said Maxine, sticking out her foot and tripping Brynner as he passed. The star fell to his knees, his face at Gielgud's lap.

"How thrilling to see you again!" said Sir John. "Do you know Maxine Audley?"

At last I was an actor. No instant success, I understudied and stage-managed on tour and in the West End with a new play, *A River Breeze*, that flopped; then a spell in repertory at the Oxford Playhouse and at the Connaught Worthing. At last, I made my London debut as a young American football player in Robert Anderson's *Tea and Sympathy,* and appeared in another play with Geraldine McEwan that closed after three weeks; I had parts on television, and months when I seemed unable to find any work at all.

Then, early in 1960, I auditioned for Orson Welles for *Chimes at Midnight*.

Two

THE DAYS THAT WE SAW

Shallow: *Ha! cousin Silence, that thou hadst seen that that*
this knight and I have seen. Ha! Sir John, said I well?
Falstaff: *We have heard the chimes at midnight, Master Shallow.*

Shakespeare *Henry IV Part II*

"My name is George" he said "did you know that?" I did not. "It's one of my names. I could have grown up George," he said late one night after dinner thirty years ago. We were sitting together in his rented apartment in the Puerta de Hierro district on the outskirts of Madrid. The meal had been wolfed down and all around us was evidence of frantic activity. Suitcases, hurriedly packed, were lugged into the room and an anxious secretary darted noiselessly in and out to check them; voices were hissing at the unseen servants. Someone was whispering on the telephone, ordering the cars to come at once and wait, lights switched off, engines running quietly.

He filled a massive armchair, sipping his drink, oblivious to the sotto voce frenzy all around us. I nursed the colossal gin he had poured me.

"This is a pleasant room don't you think?"

Indeed it was. The furniture was extremely comfortable and his wife had added flowers, books and pictures, creating an ambience of enormous warmth and style. The room opened onto a balcony, commanding an uninterrupted view of the Guadarrama hills. That night the curtains were tightly drawn. From the driveway below, there would be no sign of life.

"Did you ever meet the owner of this apartment?"

"Once" I replied. The man had stepped out of the elevator one morning as I arrived. Heavily built, gold spectacles, elegant dove-grey double-breasted suit. "Isn't he a Spanish banker?"

"He's not Spanish. He's a Grand Duke. The heir to the Romanovs. If they brought back the Tsar that would be him."

"You're full of surprises tonight George" I said.

"People become their names." He chuckled. He was a good chuckler, the best I've ever known. It would start as a rumble, shaking his whole body, sometimes erupting into an explosion of laughter that could make the windows rattle. "Bernard Shaw was George too. Can you imagine *St. Joan* by George Shaw?" Another rumble.

"And George Welles wouldn't have suited *you* either."

"You're absolutely right," said Welles.

His wife brought in her jewellery and furs. Crisis or no crisis, Paola was as elegant and soignée as ever. Her grandmother followed, ninety years old, Italian, grinning with the excitement of adventure. The governess brought in nine-year-old Beatrice. The secretary announced that the cars had arrived.

"We can go," Paola said.

"I'll get my overcoat," said Welles.

"We're coming!" called the governess to the chauffeur.

"Be quiet!" Welles turned on her, whispering furiously. "We must make no noise at all! None!" He went to get his coat.

"What about the servants?" said Paola when he'd gone. "We must say something to them. They mustn't be alarmed."

"Leave it to me," said Prince Tasca.

"For God's sake don't say we're running from the American Tax Inspectors, they won't understand!"

"Calmly, calmly," urged Sandro.

Prince Alessandro Tasca was a Sicilian nobleman of the Lampedusa family who had lived a varied life, at one time eking out a threadbare existence in New York by working as a clerk at the Aqueduct racetrack. Eventually he drifted into the Italian film industry, working for Pasolini (playing Pontius Pilate in *The Gospel According to St. Matthew*). In Madrid he was functioning as executive producer for Orson Welles. He cared nothing for his personal appearance: wearing his stained old gaberdine coat as always, and a battered Homburg stuck on the back of his head. He turned to the secretary.

"Summon the servants!"

Vicenta the cook came first, followed by the two maids, who peered nervously over Vicenta's shoulder. They stood in the doorway, a trio of suspicion wondering about their wages. Paola smiled at them bravely.

"We're going away," she ventured. Three pairs of eyes swivelled to the luggage. "But we shall be coming back." She faltered.

"I'll do this," offered Tasca. He stepped forward and told the servants not to worry.

"No se preoccupe," he began, jovially.

The eyes swivelled back and focussed on his shapeless hat, his grubby raincoat. Not a figure to inspire confidence, he had, as usual, forgotten to shave.

"Senor Welles no es un gran criminal!"

It was not, I thought, the happiest choice of words. Mr Welles had done nothing wrong, he said. He was merely going away with his family for a little while and wasn't quite sure when he was coming back. Vicenta's gaze was grim. In the meantime, on no account was the front door to be opened to strangers, no telegrams or registered mail were to be accepted. If anyone asked who was living in this apartment they were to say they did not know. Mr Welles was – pause – about to disappear! He would become Invisible! But this explanation was not going down too well. After all, the servants had been working for Mr Welles for over six months. He was six feet two and weighed 300 lbs. Invisibility was not his strong suit.

"El telefono?" said Vicenta, impassive.

"Ah si!" Tasca nodded and then – in a gesture I have seen only in movies – he yanked the phones out of the wall by their wires. This did not encorage an atmosphere of ordinariness.

Welles returned. "Let's go." And so the midnight flit began. Everyone tiptoed past the servants, down the stairs, shushing each other as they fumbled around corners. Half-way down, Beatrice stopped. "What about the animals?" Her mother reassured her, Zarco: her horse, would be perfectly well cared for at the stables nearby; Vicenta would feed the cross-eyed cat and look after the parrot. "What about Bonzo?" Bonzo was the boxer dog. "Well Bonzo would be – where is Bonzo by the way?"

"We must find Bonzo," Beatrice wailed.

"Ssssh!!!" from everyone.

"I won't go without Bonzo," sobbed Beatrice.

"I'll find him," Welles whispered.

The little group of travellers sneaked out of the back door and headed towards the cars, dodging from patch to patch of shadow in the moonlight. We looked left and right. Were there American revenue men lurking in the bougainvillea? I still had my gin. I was not going anywhere.

Suddenly bright light spilled across the driveway, and we all froze in the dazzle. When we looked up the curtains of the apartment had been drawn wide apart. Welles stood floodlit on the balcony.

"Bonzo!" he called.

Lights were flashing on in other apartments. He called again.
"B - O - N - Z - O !!!!"
So much for invisibility.

From time to time actors have to check out their careers. You open
in a play and the press-agent asks you to approve your biography for
the playbill. There, like a felon's, lies your record. Things you had to
do because you needed the money. Things you thought would turn
out well but did not. Things you thought were disaster-bound and turned
out triumphant. A few things there are of which you are proud. In my
case, playing Prince Hal with Orson Welles is one of them.

In the winter of 1960 I was very out of work in London and very
poor, washing dishes in Scott's Restaurant at the top of the Haymarket.
Not an unusual state of affairs for a young actor, but I did not know
how long I would be able to last if the Dole ran out. My father was ill
and would in fact die a few months later. In the midst of those bleak
months, I got the chance to audition for Orson Welles who everyone
knew was preparing a version of Shakespeare's *King Henry IV* histories
for a production destined for Belfast and Dublin. I thought I could
certainly get a job carrying a spear, though I hoped for a miracle and
that the great man would let me play Poins – a good supporting part.

In the event, Welles invited me that day to play opposite him as
Prince Hal, a break which altered my life for ever. Welles was the first
person to believe in me. He had such faith in his own sureness of my
ability that even when my own confidence faltered his never did. From
then on I was in his debt, a debt I was never able to repay.

By a strange coincidence I had also auditioned in the same week
for a modern-dress production of *Henry V* at the Mermaid Theatre.
Most actors approach modern-dress Shakespeare with deep suspicion,
for they sense the whim of a director who lacks any real reverence for
the text, hoping mainly to provoke a self-serving frisson of controversy.
The inspiration for the Mermaid production was encapsulated in the
first scene. The French Ambassador brings a gift for Henry calculated
to insult him. The director decided that the King would be practising
at the *cricket* nets, so that when his uncle opened the gift:
"What treasure, uncle?"
"*Tennis* balls my liege!"
The audience would gasp. Quel coup de théâtre!

I was asked to play the King. I thought I was going mad. Unemployed
for almost three months, now I had been offered two jobs playing the
same character. My mind was in a whirl. I went for a meal.

There used to be a Lyons Corner House in Leicester Square with two upstairs restaurants – The Grill And Cheese and The Seven Stars – both popular with actors. Kenneth Williams and Joan Plowright were eating together in a booth. I declared my predicament; what choice should I make? As beginners, both had worked with Welles in his unforgettable production of *Moby Dick* in London. Oh, the disasters they prophesied ahead of me if I went with Welles! The dramas! The mania! The money running out! They clutched each other, helpless with laughter, tears running down their faces. Then Joan pulled herself up, grasped my hand and said, "Oh! But seriously – you must go with Orson!"

The production was rehearsed by Hilton Edwards in the main hall of the YWCA in Holborn. As a boy of fifteen, Orson Welles had arrived in Dublin claiming to be an International Actor and a painter too. He had a donkey cart with canvasses in the back. Hilton Edwards's lover, the legendary 'Irish' actor Mícheál Mac Liammóir (actually Alfred Wilmore from Kensal Green in north London, who had learned Gaelic at night classes in Ludgate Circus), ran Dublin's Gate Theatre with Edwards. They took a look at Welles, the story goes, and Edwards said, "I think we'd better have him Hilton, there's something about him." Now, after a quarter of a century, the international actor was going to play in Ireland again.

Welles did not turn up for the first two weeks of rehearsals. He had returned to Paris where he was preparing the final cut of Kafka's *The Trial,* filmed earlier that year. It felt odd rehearsing all the Falstaff scenes without Falstaff, but one morning Welles barged through the door of the YWCA, breezily saying, "Let's get on with it," and went straight into the first scene. I was nervous of working with him, but he took pains to set me at ease and make everyone happy, though he was worried that we were such a young company. He was relieved that one of the Earls was played by a man of solid middle-age. This was a charming actor, immaculately groomed, who sat in the corner doing *The Times* crossword until his scenes were called.

"He's been at the BBC," murmured Welles. We're very lucky to have him. Such dignity!"

The night that we all assembled at King's Cross for the boat train to Belfast, I passed the Earl saying goodbye to his girlfriend. He was leaning from the carriage window, his jacket open, his tie askew, as drunk as a skunk. No one ever saw him sober again.

The night before we opened there was a press conference in Belfast at The Opera House. It was Sunday afternoon and the bar was packed.

All the Irish papers, most of the English, and some American journalists were present. Welles was in fine fettle although we were behind schedule and should have started the dress rehearsal two hours earlier. I have a picture of myself frowning anxiously beneath a mediaeval haircut. Orson introduced me: "The Worry With The Fringe On The Top."

It was five o'clock before we started the dress rehearsal and it was disastrous. Everything went wrong. Each sound cue was a catastrophe: when you should have heard bells, you heard horses neighing; when you should have heard horses, you heard a tin whistle; when you should have heard a tin whistle, you heard cheering and trumpets. Another gremlin was at work in the lighting box: when the stage was meant to be dark, it was floodlit; when it was meant to be floodlit, it was pitch; when a spotlight was meant to pick me out for a soliloquy, it darted all over the stage like the Death of Tinkerbell. The curtain fell in mid-sentence on Thelma Ruby as Mistress Quickly. "The rag's knocked my wig off!" she mumbled beneath acres of plush.

Hotspur was played by Alexis Kanner, a charismatic young Canadian actor, who found it hard to accept that he should lose his sword-fight with Prince Hal.

"*Why* do I have to lose?" he would complain to anyone he could buttonhole. "Hotspur's the best fighter in the land! Everyone says so! *Why* do I have to lose?"

Hilton Edwards pointed out that if Hotspur had been victorious there would have been no Henry V, no Agincourt, no Wars of The Roses. In vain. "*Why* do I have to lose?" No other ending to the fight was acceptable to Alexis and the Fight Master quit in disgust. But that was not the end of it. One day Alexis ran into the basement, sword in hand, fresh as a daisy and smiling winsomely.

"You're really going to like this! I've got it! You kneel here like this. I come here like that. You thrust your sword out, and – hey presto! I'm dead."

"You mean I stab you in the back."

"Well, it's an accident if you like. I mean – maybe you didn't mean to."

"In the back?"

Alexis was subdued, but not defeated.

The dress rehearsal dragged on; it was already midnight. The fight with Hotspur came just before the interval and the actors were looking forward to the break. I made my rapid costume change, clanking onstage in full armour, encased in metal from top to toe, to join Falstaff. Behind us Hotspur's voice issued his challenge.

"If I mistake not, thou art Harry Monmouth."

Falstaff and I turned. Kanner had taken off every piece of armour and unbuttoned his shirt to his navel.

Welles took a step towards him. Kanner tried an ingratiating smile.

"Gee, Mr Welles, how else can I lose this fight? What choice do I have?"

"A very clear choice. Back to the Wardrobe or back to Canada."

Years later, when I saw the brave Chinese boy in Tiananmen Square heroically facing a tank with his shopping bag I was reminded of Alexis in Belfast.

In the stalls, observing all this confusion, was Mícheál Mac Liammóir, splendidly rouged, his toupee ("my gum-pad," he called it) only slightly off-centre. He had suggested himself for the role of my father, Henry IV, but Welles had refused him – too Byronic he thought – and Mícheál had been miffed. He was surely congratulating himself now as he contemplated the chaos onstage.

Mac Liammóir's replacement as Henry IV was Reginald Jarman who gave a stalwart performance. Unfortunately, he was almost totally deaf. He got his cues by lip-reading (and in performance never missed or muddled one) and by relying on a vast hearing aid. "This is my good side," he said, patting the enormous contraption in his left ear, "can't hear a thing on my right." I must have looked doubtful for he added, "Don't worry about the machine. You won't notice it when I put on my make-up. I cover it with a cunning disguise." The cunning disguise was a fat piece of Elastoplast, taped over the whole apparatus, hidden under the steel-grey wig, which was combed forward. History does not relate whether King Henry IV had a goitre on the left side of his head, but he did in Ireland in 1960.

Apart from the lump, Reggie did not cut a regal figure at the dress rehearsal. His embroidered surcoat was still being stitched in the Wardrobe, so he was in chain mail (made of wool) which was too large, hitched up with string, had no fasteners, and was held together by a line of safety pins from neck to knee. From a hinge at the back of his massive helmet (where ostrich plumes should fly if any could be found in Belfast) dangled a long sad piece of string.

"He looks like a walking fuse waiting for a light!" shouted Mícheál to Orson. Reggie beamed, not having heard a syllable, and munched a chicken leg while they fixed the lighting. Welles supplied roast chicken and champagne for the company. Heaven only knows where he found it at two in the morning for thirty people in Belfast, but it certainly perked everyone up. It was the first time I saw how Welles, whose rages could be titanic, would summon up reserves of gaiety to lighten everyone's spirits when things were going badly.

"Jolly good Reggie!" called Hilton, through a loudhailer from the dress circle. The King of England was trying to find his light. "Just move to the left, will you Reggie? You'll find your light on the left. The *left* Reggie! The LEFT!!! Oh push him Keith, for God's sake!" Then the loudhailer gave a sort of wheeze and died.

Many years before, when Hilton was a young man grasping at heterosexuality, Reginald Jarman had been his best pal. Hilton was engaged to a girl and Reggie stole her, married her, and lived with her happily ever after. At the same time, Hilton met Mícheál. ("Fallen into the arms of the True Faith," said Mícheál.) Hilton's devotion to Mícheál was unshakeable and very touching, but he had never quite lost his admiration for Reggie whom he still perceived as a dashing seducer, no matter that his Lothario was clad at this moment in a baggy outfit of grey knitted wool held together by string and pins, topped with a huge helmet from which hung six inches of twine.

Reggie stumped around the patch of carpet. "It's no good them all shouting at me. I can't hear a damn thing when they shout." Tetchily he plucked his elbow away when I tried to guide him. His deaf-aid gave out a strange buzzing and he gave it a smart bang. The loudhailer whistled and Hilton roared again.

"Here I am again Reggie! Dear old boy! Please move to the left!"

Reggie immediately trudged a step to his right. Mícheál rose in the stalls. "You're meant to be the King of England, not the Wandering Jew!"

The rehearsal finished after four in the morning. Things did not get any better; they could not have got worse. One last irritation remained. As I was washing, Alexis came into my dressing room and gave me one of his winsome smiles.

"When I auditioned for Welles he told me it was such a pity he'd already cast Hal, since I would have been much righter. Goodnight."

Blinded by soap I turned to him, but by the time I reached the door he had disappeared.

After so many hours we were forbidden by Equity rules to rehearse next day and, in any case, everyone was exhausted. At five in the evening over High Tea at Mrs Britton's digs before the opening show, I turned to Thelma in despair.

"Whatever's going to happen tonight?"

She passed me a poached egg.

"Rag'll go up and rag'll come down."

And so it did. And when it came down at the end of the evening the applause was deafening. Every light cue, every sound cue, each of Reggie Jarman's ostrich plumes – all were in place and perfect.

Before the show I had had no chance to talk to Welles, and after the show he was surrounded by journalists. Nor had I been able to confront Alexis who had kept away from me.

Back at the digs, I was sitting in my pajamas having tea with Thelma when the doorbell rang. Mrs Britton appeared, looking awestruck. Her voice was hushed.

"There's a taxi here. Mr Welles has sent for you. You're to go to the hotel at once."

Thelma gave me a slug of whisky. I knew I had been summoned to be sacked.

At the hotel, I was sent up to Welles's suite and stood outside, summoning up courage and a brave face. I knocked gingerly on the door. It was opened by Mrs Rogers, a sensible middle-aged secretary who had worked devotedly for Welles for some years. Hilton and Welles were laughing over the remains of a late supper. They waved me in and Mrs Rogers poured me champagne. I was not sacked. I had been invited to celebrate, and that night, and almost every night afterwards in Belfast, we stayed up till four in the morning.

Welles was lonely. His wife and child were in Paris. Those nights alone with him in Belfast listening to him talk are like a dream to me now. He was a good talker, I never knew a better, and I was a good listener, I could make him laugh, and he liked the Welsh. He talked endlessly about the theatre, about art, movies, politics and bullfighting. His conversation was a whirl of anecdotes, observations and opinions. Roosevelt, Hearst, Churchill, Gielgud, Picasso, Hemingway, Manolete, Griffith and Marlene – they all flashed past, reappearing and disappearing, swept away in the torrent of his reminiscences. The energy of his mind was amazing. I was a pushover, of course; twenty-six, from a small town in South Wales, and though I had been in Korea and seen Life – and Death, come to that – and had known what it was like to be poor, I was still very much an innocent. Welles loved that. He saw that innocence in me, he saw it in my work, eventually he captured it on film, and while critics praised my Prince Hal, they were giving me credit for qualities Welles had exposed without my knowledge. But had he wanted someone merely to sit at his feet, he would scarcely have been able to find a place for me. Worldlier minds than mine were held in his thrall; Olivier and Tynan were among the crowd. I imagine that the quality of innocence in me excited him because he recognised it in himself. Many years may have gone by, but he had not left that boy in the donkey cart so far behind.

As a child Welles had been a marvel. Unlike other talented infants his prodigious gifts had not disappeared with maturity. They multiplied. He had taken to Magic and Illusion like a duck to water, but beneath the conjuror's hat, the mountebank's flim-flam, the dazzling prestidigitation, under all the glittering carapace that had grown upon him, beat the pulse of a child – a mischievous child sometimes, but always a child of Romance.

In Dublin, on a corner of a stair outside his dressing room, I met Welles's wife. He had already told me that she was Italian and beautiful, a Contessa whose father had been roughed up by Mussolini's bullyboys. Lovely she certainly was. ("Awesomely elegant" is how Maggie Smith described her, spotting Paola stepping off the train at Chichester in a forest-green corduroy suit, holding a blonde pekinese under one arm and a bottle of Harpic in the other.) She was shy and funny, and about my age. Her English was wonderfully idiosyncratic. As soon as they were engaged Welles had sent her to Dublin to stay with Hilton and Mícheál, convinced that nowhere in the world was English better spoken than in Ireland and the best speaker of all was Mac Liammóir.

In Paola's voice the language took wing. Certain words eluded her; the pronunciation of 'crocodile' was a particular bugbear, and many times would Welles lead the conversation round to Egypt, hoping to trap her unawares. She was also possessed of a quality which she shared with many women: an absolute certainty that she was always right, which seemed something of a burden to her: "It is a terrible thing to admit," she once ventured after a fierce argument – Welles and I nodding sympathetically, certain an apology was on its way – "that I am never wrong."

Dear, beautiful Paola, who would die in an appalling road accident less than a year after Welles's own death, what would she have made of another of Welles's biographers who described her as "somewhere between passive and dull." She would have laughed, I suppose, for her sense of humour was finely tuned, but it is hard to imagine two more inappropriate adjectives to describe this vibrant, energetic woman.

At the Gaiety Theatre, Dublin, the opening night of *Chimes at Midnight* was more relaxed than it had been in Belfast. At the end there was a pounding fusillade of foot-stamping and cheers. Welles stepped forward to make a speech, as he had done every night in Belfast. This was a common practice in those days, and much enjoyed by the audience who felt they had been given a little extra for their money.

Welles's curtain speeches were always witty and brief, but on this occasion he chose to be serious, aware of an internecine feud between various theatre groups in Dublin at that time. The Abbey and the Gate theatres, whose players had taken London and New York by storm, seemed to have lost their momentum. He was proud to be back in Dublin, said Welles, with Mac Liammóir and Edwards, and shouldn't Dublin honour them properly, acknowledging them as the serious presenters of theatre in Ireland, presenting international classics as well as homegrown writing, by perhaps giving them this beautiful Gaiety Theatre, and installing The Gate there as a sort of National Theatre of Ireland?

While he was making these points – with the rest of the Company standing smiling behind him – the mood of the audience began to shift. Many had been on their feet, cheering as he had taken his call. As he had started to speak they sat, ready for a few jokes and a cheery anecdote. After a few seconds, mutterings began to be heard all over the house until, by the time he reached his peroration, there was uproar. Partisans of the various sides – and there were many – rose and shouted at each other. There were cries of "Sit down!" and "By Christ I won't!"

The curtain hurriedly fell as an angry phalanx of Irish theatregoers advanced down the aisle, baying invective and shaking their fists at Welles. Next day there were headlines, and the letter pages were filled for a week with angry denunciations countered by declarations of support. One headline gave Welles much delight:

'HOW DARE ORSON WELLES BITE THE HAND THAT NEVER FED HIM.'

It was sheer joy to be in Ireland. The audiences were responsive and uninhibited, laughing and crying unrestrainedly. At most performances a clutch of priests watched from the wings, because their parishioners would not have approved their going to a theatre. In Belfast Protestant clergy ventured backstage for the same reason.

If it was a joy to be in Ireland, then Dublin was exhilarating, far more fun than London, and certainly better food. We ate in Jammet's for the French, Bailey's for the fish, and the Russell for the best blowout of all. Vanessa Redgrave and Gladys Cooper were also in Dublin, in a play at the Olympia Theatre, *Look on Tempests*, presented by John Perry for H. M. Tennent. Perry's great friend, the author Molly Keane was living in Dublin and she asked us all to lunch at the Zoo with Desmond Guinness. Guinness, authoritative and waspish on the subject of Georgian architecture, told Gladys Cooper her face had a Georgian structure which did not please her.

"Such a fool!" she complained in the taxi back to the theatre. "He may know about houses, he knows nothing about women."

Molly Keane agreed. "Imagine having one's face compared to an *edifice*! "

Around that time Huw Wheldon had put together a television programme on Welles. After dinner one Sunday night I watched it with Paola and Welles in their rooms at the Shelbourne Hotel. Wheldon was a good interviewer, neither hostile nor subservient, and he asked questions which Welles dealt with directly and honestly. A sizeable chunk of the programme was given over to clips from *Citizen Kane*. On television Welles confessed that he had not seen the film since its first release, and the camera tracked in on him watching himself, frowning with concentration. Beside me in Dublin, Welles lit a cigar; he smoked big fat Havanas – Romeo y Julietta for preference, and any room in which he moved was scented with them. None of us spoke during the programme. It was an uncanny experience watching Welles watching Welles watching Welles; a man of forty-five watching himself at twenty-five playing a man of seventy.

Paola switched off the set. Welles was fairly subdued. After a few moments he crossed to the little portable hi-fi system Paola had brought from Paris and played the recording of the *Albinoni Adagio*, a piece he planned to use as theme music for *The Trial*. This music – so familiar now – was new to me. Its sweetness and sadness filled the room.

After a while I made my excuses and left early. The flickering images of *Kane*; the amazing use of light and shade with which I was to become so familiar when we filmed *Chimes at Midnight*; the staggering performance; above all, the sheer bravura of his genius, both in its scope and accomplishment; all these things were as exhilarating as they were overwhelming.

Edith Evans once said that her criterion for an extraordinary evening in the theatre was achieved when you came out and discovered you had been walking for ten minutes in the wrong direction. That night after I left the Shelbourne I found myself walking down by the Liffey, a long way from my lodgings. The loneliness of the river was a comfort and I walked until dawn when I found a cafe serving Guinness and eggs.

The Shelbourne was an exceedingly attractive hotel, and quiet, except on the night following the Wales versus Ireland Rugby International. I had been unable to go to Lansdowne Road because it was Saturday and we had a matinee performance, but my brother had come over from Wales for the game. At lunch next day Welles said: "Two young men came into our room in the small hours. They were singing, and sodden with drink. One of them was afflicted with flatulence. Paola says it was your brother."

"How do you know it was my brother?"

"He had dark hair and a daffodil. He wore a red scarf."

"Paola, there must have been thousands of Welshmen in Dublin yesterday with dark hair, daffodils and red scarves."

"Ah! But only one of them has a brother who's acting with Orson Welles who is staying at the Shelbourne!"

Welles relished the moment. By now he was getting bored with the performances at the Gaiety, though a genuine mishap always bucked him up no end. One night as he finished a soliloquy on the forestage, Corporal Nym bustled on with his line:

"Sir! Here comes the Lord Chief Justice!"

Welles rose, as rehearsed, and started off on tiptoe, saying: "Wait close; I will not see him."

Nym was played by the diminutive actor Henry Woolf. The two of them, Woolf so tiny and Welles so vast, made an hilarious sight as they scurried upstage towards their exit. At this point their departure should have been prevented by the entrance of the Lord Chief Justice, but as I walked around the back of the set I saw the Lord Chief Justice smoking his pipe and playing poker with the Archbishop of Canterbury. I grabbed his Lordship, stuck his hat on his head and pushed him towards his entrance.

On stage meanwhile, Falstaff had metamorphosed into a very angry Orson Welles. He towered furiously over Henry Woolf.

"I thought you said 'Here comes the Lord Chief Justice!'"

Desperately Woolf improvised a line.

"He did come sir. But now he cometh not."

Then entered the dishevelled Lord Chief Justice. Woolf beamed.

"*Now* he cometh sir!"

"Right glad am I to see him too," said Welles.

There were abject apologies afterwards, but Welles's anger was dissipated in laughter.

During the second week in Dublin, Alexis Kanner tripped me up and I fell into the orchestra pit. Bored with the fight, Alexis improvised a new stroke. Caught by surprise my foot caught his, and over the footlights I went. Welles was always bored by the fight, mainly because he had nothing to do but lie on the ground pretending to be dead.

"Get on with it for God's sake!" he muttered, as usual, as we circled each other. Puzzled by the sound of this new scuffle, the last thing I heard before I disappeared over the edge was Welles growling "What the hell's going on?"

The fall was about eight feet and I was out cold for a moment. Alexis, white, ran down the steps into the orchestra pit.

"I'm so sorry," he whispered.

Beyond him a man in the audience was peeping over the rail.

"Are you alright down there?"

Several more heads popped into view.

"Would you say that's part of the play?"

Meanwile, Welles was being driven mad by the inexplicable buzzing but could do nothing except lie inert. I crawled towards my sword. Kanner, backing up the steps, died beautifully at the top. I staggered over him – my helmet badly dented – said my lines and reached the end of Act One. As I went to my dressing room, half-carried, I heard a voice asking if there was a doctor in the house. But a doctor was already in my dressing room waiting. He had been in the audience and left his seat the moment he saw me fall. There was also a bag of oranges from the man in the front row and a bottle of Irish whisky from a well-wisher. Welles sent up a message.

"If Mr Baxter doesn't feel up to it, he must not play the second half."

There was no understudy and, in any case, there was nothing really the matter, so I said bravely that of course I was going to continue. I think Welles was a little disappointed.

"What would you have done if I hadn't gone on?" I asked.

"I'd have told them a lot of good jokes."

As the doctor left my dressing room the Wardrobe mistress asked if he could have a look at my dresser.

"Why, what's the matter with him?"

"Oh doctor! He's fainted with the excitement!"

Chris was a wonderful dresser. It was the first time I had been given a dresser of my own. He was part nanny, part older brother. In front of others he was polite and quiet; alone together he was imperious, organised, maternal, and tireless. He was also superstitious, a devout Catholic who made many intercessions to Our Lady with whom he felt he was on an inside track. I was rummaging around in a cupboard one day when he came in, nursing a grievance, rattling the coffee mugs and slamming the lid on the kettle with a bang. Our Lady had not been attending to his prayers.

"It's that Blessed Saint Mary Magdalen jabbering away and distracting her." He had a soft spot for Mary Magdalen but was convinced she was a chatterbox.

"What are you doing in that cupboard?"

I had lost a medallion, only a cheap enamelled thing, but I had been given it in Venice and was miserable to lose it.

"Have you asked Saint Anthony?" Chris asked with considerable self-assurance. Saint Anthony, he avowed, could find anything. He said I had to ask him to find my medallion and promise to light a candle as a thankyou. To humour Chris while I was rummaging I said, all in one breath,

"DearstanthonypleasefindmymedallionandI'lllightacandleinreturn."

Chris was withering.

"That's no way to talk to him. Get down on your knees and say it with respect."

As soon as he left the room to get the laundry I bolted the door and, feeling rather foolish, did just as he ordered. When I rose to unbolt the door, I saw the medallion hanging on a hook. I know I checked the room thoroughly, so I accused Chris of finding the medallion and hanging it on the hook before he left the room. He looked at me with pity.

"Well how did it turn up then, Chris?"

"Saint Anthony found it. A miracle," he said. "They happen all the time but you're too stupid to see them."

Since then, Saint Anthony has found chequebooks, keys, airline tickets, notebooks, scripts, even the diary on which this memoir is founded – and I have put candles for him in churches all over the world. In New York, the playwright Anthony Shaffer lit a candle when I took him into Saint Patrick's Cathedral two hours before the first night of *Sleuth*. Shaffer's candle took a little while to get going.

"Does he know I'm Jewish do you think?"

Sleuth broke every Broadway record.

Welles informed the company that our engagement would finish after Dublin. There had been rumours of a tour to Athens, Cairo, Amsterdam and Paris, ending up with a run at the Royal Court in London. But Welles had made up his mind that the company was not up to scratch, and he saw no way of improving it. Some nights the Shakespeare was cancelled altogether and Welles put on an entertainment of his own devising. In the first half he read from Melville's *Moby Dick* and T. H. White's *The Once and Future King,* and passages from the Bible. He read magnificently without affectation. The second half was filmed. He was piecing together a TV programme to be called *Orson Welles In Ireland,* answering questions from the audience in a disarming, free-wheeling fashion.

"Mr Welles! How do you like playing God?"

"He gets to win most of the time."

On these nights the company was dismissed, the actors free to do whatever they wanted. But I had to crouch at the rear of the stalls, ready to bounce up on cue and shout: "Ahoy there! Cap'n Ahab!!" and duck back down again before the audience could spot me.

Truth to tell, I did not much care what we did. Yes, it was more exciting to play Prince Hal, but it was also a crash course in stage technique just to watch Welles. He was gifted with a superb voice, of course, and he knew just how to use it, but his stillness was immensely impressive; and there was no doubt that the performances of *Chimes at Midnight* were deteriorating rapidly. Extras were hired in Dublin to flesh out the battle scenes and to fill the stage for Hal's Coronation. Some of these extras were good actors, badly in need of work; some were not actors at all. In the first week everything went to order. But the stage door of the Gaiety is right opposite the side door to Neary's Bar. As we approached the interval many of the soldiers had a pronounced wobble. The Earl from the BBC was particularly unsteady.

> "How bloodily the sun begins to peer,
>   The day looks pale at his distemperature!"

Easy enough to say sober perhaps, but the Earl, as you will remember, had been drunk since King's Cross. Night after night, with thickening speech and reddening face, he struggled to get the couplet out, and get it out he did even though the result was gibberish. Welles would follow the laboured enunciation with childlike fascination, glancing at me, tears of laughter splashing down his beard.

"Such dignity!" he whispered.

By the time we reached the Coronation of Henry V it was nearly the end of the evening, and the extras had put in a good hour's drinking. The Stage Manager pressed a button at his desk which rang a bell in Neary's, and behind me in the wings the extras would come trooping back to form the Procession. Gnarled hands would exchange pint pots for Swords-of-State, jewelled chains and coronets. Trumpets sounded and, reeking of ale, the boozy crew would augment the recorded cheers with their own expressions of goodwill; "God Shave The King!" and "He'sh a Jolly Good Fellow!" and then would come my cue: "There roar'd the sea and trumpet clangor sounds," and on I marched to solemn music, fearfully attended while Welles knelt in front of me, facing generously upstage, trying as well as he could not to glance at the shambles behind me.

One night I paused to look around. The entire company, who had been on a tour of the Guinness works that day and had been drinking all night, swayed in tipsy unison across the stage, coronets dipping crazily over their ears, tongues lolling stupidly, banners sagging as the Peerage clutched them for support. Lest you should wonder whether anyone remarked on this baffling spectacle, a lecturer from Trinity College sent me a letter commenting on the brilliant dramatic stroke which "illustrated so succinctly how Prince Hal merely exchanged the honest ribaldry of the Tavern for the venality of the Court." Truly there is one born every minute.

It was early spring and the Irish countryside was at its best. I packed a bag and drove to Galway, hardly passing a car on the journey, stopping at small bars for enormous lunches. We picnicked at Howth Head and took a train through Killiney and Bray down to Wicklow, and when we were waiting at the tiny station to return to Dublin I asked the porter if the train was always late. "It isn't late at all," he said "it just hasn't arrived."

We had only a week left and the sense of running-down was depressing. Actors gathered in corners backstage and discussed The Future. I had no future; it would be back to washing dishes and the Labour Exchange for the dole. Welles was involved with plans for Ionesco's *Rhinoceros* which he was going to direct at the Royal Court with Laurence Olivier. Olivier came over to Dublin and saw *Chimes at Midnight.* As I went up to my dressing room Alexis grabbed me on the stairs.

"Did you see him? Did you see God?"

I was in the shower when I was summoned to meet Olivier and I ran down in my bathrobe to Welles's dressing room to see the great man. What impressed Olivier the most was that I had fallen into the orchestra pit. He told me that his body was covered with old scars from torn cartileges and vicious stage fights. "If you see John Gielgud coming towards you with a sword, run!" And was I marked from my fall? He made a little moue of disappointment when he saw only a nasty bruise. Did I have no other wounds? I told him that I once slept on the floor of Gary Raymond's flat in Brixton and a spring burst through the mattress and slashed my left buttock, leaving a scar.

Olivier asked whether he could say something about my work, but Welles interceded: "Now Larry," he rumbled. "Don't start that actor-laddie stuff."

Olivier turned to Welles wide-eyed. Welles laughed and said: "You love giving actors notes guaranteed to screw them up."

"I was merely going to say," said Olivier, turning all his charm on me, "you have Welsh knees. Your legs are better than mine. You don't need to pad them, but when you walk across the stage holding the crown, this is what you look like. Watch your knees."

He then did a cruelly accurate imitation of my bent-kneed walk, and followed it with a dazzling smile.

"You don't mind my telling you, do you?"

Thereafter I became obsessed with my knees. Welles would often stare fixedly at them during our scenes together until I had learned to laugh off Olivier's gibe. But I never forgot his advice and my knees have been straight ever since.

Sometimes Welles could be impossible to fathom. One incident during the Irish season brought out the explosive side of his personality. It was, if you like, 'the ordeal of Anne Cunningham'.

Welles had accumulated a lot of film footage for his *Orson Welles in Ireland* programme, which he wanted sent to laboratories in England. He needed a courier. Anne Cunningham, a pretty girl and a talented actress, had little to do in the play and we were closing on Saturday. She was given a ticket to London. Everyone was pleased for her and off she went. On Friday night the performance went well, marred only by Reggie Jarman's hearing aid emitting a piercing whistle as he announced: "Here's more news!"

"From radio Cairo, I dare say," whispered Welles.

We duly trooped into the wings in high good humour. Anne Cunningham was there, smiling. She had been to London, delivered the film, but had come straight back to be with us for the last performances. Welles froze.

"What are you doing here?" he thundered.

There ensued a terrible scene as he berated her. No one could understand why. The company slunk away, and as I moved to follow Welles, he stormed off to his room, slamming the door and shouting.

"Stay away!"

Moments later, Anne came to my room in tears; what on earth had she done to upset him? I went down to Welles's room again, but by then he had already left the building; and when I telephoned the Shelbourne Paola could say only that he had arrived in a rage and disappeared to the bedroom without giving any explanation.

Next day, our last at the Gaiety, Chris, my dresser, firmly ticked me off. I was to go at once to that old devil and plead Anne Cunningham's case. Obediently, I ventured down to Welles's room, but not without some trepidation. It was the first time I witnessed such roaring anger in him, and the wildness of his fury reminded me of my father.

He was expecting me. He was calm, but implacable.

"It's no good, Keith. I cannot and do not forgive her. I gave her a ticket and she came back!"

Useless to argue that she wanted to come back to be with the company – his company – for the last day. To be onstage with him was more important to her than anything. He would not discuss it. She had been given a ticket. She had wasted it. There was nothing more to be said.

The company were booked on the Sunday evening boat from Dun Laoghaire to Holyhead. Early on Sunday morning I made my way to Geraldine Fitzgerald's house near the port. Geraldine, a graduate of the old Gate Theatre, had acted with Welles in his pre-Kane days at his famous Mercury Theatre, New York. Her son Michael Lindsay-Hogg, soon to be a fine director himself, was walking-on in our production. It was a beautiful day and a happy lunch. Welles was his ebullient self, and for a while I could forget that this was my last day in Ireland. We travelled in a convoy of cars to the port. We clambered up the gangplank to embark, Welles in the lead. Waiting for him at the top was Mrs Rogers, and beside her Anne Cunningham, hoping for a reconciliation, but Welles just scowled and ignored her, and went to his cabin. Paola followed with Beatrice. I had not even said goodbye to him.

Feeling sorry for poor Anne Cunningham I took her for a drink. Rightly, she was terribly hurt, as well as puzzled by the whole incident, and I said all that I could to console her, which was not very much, before going up on deck to be alone.

We cleared the harbour and I sensed the sea was going to be rough. There was a stiff breeze but no rain. I felt utterly miserable – sad for Anne, angry at Welles – but, most of all I was depressed because the Irish adventure was over and with no prospect of work I was going back to a room in Battersea that I had begun to loathe. I watched the sea slipping by. It was already dark, the Irish coast was disappearing, and I allowed myself to sink into a Celtic gloom. The few passengers watching the last lights of Dun Laoghaire fade went below. It was cold and the boat began to pitch quite violently.

"When they announced the *Citizen Kane* nominations at the Oscar ceremonies in 1942, every one of them was booed."

Welles was standing a few yards from me, leaning over the rail, looking out towards the dark. I couldn't see his face clearly, nor make him out in detail – he always wore black – against the night.

"That girl. I behaved badly."

"Yes," then a great sigh, almost a cry of pain. "When I'm angry. Never ask me why."

He cupped his hands and relit his cigar.

"It's been quite an engagement," he said.

"Put like that it sounds like a battle."

He chuckled.

"The War of Jarman's Ear," I said.

He puffed on his cigar, guarding it from the wind and for a moment in the glow I could see him grinning. He said good things to me then, and we walked round the deserted deck to find a bulkhead sheltered from the spray whipping over the prow of the ferry. Welles revealed that the stage version of the Histories had been just an experiment, a test run for a script that one day he would film. He asked for my hand.

"I'll never make the film without asking you to play Prince Hal," a promise he would keep.

In the four years since Dublin much good fortune came my way but there was never any doubt that the handle which first opened all the doors was the name of Orson Welles. For Welles, things were up and down as usual. Between Dublin and Madrid he had made several attempts to get other films off the ground. There had been a particularly intriguing plan to film *Julius Caesar* recreating the spirit of his old production at the Mercury Theatre, New York. It was set in the era of Fascism, of jack-booted, goose-stepping dictators, and Welles's modern-dress production had caused a sensation. The design of the play and the Nuremberg Rally-style lighting took the critics' breath away in 1937 and the costumes – peaked hats and tunics – were equally admired. (Except by the actress Mrs Patrick Campbell. "I felt," she told Welles, "as though I've spent an evening at a convention of chauffeurs.")

In 1960 Rome was the host city to the Olympics, and it was Charlton Heston who came to London to talk to Welles about putting *Julius Caesar* on film. Welles talked brilliantly of using a roving camera to shoot the Olympic crowds thronging the city against the classical ruins – as though the modern mob had vandalised them – so that the play would have a double 'time-image'. Nothing came of this project.

Then in 1963 Dino De Laurentiis announced his plan to film *The Bible*. Various directors were assigned separate segments. Ingmar Bergman would be responsible for *The Creation*, Luchino Visconti for *Joseph and His Brothers* (following *Rocco E Suoi Fratelli*), and Orson Welles would direct both *Abraham and Isaac* and *Jacob and Esau*. Welles prepared a script and wanted me to play Jacob. I flew to Rome for make-up tests – Jacob had to age from seventeen to ninety – and Welles supervised my make-up himself, glueing on beards and eyebrows, waxing out hair on my scalp for the old man, curling and highlighting and lavishly slapping on eye-shadow and false eyelashes for the teenager.

"The thing about film, Keith," he said, wielding the make-up sticks like a painter, "is that you can get away with a great deal more than people think. Confidence is all that matters." The rushes proved him right. He lit me carefully, and the boy's unlined face was as real as the aged patriarch's frailty.

It would have been the first Biblical film with a sense of humour. Welles's script never departed from the traditional account in *Genesis*, but his handling of the material was dynamic. Jacob's transformation from a really odious teenager on the make into the archetypal Jewish patriarch – into Israel himself – was both moving and hilarious, and always reverent. The meeting with the Angel at Peniel, when Jacob wrestles with the Angel of God, would have been both frightening and dazzling.

Welles wanted Nureyev to play the Angel and he was invited to the Ritz. When Nureyev arrived I was lunching with Welles and Paola. Welles decided Paola was over-excited and would I take her out to tea? As we left, Nureyev was coming up the Ritz staircase. Paola pulled me behind a pillar.

"My God. So beautiful," she whispered. And he was. Twenty-three years old, sensationally callipygous, with a mane of untidy blond hair, the physique of an athlete and the movements of a tiger, he would have made a very remarkable Angel indeed. Welles planned to shoot the sequence against the sun's rays through a whole day, from dawn until sunset. Nureyev listened carefully while Welles explained his plan. When he had finished he had one question.

"How much speak?"

Welles explained it was a magnificent part, dominating the story, but silent, and he wanted Nureyev to be naked. Nureyev thought about it for a moment.

"Agreed. But no speak?"

"No speak."

"You want me to make with muscles only?"

The treatment of the Abraham and Isaac story would have been equally startling. Welles wanted to shoot the picture on the barren slopes of Vesuvius, in that ashy ominous landscape, with Isaac running for his life, falling, stumbling, screaming in terror as his father pursued him with a knife. I queried whether Welles had not let his Freudian impulses run away with the plot?

"You think the boy would lie there smiling as his father tries to cut his throat?"

But Welles and the other directors never got to shoot their segments. De Laurentiis sold the entire idea to Cinerama. It was turned into a dull film by John Huston. Two years later Nureyev told me that the only director he had ever really admired was Welles, and the one part he hated losing was the Angel at Peniel.

When the project finally collapsed I was engaged to play in the stage version of E. M. Forster's *Where Angels Fear to Tread* in London. I had almost given up hope of working again with Welles, but he kept faith and in June, 1964, a letter arrived:

> Dearest Keith,
>
> Why don't we go quietly ahead sometime this year with our own family-sized production of "Chimes"? There probably wouldn't be sixpence in it for any of us, but it would certainly be fun and, I think, worthwhile…What are your plans?'

Four months later I received a telegram from Welles:

HAVE JOHN GIELGUD AS THE KING STOP MARGARET RUTHERFORD
AS MISTRESS QUICKLY STOP JEANNE MOREAU AS DOLL TEARSHEET
STOP I AM PLAYING FALSTAFF STOP PLEASE COME LOVE ORSON.

In October I flew to Madrid.

From Barajas Airport a car took me directly to Welles apartment. The air was scented with Romeo y Julietta cigars. I stepped with a smile from the elevator only to be grabbed by a grim-faced Mrs Rogers and yanked into an ironing room. With a finger to her lips she pressed her ear against the wall.

"He's with the producers," she whispered. "They've been here all morning. I think the film is cancelled."

Then there were farewells and the noise of the front door banging shut. Welles and Paola were shouting my name and I emerged into the hall. As they hugged and kissed me Welles said, "The film's back on again!"

Slightly stunned, leaving my bags in the hallway, I followed Paola to the balcony with its breathtaking view of the Guadarama Hills. It was a beautiful day, warm and sunny. She had prepared baby squid, cooked in its black ink sauce. Welles poured me a huge drink. As Paola served the food and Welles talked, a feeling of contented wooziness began to creep over me, induced no doubt by a combination of the warmth of the day, the wine, the dazzling view, the pleasure of being with them both again – but most of all by the sense that here I was, embarking on another adventure with Welles. It was an adventure that would lead me up and down, round and round, now juddering to a halt, now jerking forward again, sometimes chugging in the doldrums, sometimes surging smoothly ahead, always pulsing with the energy of a man driven by a passion that was overwhelmingly seductive. There would be times when I would wonder – often wonder – whether we would ever reach the promised shore in the distance; and when we did finally arrive, would the landfall seem miserably flat and dull after such an exhilarating passage?

As I was recovering from the hurly-burly of my arrival, another surprise greeted me; I had come to Madrid not just to play Prince Hal in *Chimes at Midnight*, but also Dr Livesey in *Treasure Island*.

The producers had approached Welles with an offer to direct *Treasure Island* and to star as Long John Silver. He undertook to assemble an international cast, but only if the producers would also fund *Chimes at Midnight*, to be shot concurrently. Since *Treasure Island* was not made, it is unlikely that John Gielgud ever knew that when he signed to play Henry IV he had also been booked as Squire Trelawney. At the last moment, however, the producers had got cold feet, or smelt a very large rat, hence the visit that morning at Welles's apartment to be reassured of his intentions. He convinced *them*. He did not convince me. Even with my limited experience of movie-making it was the maddest idea I had ever heard; the logistics were impossible. Nevertheless a set was being built – Mistress Quickly's tavern in Eastcheap would double as the Admiral Benbow Inn – even a boat had been hired and was this very moment bobbing at harbour in Alicante.

I was sent to Cornejo's, the costumiers in Madrid, to be measured and fitted for the Prince Hal costumes. They had been designed by Welles and were indeed elegant and simple and, thanks to Welles being an actor too, extremely comfortable. A cocky young English boy wandered in and looked me up and down. He had been hired to play Jim Hawkins. He pushed his tricorn back and said languidly, "Are you going to be in *my* film?"

That was the last time I ever saw him.

This is how Welles bamboozled his producers into believing that he could pull off both projects at the same time.

One: he would go to Alicante and oversee the launch of *Treasure Island*; two: leave a second unit to accomplish necessary sea footage while he started principal photography on *Chimes at Midnight*; three: when *Chimes at Midnight* was underway, and a scene being lit, he was to seize moments to film a page of *Treasure Island* on a different corner of the set; and four: and when *Chimes at Midnight* was finished he planned to devote all his energies to completing *Treasure Island*.

Would anyone have believed it possible? The producers did, and so the adventure began with Welles collecting me in his car, the two of us being driven across the breadth of Spain, through la Mancha, towards the coast. On the quay side at Alicante was a merry group. The Spanish producers were in festive mood and Jesus Franco, heading the second unit, was assembling a shot. In the background, pennants streaming in the breeze, lay the good ship Hispaniola. This modern copy of an eighteenth-century schooner had previously starred as the man o'war in *Billy Budd*. The ship was manned by an English crew, handling the sails as well as the hidden engines. They wore costume to augment the actors, who at this moment numbered one: Tony Beckley, engaged to play Poins in *Chimes at Midnight*, though at this moment dressed for Israel Hands in *Treasure Island* and none too happy; and all too ready to confess that he was a rotten sailor, and the weather forecast was for rough seas, while he would be on board, filming as the ship sailed up the coast to Calpe. Worse still, they would be shooting a scene in which he had been wounded. Even as we were speaking a props man was liberally daubing him with fresh chicken blood, holding the dripping carcass as he worked. I felt as nauseous as poor Beckley, and I wasn't sailing anywhere.

Welles changed the position of the camera and called, "Action!" A few seconds later, "Cut!" Then everyone thronged round the camera, congratulating each other, celebrating the fact that the project was under way. I took a glass of champagne to Tony Beckley to cheer him up and sat on a bollard to watch as the Hispaniola, second unit aboard, sails swelling, moved out to sea.

At the end of that first session Welles and I drove up to Calpe. In those days, and I have never returned, it was a little bay of infinite charm. Now I hear it has been turned into Miami Beach, Spanish-style. As we drove along the coast Welles explained there was nothing he could do until the ship arrived. He had brought me along for company, and he thought we might rehearse some of Prince Hal.

The hotel overlooked the cove. It was out of season and we had the little restaurant all to ourselves. Before dinner we walked up and down the little terrace as I practised my first soliloquy. A year later Welles said it was the thing I did least well during the making of the film and he wished he had never asked me to rehearse it.

Mrs Rogers was waiting in the dining room with papers for Welles to sign. At dinner Welles began to talk about his vision for the film, and the story of Prince Hal and Falstaff which would be the focus of the narrative. Although he was planning the early scenes to be shot in summer lanes, under trees laden with blossom, and in meadows sprinkled with flowers, the inescapable climax of the film was Death; not just the death of Falstaff, and the death of Hal's carefree youth, but the death of a kind of England too.

Modern audiences tend to lump all the historical plays into one Shakespearean period, forgetting that the England that Shakespeare celebrates in the *Henry IV* plays had disappeared two hundred years before he wrote them, and was as remote from Elizabethan England as the American War of Independence is from us today. Just as we look back to a golden age of elegance, before the Industrial Revolution, so Shakespeare was remembering an England he knew only from Romance and legend; a quieter England, the England of Chaucer, an England of castles. Gunpowder had barely been invented. It was possible to believe in chivalry. Nobles might skirmish, but War was fought abroad. No wonder this was the England in which Malory had set the tales of King Arthur though the Arthurian age had been centuries earlier. At that time too, the Church was securely Roman, and any schism would have been beyond comprehension. The Crown might change hands, but the people's lives went on unaltered. By the time Shakespeare wrote these plays Church, kingdom, throne, country – all had been savaged, changed utterly. The mirror of that other, earlier England was Falstaff, the contemporary of Chaucer: Chaucer – a page at the court of Richard II whose Plantagenet inheritance stretched back directly to the Normans. Welles felt that the story of Falstaff was the story of the last years of that England – merrie England. Indeed Falstaff was himself merrie England, and with Falstaff's death merrie England died too.

"The film is a love story. Never, ever forget that. Everything else – the politics, the comedy, the battles – they all drop into their place. What the film is *about* is Love, and love betrayed. I want to call down the corridors of time with this picture."

The three of us sat alone in the empty restaurant. His eyes glistened. It was the only time I saw him become emotional about his work. He pushed his chair back and rose from the table. I walked him to the door of the restaurant and as I turned back to Mrs Rogers I saw that she was weeping quietly.

I am certain that Welles never meant the film to be as bleak as it turned out to be. He wanted the beginning to be light-hearted and gay to contrast with the sadness at the end. Certain things happened, accidents some of them, so that the joie de vivre he aimed for was never achieved, or when it was attempted did not really ring true. Yet the elegiac texture of the picture is what gives it its overwhelming impact, and by the time Welles realised what he had done he made no attempt to rectify it. He must have known that some instinct had driven him towards the way he had shaped the images, and I believe as a piece of filmed Shakespeare it has no equal.

Let me make myself plain. The Zeffirelli versions of Shakespeare, the Olivier movies, and the Branagh movies too, are superb records of some stunning performances: they are though, all of them, imprisoned in stage technique, filtered through the prism of minds whose discipline is primarily theatrical. In the case of Olivier's *Henry V* and *Richard III* (and Ian McKellen's) this is amusingly deliberate; in the case of Joseph Mankiewicz's *Julius Caesar* the rhetorical style, the bewigged actors, the hammy performances now seem risible. In spite of its manifold flaws – an out-of-sync soundtrack at the beginning is a serious one – *Chimes at Midnight* has a vitality and dynamism that is as powerful today as it was when Welles completed it thirty years ago. In 1992 a print of the film surfaced in New York and was shown at the Public Theatre, eliciting rave reviews. The *New York Times* critic went straight to the point:

> "Next to Olivier's Shakespeare films, with their comparatively big budgets, studious attention to text and speech and clearly seen associations with England's mainstream theatrical heritage, Welles's films look raffish, at least in part because they are so alive, vivid and pertinent. They are bloody entertaining. Welles was a very good actor and a great filmmaker. Olivier was a superb actor and a good filmmaker, qualities that somehow result in films that today play as if encased in aspic."

The New York critics also put their fingers on the film's especial quality when they asked their readers if they had ever been *moved* by any other Shakespeare film? The kind of feeling that makes you reach for a handkerchief as audiences do at *Chimes at Midnight*.

It is certainly the most powerful of Welles's three Shakespearean essays on camera. Why should this be? In the first place, it was a period that Welles responded to emotionally and pictorially. He was always a Gothic director. The rays of light, slashing from the arc beam across the projection room at the beginning of *Citizen Kane*; the tall windows of Xanadu; the stark white shaft of light illuminating the echoing vaults of the library where the reporter tries to unravel the mystery of Kane – these were the first compelling strokes of a young artist exulting in the dramatic use of light and shade, and they would become his trademark, seen again in *A Touch of Evil, The Trial* and indeed in all his films. In *Chimes at Midnight* on a fourteenth-century canvas, he was justified in painting Gothic images of amazing pictorial strength. Incense was burned to isolate the light more sharply. The mist circling the trees, during the Gadshill robbery, catching Hal disguised as a Friar running through an autumn cathedral of birches shedding leaves; the great window behind the young crowned King, and the ray of light falling across the throne of his father; the massive stone pillars framing Falstaff as he walks away into the night, his shadow looming up across the deserted gateway; all these are masterly strokes by an artist at the height of his craft.

But sheer visual artistry is not what gives *Chimes at Midnight* its unique poignancy. Once when I told Welles I should have liked to have played Henry V he looked at me with astonishment.

"He's a terrible, terrible man."

In his view Prince Hal's metamorphosis from heir apparent into absolute monarch was not a matter for celebration. The film mourns the loss of innocence, the abandonment of love. When, mildly, I offered that, in assuming his responsibilities Hal had necessarily had to make sacrifices, Welles scoffed.

"His friends for his country?"

A letter from Cambridge lay on my chair.

"Tell that to Morgan Forster," he said.

In *Chimes at Midnight* betrayal of friendship underpins the whole picture. It is foreshadowed several times and the narrative moves towards it without deflection. The old King, sick and haunted by guilt – played so memorably by Gielgud – claws his son to him in private conference. Confessing "God knows by what crook'd ways I met this crown," he whispers secrets to his son, in an ice-cold castle like a prison. When we see Hal next, he has turned into a facsimile of his father. The Prince, who lamented Hotspur's death so eloquently, has become the King who will order his prisoners slain. The nimble-footed madcap Prince of Wales is now the war-like Harry. Death is in his bearing as it has entered his heart.

Welles brought to his performance of Falstaff a sense of loss, far beyond the straightforward demands of acting. Consciously or not, it is this emotion that informs almost every frame of the picture. His Falstaff is a man who refuses to acknowledge pain even when he receives a great deal less than his just deserts. That this Falstaff realises he will be mocked as a buffoon and a charlatan, that men of all sorts will take a pride in girding at him, that his plots and schemes will usually come to nothing, that he will resort to tricks, even dishonesty, to live, that he must go on and on, even when he senses there lies nothing ahead of him but rejection – how much of all this did Welles recognise in his own life as he played out the scenes?

A few years before Welles's death a gargantuan junket was held in Los Angeles in his honour. He had returned from exile in a Europe that had revered him to his own country which had rejected him. He believed at last he might take his place again in Hollywood. Today's, and yesterday's, megastars arrived for the banquet. Money was lavished on the proceedings. A first-class round-trip air ticket was offered to me and accommodation in the Beverly Wiltshire Hotel, but I was working in a play. Beatrice telephoned me. Studio heads had been there, she said, executive producers and money-men. Welles spoke brilliantly. The audience clapped frenziedly. There was the obligatory standing ovation. He described himself as the friendly neighbourhood cornershop competing with the giant supermarkets. Everyone laughed. He showed a clip from his latest film *The Other Side of the Wind;* rapturous applause. But it was unfinished. He needed money to complete it, but the film was never completed. The celebratory dinner cost a fortune.

In mid-October the filming of *Chimes at Midnight* begins. We assemble in Barcelona, ready to proceed to the location where we are to start shooting, and the first snag occurs. Welles has chosen a deserted monastery for the royal interiors, high on a hill near Andorra. There is a small hotel forty minutes away, just large enough to accommodate the actors as long as some of them agree to share. But the production department has forgotten it is a summer hotel, with no heating and the nights are already cold. Heaters will take a week to arrive and Gielgud's arrival is imminent.

"Change the schedule! We'll come back next week. Film Gielgud and Baxter and Beckley in the cloister in Barcelona. Change Gielgud's flight! Get Beckley off the ship."

Beckley is duly brought from the Hispaniola. He discards his Israel Hands costume (which he will never see again), puts on his Poins clothes, and we go straight to the location, an exquisite thirteenth-century pillared cloister on the edge of a lake. But the new schedule means we collide with a Festival. Crowds fill the cloisters and filming is not permitted.

"Wait a few days the crowds will be gone," they say.

Impossible to wait. Welles is too pushed for time. It is Friday, and Gielgud is due on Sunday, and can only stay three weeks before starting rehearsals in America for Edward Albee's new play, *Tiny Alice*. New orders are issued.

"Change the schedule! Back to Madrid. Shoot the battle scenes with Gielgud, and come back here later. Change Gielgud's flight! Everyone back to Madrid!"

Problems escalate, it seems with our every move. After driving all night, we arrive on Saturday morning ready for action, only to find there is a shortage of hotel rooms in Madrid. At such short notice it is impossible to find proper lodgings for the actors. But we are not entirely out of luck; behind the Welles's impressive apartment building in the Puerta de Hierro there is a modest block of flats. Welles has rented one of them, and has already installed his Moviolas and sound equipment in the reception room where he will eventually edit the picture. The rest of the apartment is deserted. No carpets. Nothing.

Energetically Paola Welles leaps at the chance of doing up a couple of rooms, and Norman Rodway (Hotspur) and I arrive at the same time as the furniture van. It would be difficult to find anyone more amiable than Norman, and we rattle around the empty rooms very happily together. But one could hardly ask Gielgud to do the same. And he was due to arrive next day.

"We'll find him something," said Welles.

More problems ensue. We discover there is no armour. The armour is not on schedule for another two weeks and so it is not ready. How can we shoot the battle scenes without armour? Especially the King; he, of all people, has to have armour.

"There must be *one* suit of armour in Madrid!" Welles says to the Wardrobe Supervisor who has flown in from Crouch End.

"Yes!" replies the wardrobe supervisor. "One!"

"Thank God."

"For a man of four foot six."

Gielgud is a six-footer.

"Fine," says Welles. "We'll stick it on a wooden clotheshorse outside his tent and no one will know it is for a midget."

"But what is Sir John to wear, Mr Welles?"

"Whatever we can find. And that goes for Mr Baxter too."

It is Saturday night.

At ten on Sunday morning Paola cooks breakfast for all the conspirators. Welles is about to drive to the countryside to choose a spot for Monday's shooting. I am to go and meet Gielgud's plane at Barajas Airport.

"We'll find something for you to wear when I get back. For Christ's sake don't tell him there are no costumes!"

Welles asks me to apologise to Gielgud for not meeting him. I am to keep him cheerful, to distract him, and take him to his hotel. When they find him an hotel, that is. When will that be? Welles has no idea. The producers have been on the telephone all morning, trying to pull strings. I have to apply delaying tactics until a room is found.

"What shall I do with him?" Give the photographers a free hand, suggest different set-ups for their shots. A reporter is also at hand who is told to ask a lot of questions. And afterwards?

"Take him to the Prado," says Norman.

"He'll have seen the Prado," Paola observes.

"Take him to a bullfight," says Prince Tasca.

"Are you mad?" Welles retorts.

"Afternoon tea of course," adds Mrs Rogers.

Gielgud's plane lands on time. The producer, Emiliano Piedra, and I are waiting on the tarmac as he comes down the steps.

"Hello Keith. How kind of you to meet me."

One of the reasons that Gielgud is so loved within the profession is that he has the sweetest manners possible. He is without malice; his famous gaffes are never aimed to hurt. He never grumbles. He is almost always bright and full of fun. Almost always. On this eventful day in Spain, however, he has a runny nose and is obviously tired. Behind him follows his companion, Martin, an extremely attractive Hungarian. Martin has a handkerchief pressed against his face. The photographers move forward to take a few shots.

"Would they think it very rude if I said that's enough?"

"He had stinker cold," says Martin. "Now he give it me."

"A few questions, senor Heehee –" began the reporter.

The Spanish have a problem pronouncing the letter 'g'. If you want ginger ale, you ask for Hinker Ali. 'Gielgud' foxed them.

"Geelglo," our producer corrects carefully.

"What you think of Madrid?"

"Oh please," said Sir John. "I'd rather not. I don't feel quite up to it."

The reporter has his pencil ready, a battery of questions as ordered, and notebook as thick as a telephone directory.

"Another time perhaps? I'm a little under the weather."

"I tell him not to come," says Martin gloomily, blowing his nose with force.

"I'd like just to go to my hotel," Sir John pleads.

"Tea first," I say firmly. "That'll buck you up."

We drive – very slowly – the long way into Madrid.

"Strange to be so far from the city," Sir John wonders, "it must be further out than Heathrow."

When we eventually crawl up the drive to the Hilton, he cheers up at once.

"I don't usually care for American Hotels outside America, but at least one can be sure the plumbing works. Do look at those mosaics Martin!"

Martin blows his nose.

We sit at a table in the lobby. In the background, by a bank of telephones, I can see Juan Cobos – an assistant director – shaking his head at me. He is in touch with Mrs Rogers who is to call him the minute she finds a room.

Sir John is already feeling better.

"What about a cake, John?"

"I am rather greedy. They're such gaudy little things."

He helps himself to two. Things are looking up.

"Now you will be sick," Martin says.

Gielgud has got it into his head that he is booked into the Hilton and is just sitting there while they prepare his room. I do nothing to disabuse him of this notion. He starts on his cake.

"Are the costumes pretty? It's such a charming period. When I did *Richard II* for the first time at the Old Vic, I had the robe that I'd seen Ernest Milton wear. Black velvet with an ermine collar. It looked so opulent from the front, but up close it was very shabby. The ermine was moth-eaten white rabbit and the black velvet was almost green with must. Michael Redgrave, when he played Bolingbroke with me, the Motleys did a magnificent job. What am *I* going to wear?"

I look at him despairingly.

The hotel manager, smiling effusively, advances across the lobby. He has no rooms to offer, the Hilton is packed, but he wants to pay his respects to the great actor, and besides he has a plan. Gielgud whispers to me as he drew near.

"Who is this man? Why does he smile? Do I know him?"

"I think it must be the manager."

"Is he taking us to our rooms?"

I giggle helplessly. The manager bowed.

"Senor Gluegill?"

Gielgud put down his cake. The manager beamed. He put one hand on Gielgud's shoulder and leaned forward conspiratorially.

"Come with me to the Sauna."

"I really – " begins Sir John faintly.

"I make two mattress. Plenty sheets and towels."

"What you talk?" says Martin through his handkerchief.

Quickly I explain that Sir John is not being propositioned, that the manager is merely trying to offer some accommodation.

"You mean," says John frostily, and who could blame him, "we've come all this way and there is no room for us!"

By a stroke of luck Cobos signals to me at this moment. A room has been found, and before John knows quite what is happening he, Martin and I get in the car and off we drive.

I would like to emphasise here, dear reader, that it says a great deal for Sir John that he never once complained, to the press or in private, about the manner of his arrival, or when things did not go too well for him later that night.

The magnificent palace built by Philip II at Escorial is in a village twenty-five miles northwest of Madrid. It was an easy hour's drive and Gielgud's innate buoyancy had recovered itself. I was happy to tell him that it was all for the best; he was staying close to the location. The hotel itself was comfortable and we went straight to the bar for a drink. I left the two of them, Martin and John, sitting happily together on a pair of bar stools, their luggage at their feet, and returned to inform Welles that all was accomplished and that Gielgud was in high spirits. Quarter of an hour after I left Escorial, there was a power failure, the elevator went out of service, and John and Martin had to carry their bags three flights upstairs while the porter tried to find the fuse. But none of this did I discover until next day.

Back in Welles's apartment a real feeling of excitement was in the air. Welles had found, he said, a splendid location for the first day's shoot. The King's camp was to be sited on top of a hill and the wagons and canvas and banners had already been unloaded.

"Now we must find you a costume."

Since we had no armour, we were to shoot the scenes as though we had been interrupted just before dressing for the battle. We had therefore to find a costume for me that would look like 'undress armour'. No one knew what that would be.

"Improvise!" said Welles gaily.

Norman handed me a drink. A dresser passed me a jockstrap. A wicker skip from the Samuel Bronston Studios stood open in the centre of the room filled with anything the wardrobe supervisor had thought might come in handy. Orson, drink in hand, pulled things from it like a Lucky Dip, chucking them across for me to try. In the end this is what I wore: knitted 'chain-mail' pants and a soldier's tunic from *El Cid;* over it a suede jerkin that Jayne Mansfield had worn in *The Sheriff of Fractured Jaw*, embroidered with piping from Stephen Boyd's horse's harness from *The Fall of the Roman Empire*.

It looked great.

Very early the next morning I was called to Welles's apartment. I was in my improvised costume. Welles was in cracking form, about to leave. He wanted me to go to Escorial while Gielgud dressed and stay with him until the car came to take us to the location. Gielgud was to do the first shot of the picture. Welles knew that most actors are nervous of their first moments in a film, so he hoped I would keep Gielgud cheerful while the shot was prepared. The moment Gielgud arrived, he would step in front of the camera and say: "How now, my lord of Worcester!" and the film would have begun.

They had tried to telephone Gielgud at the hotel to tell him that I was coming to bring him to the set, but they had been unable to get through. Welles collected his script and a box of cigars and said: "This is where the fun starts."

We left his apartment. In the elevator Welles lit a cigar. I reached to press the button to descend but he pushed my hand away.

"Do you think John will think me a fool?"

It had never occurred to me that Welles might be nervous.

"I'm in such awe of him you see. No actor can touch him in Shakespeare. I don't want him to think me just a trickster."

I had no idea what to say. He sighed and pressed the button, the lift started to descend, and then a thought struck me.

"What is John to wear?"

Orson cheered up.

"Find him something that he'll like."

At nine o'clock early-risen American tourists munching croissants at the hotel looked up in surprise as I, dressed as the Prince of Wales, strolled past them purposefully.

Gielgud was in his room, sitting on his bed in a silk dressing-gown, looking miserable.

"It's been a dreadful night. All the lights went out. We had to carry our bags upstairs. Martin's feeling rotten. Rather a poky room."

It *was* a poky room.

Martin, smoking furiously and gulping down black coffee growled through his cold.

"The telephone, she don't work."

"Yes. Orson tried to reach you."

"Is lousy place."

Sir John had stopped listening. He was studying my costume.

"I must say Keith, you look very larky!"

I explained that he would be in the first shot, that we would be called as soon as Welles was ready, and that he just had to say one line to Worcester.

"But that's in the Battle. Shouldn't we be in armour?"

Taking a deep breath, thinking on my feet, I said Welles was convinced that full armour deadens an actor's performance and destroys the individuality of the character. It would be more interesting to shoot in costumes that were 'undress-armour', but robust. Gielgud swallowed it whole.

"He's so brilliant. What shall *I* wear?"

A knock at the door, and the wardrobe supervisor appeared, a Scotsman who later fashioned an ingenious mask for me in *Sleuth*. Talented and painstaking as he was, it has to be said that he was also dour. He dragged a knotted dirty sheet behind him, untied the bundle, and said, "That's it."

Gielgud stared, unbelieving, at the wrinkled jumble at his feet.

"We go home," said Martin.

Using his fingers as tongs Gielgud extracted a pair of tights from the ragbag, studying them with alarm. They drooped, concertina-like, from his hand. I was talking wildly, praising the innovative genius of Welles, when Gielgud spied a tunic and poked it gingerly, a glimmer of hope in his eye.

"Such a rich colour!"

"Is black-and-white movie," said Martin.

"Try it on, John," I urged.

"I might as well. It's what I'm here for after all. I'd better take these tights."

He went to the bathroom, chattering all the while.

"These tights are a bit smelly. Maybe it's just mildew. Shall I catch something from them? I've never had Spanish Fly and I don't want Spanish Crabs. I've always had good legs. Larry's are spindly, but he has hair. How do I look?"

He came out, buckling his tunic. Like all actors he had begun to psych himself into his work.

"You look great John. Wonderful legs."

"I'm the Dorothy Ward of drama. Dorothy Ward has wonderful legs. The best Principal Boy I ever saw. These buckles are very fiddly. I know all my lines. Marvellous part. So kind of Orson to ask me. Will he think me old hat? He's so brilliant and I'm an old warhorse. I want to make Bolingbroke monkish. Will he agree? An old wicked monster, clutching the crown with bony hands. Shall I wear the crown? I look good in a crown."

"The crown hasn't arrived from London yet."

"What about a cloak? A large cloak. Ah, there's a good one!"

He pulled out a cloak and, with the practice of years, spread it across his shoulders, studying the effect in the mirror. Majesty was growing on him every second.

"Maybe a big brooch? What do you think?"

"I'm sure they can find a brooch."

A waiter knocked at the door. The car was waiting for us. As we moved through the lobby the American tourists boggled.

It was a magnificent morning, brisk and sunny, and the car sped through a wild, deserted landscape. Suddenly Gielgud gripped Martin's arm.

"Look Martin! The flags!"

In the distance, on the crest of a hill stood a row of tents. Behind them, against clouds scudding through the blue sky, was a line of banners, all cracking in the wind.

A grin lit up Martin's handsome face.

"Beautiful!"

We arrived at a farm gate and got out of the car. Some mules were tethered nearby, and an assistant director asked Gielgud if he would like to ride a mule up the hill.

"Certainly not. They bite."

Gielgud set off at a brisk pace. Martin and I followed. Soon we found ourselves in a cornfield. The crop had been reaped and we picked our way through the stubble. On the skyline Welles stood waiting, his black coat billowing around him. He opened his arms wide and roared a welcome.

"John!!!"

Gielgud, smiling shyly, stood amongst the corn stalks.

"Hello Orson. I feel just like Ruth."

❖

When actors speak of bad experiences with directors, or when directors describe actors as difficult, it is because the trust that should be between them has broken down. I am always being asked what it was like to be directed by Welles, but I have never been able to give specific details, or indeed recall a single instance of his shaping any of the actors' performances. This is not to say we were not directed. His inimitable imprint is stamped across our work. It is simply that he created such a relaxed atmosphere. The actors put themselves unreservedly into his hands, accepting quickly his vision of the scenes.

After Gielgud went to New York he wrote to me to say how grateful he was to Welles for having made him feel so at ease. I believe it was the first time Gielgud allowed himself to be persuaded that he actually had something very exciting to offer to the cinema. Now that we have become accustomed to seeing many fine Gielgud performances on the screen, it is difficult to believe that there was a time when he lacked confidence before the camera. Over the years he had convinced himself that his style was not suited to the screen.

In his autobiography, *Early Stages,* he virtually admits as much when he writes of his work in films in the Thirties. His great rival, Olivier, did nothing to encourage him. When Olivier was casting his *Henry V* film, Gielgud wanted to play the Chorus. Olivier pooh-poohed the idea. The cinema, he said, was not for Gielgud, though he could play the tiny part of the King of France if he wished.

Welles, however, did encourage Gielgud to use his imagination as freely as he might if he had been playing Henry IV in the theatre. This was a tremendous psychological release to Gielgud, who chattered away with suggestions to Welles all the time. It was not a question of whether Welles used Gielgud's ideas that mattered – sometimes he did not, but sometimes he did – it was the fact that Gielgud's creative juices had not been fully stimulated until then. Welles knew that Gielgud's innate taste and instinct would discipline his talent and that he would adapt his performance to the less familiar medium. Nothing was more moving than seeing these two extraordinary men working in tandem so happily together, laughing unrestrainedly, so full of respect for each other, especially after they had both been so nervous of not coming up to each other's expectations. No wonder that Gielgud, in his letter to me from New York, wrote: "Oh! I do miss Orson's brilliance and all the fun!"

It was the same for everyone. Welles took great pains to smash any idea that there was some mystique about acting for the camera. He never postured as The Great Director. The atmosphere on the set was always light-hearted. Everyone was encouraged to see the rushes of the previous day's filming as soon as they came back from the laboratory. These screenings in some local flea-bitten cinema were happy occasions, with a great deal of good-natured heckling and laughter. No one laughed louder at a miffed performance than Welles would at his own. The result of all this was that the actors gave themselves to him unstintingly. At the height of her fame, after making *Jules et Jim,* Jeanne Moreau came for a week to play the small part of Doll Tearsheet. A journalist asked her why she had bothered to fit it into her crowded schedule. She looked at him, puzzled.

"Orson Welles asked me," she said.

Margaret Rutherford, playing Mistress Quickly, summed it all up very well. She was huddled under a hawthorn bush against the bitter November chill when Welles sent me over to her with some coffee laced with brandy.

"Are you cold?" I asked.

"On no!" She shook her head. "Working with him is like walking where there's always sunshine."

He worked fast. Compared with other directors he was Speedy Gonzales. We shot without proper sound equipment which meant that every word would have to be dubbed into the film in recording studios and, of course, this would create technical problems; but we were able to shoot in locations of total authenticity. No studio set could reproduce the patina of that massive medieval throne-room, or the reality of its coldness, so that even indoors, when the characters addressed each other, their breath steamed in the icy air. When we worked outside and the shot was finished, Welles would march off carrying a viewfinder, calling: "Follow me!" The camera crew would leave their equipment to run after him while the actors lay around on the grass. After a few minutes there would be shouts and we dutifully assembled at the next spot Welles had chosen.

Quite often he decided to rehearse on camera, filming as soon as the actors were in place and lit, and the dialogue was fresh and unforced. When the time came to shoot Gielgud's 'Uneasy lies the head that wears a crown' soliloquy, Welles led him to a tall, barred window and showed him where the light would strike his face and catch his eyes. This was shot simultaneously on two cameras, one in close-up and the other in a longer shot. Gielgud did the speech thrillingly, without rehearsal, the first take. The Spanish technicians and crew applauded. They had never heard a film actor speak at such length without interruption. John grinned at them.

"I said all the words in the right order!"

A second take was filmed in case the first was flawed, for by the time it had been processed in the laboratories Gielgud would be in New York, unable to return.

There were no flaws. The first take was used.

When Welles came to shoot Mistress Quickly's account of Falstaff's death, he asked Margaret Rutherford where she wanted to sit.

"On this step perhaps? With the coffin over there."

She agreed it was the perfect choice. While they were lighting her I went to get a beer, and by the time I returned the scene was filmed and I had missed seeing it. Welles's confidence in his actors spread like a benediction over the company. Scenes were rehearsed when camera movements were complete, or if many actors were involved, or if Welles planned a particularly long take. He wanted, for example, to shoot the whole sequence with Justice Shallow, when Pistol brings the news that Hal is to be crowned King, as one uninterrupted scene. Three days were spent rehearsing meticulously and it was indeed shot in one take lasting over five minutes. If he was not satisfied he would shoot until he was.

"Time is precious" Welles declared. "Film I can waste."

One day Welles talked of the Seven Deadly Sins. He believed that all of us are susceptible to one Sin above the other six. I thought I might guess his own particular vice but I was wrong. "Sloth" he said. Yet there was nothing sluggish about him at work. Sometimes this rapid pace was necessary because he had the actors for such a short time: Gielgud for three weeks; Moreau for one; Rutherford for four.

On his last day Gielgud finally got to do some of his battle close-ups. His armour was still not available but a breastplate was found in an antique shop in Barcelona, and an ill-fitting helmet. This is why in the film you only see the helmet at the moment Gielgud pulls it from his head.

A horse was brought. Gielgud looked at it with suspicion – he does not care for horses, so he mounted carefully. It was a very old horse; out of camera shot a man held the poor old nag by the bridle. A slight breeze ruffled Gielgud's hair.

"Look to the right John. Now to the left."

"Bear Worcester to the death!" cried Gielgud.

The horse munched some hay and yawned.

"Look furious John!"

The horse quietly regurgitated out of shot.

"Have a heart attack John!"

Gielgud drooped over the horse's mane and the ostler, unseen, jerked the old pair, the King and his beast forward.

"That's it John. Off to New York with you!"

Everyone applauded, and Sir John said goodbye.

When the rest of the shots that surround this scene were added, they create a montage of amazing tension as Henry IV orders Worcester's execution, dismisses his son's valour, collapses on his horse, and rides away at the head of his troops. But those additional shots were filmed in Madrid, three hundred miles away six months later, and by then Gielgud was appearing eight times a week on Broadway.

Gielgud's terror of horses was shared by Norman Rodway who was playing Hotspur. Since Hotspur had to be seen in full armour, it was possible to use a double, except for the one moment when he had to pull off his helmet to make his challenge: "If I mistake not, thou art Harry Monmouth!"

The close-up was achieved by seating Norman, dressed from the waist up, on the shoulders of two sturdy extras who jiggled him as he spoke while the camera shook with Welles's laughter.

When it came to the use of doubles Welles's audacity was no more remarkable than one might expect from a man who had mastered magic at an early age with some help from Houdini. During the war, Welles had performed a magic act sawing up Marlene Dietrich before the troops at the Stage-Door canteen, Los Angeles. The gifted illusionist knows how to make his audience see only what he wants them to see. Every time Gielgud is seen in long shot, it is a double. Every time Walter Chiari (Justice Silence) is seen in long shot it is a double (me in Walter's costume). Every time Margaret Rutherford is seen in long shot it is the male assistant director in her clothes.

No one has ever noticed. Nor have they spotted that in one quick shot, when Hal is riding to his Coronation, the crowd is mostly cardboard-cutouts with bits of material attached to blow in the wind.

My horse was a handsome chestnut of amiable disposition, but with one particular quirk. His equanimity was disturbed if he was placed alongside a mule or a crossbreed. To be blunt, he had an erection.

This was a source of great amusement to the crew. Between sequences in the battle sequence, when it was simpler to stay in the saddle, if I was not paying attention the crew would persuade some innocent extra to lead a mule behind me and tether it near my horse. It is a strange sensation sitting on a horse when it is sexually aroused. It gave me no pleasure, though I cannot speak for the horse.

Welles's gift for improvisation was stimulating. We were in Madrid, filming battle sequences in the Casa de Campo, a big park – some four thousand acres – on the west of the city. The weather was good and Welles wanted to film the trees while they were still in leaf, indeed to catch the leaves as they fell. We finished a shot and suddenly he strode off out of sight. An assistant came racing back screaming, "Senor Beckley! Where is Senor Beckley?" He turned to me. "Senor Welles say you put on your grey dress!"

I cast off my armour and was pushed and pulled into my grey velvet court costume while a taxi raced to get Tony Beckley, playing Poins. Remember, we had not been able to pick up the shot planned for that lakeside cloister, and there was no chance now of going back to Barcelona. Welles always thought there should be water in the scene, perhaps a shot of Hal and Poins on a boat drifting through a meadow, something to catch the melancholy of Hal's mood. Now, here in the middle of Madrid shooting battle sequences, Welles had wandered away to find the next angle when he came across a pond. We had all seen it countless times. It was an ugly pond, about two feet deep for children's sailboats, and the cars drove past non-stop. But it was an early morning in November, and though you could still hear the cars, they were shrouded from view by a thick mist over the water giving the whole scene an eerie greyness. Beckley and I sat on a parapet with the misty water behind us and shot the scene in five minutes. The steady drone of the cars never ceased. By the time the camera moved to shoot the reverses the mist had lifted, and the whole ugliness of the place was revealed, but not to the camera.

When it rained we had a cover set. Mistress Quickly's tavern (alias the Admiral Benbow Inn), brilliantly designed by Welles and Jose Antonio de la Guerra, was erected in a warehouse in one of the poorest quarters of Madrid. It was an amazing set with many different levels and steps, a huge fireplace, and a flagged floor.

In a touching 'homage' to Welles, the director of the cult nineties film, *My Own Private Idaho,* uses a series of shots in a set exactly like the tavern in *Chimes at Midnight,* showing the Falstaff character dressed in a replica of Welles's costume, and a dog running past the camera as it does in *Chimes*. To the best of my knowledge, these references were not spotted by a single critic.

On the evening before shooting in the tavern began, people were invited to come and watch. Omar Sharif was in Madrid to start *Doctor Zhivago* and he came too. Jeanne Moreau had just flown in from Paris and Welles brought her along. There was wine and a table of tapas, and everyone was handed a hammer, or a blow-torch, or a bucket of dirty paint and told to 'distress' the place. We set to with a will.

There were no dressing rooms, and room for only one 'star' caravan in the yard. Although this had been allocated to Jeanne in compliance with her contract, she insisted Margaret Rutherford should occupy it – and insisted, too, that Margaret should never know. I dressed in a house outside the yard where I could catnap between shots. There were five children in this house, and sometimes I would wake to find them standing in the doorway staring solemnly at me, the baby in the elder brother's arms. Their mother brought me soup, and I played Snap with them, and let the black-haired baby stroke the coloured glass on my sleeves. Jeanne sang them the song from *Jules et Jim*.

Outside Margaret's caravan the afternoon sun warmed a patch by the steps. Margaret sat there between shots with a woolly cardigan round her shoulders while her husband, Stringer Davies, read to her, poetry and Chaplin's autobiography. Margaret held Stringer's hand as he read. She was no fool. She was aware that her looks made people laugh, but she never thought of herself as a clown. If you bothered to observe her, you noticed at once her aching femininity. They had met, Stringer Davis and she, in an air raid during the Blitz.

"I was a War Bride," she said tenderly and proudly.

We moved to Avila to shoot against the city walls, like the walls of old London. I rode on my horse and waved to Welles: "Farewell, all-Hallown summer!" and turned to confront the winter of the King's death.

Eventually, Margaret left. Then Jeanne went too, and then the cold set in.

Not far from Avila there is a mediaeval village where cobbled streets straggle up a hill. There were no television aerials then. The people who lived there, farmers mostly, eked out a meagre existence tilling unfertile soil. Centuries had come and gone without leaving their mark. Villagers were content to earn a few pesetas as film extras; the men marching off to war as soldiers, the women leaning from the windows waving farewell. Their workaday clothes were so simple they hardly needed costuming. Many of the houses had stables at ground level, and donkeys and cattle lived with the people in their front rooms.

At dawn the location canteen arrived, bringing hot coffee and rolls. Welles had kept me on a strict diet. No carbohydrates, but if I arrived very early, before he did, I could steal bread and cheese and hide them in my saddle cloth. As I rode through the village in costume it was an eerie sensation clip-clopping up the cobbled street in the half-light as the village came to life, people tending animals, fetching pails of water. The street opened onto a plateau overlooking a bare plain which stretched into the distance. My driver once told me that the Christian kings had fought a great battle there against the Moors. The plain had been drenched with blood and now nothing would grow there, he said: "Ni siquiera el amor," not even love. But I was drawn to the place. It fascinated me, though one morning, as I sat there watching the sun rise, the wind from the plain below sang wildly in my ears, tugging me to the very lip of the precipice. For a moment I was gripped by a feeling of menace so overwhelming that I jerked the reins, pulled my horse round and cantered safely back to the braziers set up outside the church.

Then we moved north to Soria to find snow. Hilton Edwards, arriving to play Justice Silence, was already exhausted by his flight from Dublin and the long drive to the location. Alan Webb arrived the same day from London, to play Justice Shallow. Welles was staying in Logroño but motored over to welcome his old friends, bringing bottles of Tequila. He passed them round as he watched Edwards and Webb check into their rooms. We all went down to the little hotel bar to celebrate their arrival. More bottles of Tequila were ordered. Tequila was not a drink familiar to many of us in those days but Welles had developed a fondness for it in Mexico years before, and now suddenly had a hankering for it. In honour of Hilton and Alan it was to be 'a Tequila festival'. Andrew Faulds – soon to be a Labour Member of parliament – and Prince Tasca also joined us. Lemons were brought in, plus whole canisters of salt and we all learned the Tequila ritual.

The hotel was small and the bar, a little below street level, had one window opening onto the street. While we were drinking a storm was gathering outside. Whether it was the drink, or the exuberant expressions of friendship, or simply that the heating had been turned up against the cold outside – or a combination of all three – the little room soon became stifling. Lulled into inactivity by the heat, conversation petered out, and we sat slumped like discarded rag dolls, in a mess of spilled salt and sucked lemon-quarters. Suddenly Welles stood up, eyes staring.

"Air!" he gasped. "I must have air!"

He lurched through us all towards the little window, but it had not been opened for years and was stuck. Frantically he pushed at it. He seemed especially huge in the tiny room, pounding at the window like Kane smashing the room at Xanadu. At last the window flew up, and at that very moment the storm broke. Thunder reverberated through the street, rolling over the hotel, shaking it. Every light went out, plunging us into darkness. As Welles staggered back from the open window like a giant, arms flailing through the air, a lightning flash lit him surreally. There was another crescendo of thunder and Welles fell headlong to the floor and lay inert. Tasca and I rushed to him. The lights flickered and came on again, as the storm withdrew, but outside the rain was lashing down. Suddenly, Welles sat up like a jack-in-the-box. I offered him my room and said I would move in with Alan for the night but he refused. No, he would go back to Logroño. A final distant roll of thunder and Welles walked out into the rain, his jacket whitened with salt, smelling of lemons. We stood silent, watching him get into his car. Alan turned to me wide-eyed.

"Is it like this every night?"

Next day, we were filming in a village in the Basque country, not far away. Welles arrived in good spirits. It had been a liver attack he said. He was fully recovered, but had decided to go on a strict diet. This was especially disappointing for him, since the local taverna had such an excellent kitchen. Welles had ordered a wonderful meal for the company: baby eels and sea bass.

"All I shall eat" he said sadly, "is boiled chicken."

And so he did. He ate boiled chicken. Five of them.

We moved further north to the next location in the heart of the Basque country. The snow was knee-deep in the fields and Welles was delighted. He wanted snow for the Prologue, as the three old men – Falstaff, Shallow, and Silence – tottered across a winter landscape talking of the days that they had seen. But Hilton Edwards had a bad cold and it was worsening. He begged Welles to release him from the picture and Welles agreed at once. Certainly he needed Edwards badly for the sequence, but now he had to shoot it with only Alan Webb in case the snow melted before Hilton's replacement could be found. Imperative to find someone quickly; without a Justice Silence shooting would have to stop. It was the weekend. Welles needed someone by Monday. Undismayed he announced: "Let's go to Pamplona."

Cheered by the knowledge that there was a good hotel in Pamplona with a superb restaurant – and, most importantly, a telephone with direct dialling to London, we crowded into cars: Welles, Mrs Rogers, Alan Webb, Michael Aldridge (Pistol), and I, and set off. Welles took a suite. Mrs Rogers had a list of actors and agents but no one seemed to be at home in England.

"This is ridiculous!" scowled Welles. "What we need is *one* contact in London who can do the telephoning for us. An agent."

But it was Saturday and all the agents' offices were closed. Alan Webb suggested John Perry, a director of H. M. Tennent. We called Perry's house in the country; we called him at his London home. A servant answered. Mr Perry was at the theatre. H. M. Tennent was presenting Dietrich at the Queen's Theatre and it was her last night. Welles perked up.

"Marlene's a friend of mine. She'll get us an actor. Call the theatre!"

He got her on the line backstage at the interval. She was speaking from the Stage Manager's desk and promised to arrange everything.

"Call me in two hours."

"I love you Marlene!"

"I love you Orson! Listen, can you hear the applause?"

At ease again Welles turned to us, his loyal band of followers, and said: "Let's eat." We had a gargantuan meal.

Two hours later as good as her word, Dietrich was on the phone with John Perry and by midnight we had an actor. Welles spoke to the actor; Michael Aldridge, who knew him, took the telephone and put his ha'p'orth in to reassure him. Our new-found actor had to fly to Paris the next morning, then take the overnight train to the border. He would be met and driven to the location. But since it was already Sunday and all the banks were closed, there was no way of telegraphing tickets or fare; so the actor would have to pay his own way and be reimbursed when he arrived. With that settled, and knowing that he would not arrive until Monday, there was nothing to do but wait.

On Sunday we ate a lazy lunch at another splendid Basque restaurant that Welles had found in a forest.

Monday came. No actor arrived. He had called his agent. The agent told him not to leave without a written contract. Cautious advice; obviously sensible, but it cost him the job.

Welles telephoned Paola in Rome, where she was on a visit to her family.

"What about Walter Chiari?" she suggested.

Chiari, an immensely gifted actor, a huge star in Italy said he would come at once. There were no direct flights from Rome, so he would fly to Bordeaux and take the train to Hendaye. The platform at the station crossed the border; one end in France at Hendaye, and the other end in Spain at Irun. Passengers travelling between the two countries had to walk the length of the platform with their luggage and their passports. We travelled to Irun to wait for Walter's arrival on Tuesday. I took my passport and elected to go along the platform and wait in Hendaye as his train came in. Prince Tasca offered to accompany me. He did not have his passport with him but he was after all an aristocrat, and the customs officials were merely petits bourgeois, so they would wave him through. Welles bet him a magnum of Krug he would never get across the platform.

Next morning, an adroit mixture of hauteur and swift talk took Tasca past the Spanish police. Twenty yards further the French gendarmes were stony-faced.

"Non. Absolument pas." Monsieur had no passport.

He explained that he was a high executive working for Orson Welles. They did not budge.

"Mais je suis le Prince Tasca!"

They looked at the Prince, they looked at the unshaven face, they took in the battered Homburg and the shapeless gabardine. They asked for a document of any kind to prove his identity. Tasca produced a card. It was torn and crumpled. It identified him as a clerk at the Aqueduct race-track.

"Non. Absolument pas!"

That night we dined in splendour just down the coast in the old port of San Sebastian and drank Walter's health in Tasca's champagne.

A week later location shooting was finished. One by one, the actors finished their roles and began leaving to go home.

There were still long chunks of scenes to be completed which needed only Falstaff and Prince Hal.

By now rumours were flying around that the film had run out of money and in late December it was announced that the picture would shut down for Christmas. I was alarmed, but Welles explained that, by closing the picture, all contracts for the crew would be terminated. He could start again in January, with a much smaller crew. He begged me not to go back to England and I spent Christmas with Welles and his family. On Christmas Eve Paola produced all the tree ornaments she had made over the years; little figures made with great skill, representing fairy-tale characters. On an upper branch, the princess's long golden hair reached down to a lower branch where Rumpelstiltskin lurked. On another Alice hid from the Queen of Hearts. Paola's ninety-year-old grandmother sat by the fire, chasing a mince pie round her solitary tooth while Beatrice and Welles decorated the huge tree. Paola and I made knock-out cocktails in the kitchen. She tried to hide a sweater she was knitting for me.

As Christmas scenes go it was ordinary enough, but since Welles's death the biographies have been coming thick and fast, and in none of them is Welles pictured in the tranquil domestic surroundings to which I bore witness, and that Paola so lovingly created for him.

January soon came and the Moviolas installed down the corridor from my bedroom were switched on. As it happened, I had been alone in the flat for some time. Norman Rodway had left weeks earlier. Fritz Mueller came from Switzerland to work with Welles on the editing. I wandered to my room through festoons of film, and would wake to the sound of my voice booming out at Gielgud, or Welles shouting to one of his young assistants. As always, it was thrilling to watch him work. I had never been in a cutting room before and Welles encouraged me to wander in and out as I pleased. This was another unique facet of his character – he never showed off in the cutting room either as "the Director".

There have been many tales told of the cruelly manipulative behaviour of David Lean, John Huston, Otto Preminger – and other directors of infinitely less talent – during the course of making their films. Perhaps this need to demonstrate authority, by instilling fear on the set, is triggered by some terrible emotional insecurity within themselves. Welles was immune to the virus of that kind of insecurity and never needed to practise intimidation to demonstrate his skill. He never pretended there was something remarkable about the way he put his films together. He worked with a furious energy, but the atmosphere on set was always calm and happy. Laughter echoed round the camera. Since I had had so little experience of working in films, I assumed the way we worked on *Chimes at Midnight* was the norm. As the years went by, and I stood on sound stages on both sides of the Atlantic watching directors of minimal talent flexing their authority, posturing arrogantly in front of the unit, my mind has often returned to Welles. By any standard, he was the greatest director with whom I ever worked; he was, by leagues, the least affected, the most open. And, aside from his great talent, that was the most remarkable thing about him.

As soon as there was more money, Welles resumed shooting at the Casa de Campo. One hundred and fifty horsemen were called, and filmed galloping in armour, charging with lowered lances, banners streaming. By skilful editing, and reversing the negative, Welles was able to give the impression of thousands: a commonplace process in these days of digital enhancement, but much more difficult to achieve thirty years ago. Weather permitting Welles rushed to a field to film the short sequences that he would add to the battle montage, already worked out in his mind. He was using a very small unit now, which pleased him, just three around the camera and three more crew, and perhaps a dozen extras. He shot sequences of men fighting, men struggling, men falling, men writhing in death agony, men lost in a sea of mud. An accumulated sense of dread is created. There are no sustained scenes of butchery, hardly a shot of detailed violence, yet by brilliant editing, the shots coming so sharply one after another, interspersed with scenes of poetic grandeur – the duel between Hotspur and Prince Hal is presented as a tragic idyll, set apart from the main horror of the battle – it is far more affecting than if Welles had resorted to precise shots of brutality and slaughter.

The battle sequence in *Chimes at Midnight* has been acclaimed as the definitive film interpretation of a mediaeval battle. (One can see its influence in the Agincourt sequence in Kenneth Branagh's *Henry V.*) It would have been extraordinary enough if Welles had had access to limitless resources; that he accomplished it on a shoestring is a cinematic miracle.

Luckily, I was on salary and could idle my days away until we were ready to shoot my Coronation. Life in Madrid was very cheap in those days and £150 a week was a fortune. I sent oysters by the bucketful to Welles and rosetrees in tubs to Paola. I mooched around the city and explored the Prado, leisurely allotting myself the luxury of one week to see the Goyas, another for the Velasquez, another for Hieronymus Bosch. I went to Toledo nearby.

To kill more time I went riding, with Beatrice on her new pony, Zarco. I saw boisterous operettas. I sat in a grand restaurant, La Puerta de Moros, eating caviar by myself and sending champagne to the pianist. I was bored to distraction, except on Sundays.

On Sunday afternoons I went to the bullfights. The season was over. The star matadors were in Mexico for the winter, earning big money in the huge rings there, but in the small rings in the countryside around Madrid, the novices were putting themselves through their paces. In Alcala de Henares one bleak afternoon I watched a brilliant novillero, Aurelio Nunez, bring the little town to its feet.

This obsession had been a long time growing inside me. At first I had gone to the Plaza de Toros in Madrid only to fill an afternoon. Like many newcomers, I found it sickening; the gushing blood, the baying crowd, the extravagant narcissism of the toreros, and an English tourist next to me was sick all over her sandals. I knew Welles was an aficionado, but he never tried to convert me. When I murmured my disapproval he merely shrugged. What point was there in trying to persuade someone who had a deep-rooted prejudice against it? The blood was part of the ritual. Ferocity was bred into the soul of Spain. The bull had to die. It was like a play Welles said, rigidly structured. The First Act, the picadors; the Second Act, bandilleros; the Third Act, the death.

"How could there be a production of *Julius Caesar* without Caesar's death?"

At the time we were lunching with our producer, Emiliano Piedra.

"He's right," said Emiliano, "Caesar has to die."

"But an actor isn't killed every performance!"

"Ah," sighed Emiliano "if only..."

In the parks boys practised veronicas with improvised capes, swinging them in a graceful arc as their friends with bicycle handlebars, pretending to be young fighting bulls, charged past grazing their thighs. By chance I stumbled into a small club, El Duende, in an alley behind the Plaza Mayor. The air swirled with pungent tobacco smoke. Toreros who had fought that day were drinking with their managers and girls, shouting across the tables to one another. Andalusian gypsy women danced with their partners to passionate flamenco music, and the toreros, clapping in staccato accompaniment, cried out their encouragement. I was hypnotised.

Next morning I described the bar to Welles. He laughed.

"No one finds El Duende by accident. You were led there by a spirit-guide."

From then on I accompanied him to the fights.

Welles was welcomed by toreros and their managers as a compadre, sitting alongside them at the barrier. As a young man he had himself fought in small rings in the South. An elderly bandillero who worked with the legendary Antonio Ordonez claimed to have seen the teenage Welles in action in a small town outside Seville. Welles had fought with courage, but without style he said. Nevertheless, it was something for which Ernest Hemingway never forgave him, that Welles had actually fought in the ring, and he, Hemingway, had not.

I had never been taken by Hemingway's writing, his style seemed affected to me. Welles defended him fiercely, and gave me a copy of Hemingway's short stories for Christmas. His admiration for Hemingway had never been reciprocated, but Welles dismissed the older man's jealousy with affection. Welles particularly enjoyed telling the story of their fistfight in 1937. Welles was asked to narrate a documentary about the Spanish Civil War. Hemingway wrote the script and wanted to record it himself. The studio found Hemingway's voice squeaky, oddly effeminate and so, to Hemingway's fury, Welles the wunderkind was hired. On the first day in the studio an operator started the projection, with Hemingway glowering in the shadows, while Welles began reading the commentary. Hemingway shouted "Every time he says the word 'infantry' it sounds like a cocksucker swallowing." Welles asked if Hemingway was speaking from experience, and before anyone could prevent them, the two men were hurling blows at each other in front of the screen as the images of war flickered over them.

Often we ate in a quiet restaurant El Callejon, also popular with the bullfighters. Hemingway, Welles said, had liked it too, and there was a signed photograph of him amongst the other pictures on the wall. One night, as I went to pay the bill, a Frenchwoman beckoned me. She asked if it was Hemingway I was having dinner with.

"Ernest Hemingway is dead madame. He died four years ago."

She looked again at Welles.

"I was thinking how well he looked."

I went to Morocco and idled my days away until the producers found more money and we could resume shooting; close-ups, bits and pieces, inserts of dialogue between Falstaff and Hal, all for scenes we had finished months earlier. We finally shot the Coronation scene and Welles took infinite pains to help me, acting with heart-breaking simplicity off-camera. Then more inserts for the battle sequence. By now it was early spring and the days were sunny and cloudless.

Driving to work one morning Welles was in thoughtful mood. He had been working hard in the editing room. Four-fifths of the picture had been assembled in a rough-cut.

"The film is so bleak," he said. There was no pastoral, unhurried, summery scene in it. It was not how he had imagined it a year ago. He looked out of the window. We passed a magnificent tree standing by itself in a field. It was covered in blossom, and as we turned down a lane he ordered: "Stop the car!"

We got out where the hedgerows were in bloom. Instantly Welles decided to add a sequence. He would shoot Falstaff and Prince Hal riding down the lane before the robbery scene. The sequence would be shot 'day-for-night': filmed in sunshine to appear as moonlight, a quiet lyrical scene as the two men ambled along on horseback, with Falstaff setting out his plan.

"Let us be Diana's foresters, gentlemen of the shade,
minions of the moon..."

It was a long speech and a complicated one, which Welles had not learned. I had no lines and all I had to do was amble happily alongside him on my horse.

We found the crew. Welles cancelled the scheduled shot and we went back to the lane. Welles believed Falstaff should have a horse that matched his bulk. An enormous carthorse was brought from a farm – the nearest thing to a shire horse Madrid could supply. The creature was tethered nearby while the camera was mounted on a dolly. Welles did not want to mount the horse while he rehearsed.

The plan was for a simple shot, riding towards the camera, which would retreat as we drew near. To rehearse it, Welles walked beside my horse as I rode. Crouching below the camera a script-boy had Falstaff's lines written on large boards, which he had to shuffle as Welles proceeded through the speech.

All did not go smoothly.

Welles was attempting the impossible, a Falstaffian expansiveness, while at the same time focussing on the boy walking backwards under the camera. The boy was Spanish; he did not read English and sometimes the boards came out in the wrong order. Sometimes the boy's back nudged the camera into a hedge.

Up and down the lane we went, never getting out of the mess. The sun had risen and Welles's temper rose with it. It was going to be a hot morning.

In desperation Welles had another idea. Since we were shooting without direct sound he would have – as well as the boy with the boards – someone to shout the words *one line ahead of him* out of shot.

So Mickey Knox, a young American dialogue coach, was handed a Shakespeare and instructed to walk backwards shouting the lines behind the hedge. With renewed confidence, another rehearsal was attempted. The camera moved backwards, the boy moved backwards, and behind the hedge a shouting Mickey Knox moved backwards too. Occasionally a red-faced Welles would interrupt with a "can't hear," followed by a "too loud," but all in all it was the best we could manage.

"Let's shoot the damn thing" shouted Welles.

Knox took a surreptitious slug of brandy, the boy with the placards was trembling, and Welles, in a bad temper, pulled on his costume. He called for everyone's attention.

"I'm going to do this goddamned shot in one take. Just keep the camera rolling as we walk up the lane. If I screw up a line, I'll repeat it. I'll shoot cutaway shots of blossom later to cover any mistake. Where's my horse?"

He mounted with difficulty. A most fastidious man, his movements were always delicate and precise, and he hated to be reminded of his bulk. He was aware that he cut a foolish figure as he struggled to get his foot into a stirrup. Three men were under his rump to hoist him up. If he had ever filmed it – 'Falstaff mounting his horse' – he would have enjoyed his clumsiness. But this was simply fat Orson Welles, whose girth was a source of jokes behind his back.

"Action!!"

We moved slowly forward.

"'Let us be Diana's fo –'"

"Shut up Knox! For God's sake, I know this bit! 'Let us be Diana's foresters, gentlemen of the – of the –' What is it –?"

"'Gentlemen of the shades!'"

"I can't bloody hear you!"

"'GENTLEMEN OF THE SHADES!'" yelled Knox, stumbling back.

"'Gentlemen of the shades.' Look at that fool, dropping those cards – Line Mickey! Line!"

"'Minions of the moon!'" called Knox, climbing out of a ditch.

"'Minions of the moon; and let men say we be men of good government, being governed as the sea is...'"

Then it was my turn. During the rehearsals my horse had behaved beautifully, but it had never met Falstaff's horse. Now, as this strange animal lumbered close alongside, the old sexual sap began to rise. Whinnying softly, my horse nuzzled and pushed at Welles's horse.

"What are you doing Keith, for God's sake!"

Welles's carthorse – and who can blame it? – had had enough. Confronted by madness, disturbed by the shouting, sexually intimidated, with a fat man bouncing on its back, it did what any sensible self-respecting beast would do. It ran for its life. Turning its back on the camera, it took off down the lane, out of sight, with Welles bobbing up and down helplessly.

The scene was abandoned. It was never referred to again.

The truth is, Orson's heart had never really been in it from the start. Had it gone like clockwork, had he known the lines, had the sequence acquired all the sylvan charm imaginable, I am convinced he would have cut it from the picture. It was a relic from the back of his imagination, from an earlier conception. By this late stage he knew in his heart that the tone of *Chimes at Midnight* was wintry; and that would be its haunting quality.

Welles was ruthless in his cutting, abandoning anything that disturbed the pattern of the film's emotional drive. Among the casualties was a sequence he had filmed in our first days at Colmenar Viejo. Against a turbulent sky, a procession of priests brought the dead body of King Richard II to Gielgud. When we saw the rushes, we marvelled at the composition of the images. Now the sequence was discarded. Why? It was beautiful, Welles agreed, but sentimental.

"You must kill your babies."

Biographers have said that Welles hated to complete a picture; that he dreaded exposing his work to critics; that he deliberately left projects unfinished. There was no evidence of that this spring. While he waited for money to continue shooting, he worked with a focussed energy in the cutting room with Fritz Mueller. Darryl Zanuck came to Madrid to see an early cut, and the word was good. Favre le Bret, President of the Cannes Festival urged Welles to let him open the film at that summer's Festival. Welles returned every night after shooting and went directly to the Moviola without bothering to change out of his costume. Nothing was allowed to disturb him. There was no telephone in case the noise interrupted his concentration.

One night after work I sat playing cards in the main apartment with Beatrice and her great-grandmother. Paola asked me to tell Welles that dinner would be at nine. As I walked to the foyer of the other building I saw the concierge in conversation with two men. They spoke no Spanish and he had little English; he asked my help. The men had come to speak to Mr Welles. One was American, the other was silent. An interview was what they were after. Knowing that Welles guarded his privacy, I would not confirm that he was at that moment in the apartment upstairs, though his voice could be heard issuing from the Moviola. I said I would give a message to his secretary if they would like to leave me their names and a telephone number. They declined.

I went upstairs to the apartment, found Welles and gave him Paola's message that dinner was almost ready. He grunted an acknowledgement, hunched over the Moviola. As I went to my bedroom to change my shirt I mentioned the two Americans downstairs who wanted to speak to him.

"What!!!"

The explosion stopped me in my tracks.

"Did you say I was here?"

"No, of course not."

"How did they find me?"

I reminded him that journalists seem able to find anything they want.

"They're not journalists! They're American tax officers!"

He was convinced the US Internal Revenue men had found him. One of the reasons he lived as he did, always on the move, was to avoid American tax authorities who were demanding a walloping sum of money; and since he always invested any profit he had ever made in new projects, he could not possibly settle with them.

He ordered me to go downstairs and in a whisper he told me what I must say: "Mr Welles is not here. He is not in Spain. I don't know where he is. He does not live here."

I was flabbergasted. Behind me his recorded voice thundered from the machine. Nevertheless I went downstairs obediently and repeated his message word for word, as inscrutably as I could. I tried not to catch the concierge's eye; English-speaking he may not have been, but he could detect a whopping lie in any language. So could the Americans. The machine had fallen silent upstairs. An unmistakable voice was calling:

"Fritz! Bring me the next reel!"

The Americans left.

Later that night I watched the Welles family drive away into hiding. Initially they took refuge in the same Escorial hotel in which Gielgud had stayed so many months earlier.

The luckless Americans were in fact film fans from Minnesota who wrote to me when the film came out asking for a signed photograph and apologising for having invaded Welles's privacy.

❖

The day came, unbelievably, when filming was completed. It was April, seven months since I had flown to Madrid, and five years since Welles had summoned me to the front of the New Theatre and asked me to play Prince Hal. My life had been so knitted into the pattern of his, it was strange knowing that the Adventure was over. The family had left Escorial and were staying in the city. Antonio Ordonez, Hemingway's hero, was in Mexico and had lent Orson and Paola his apartment. We went back there for dinner, the three of us not knowing how to say goodbye, and each of us wanting to delay it. We sat among the trophies: gold-mounted hooves and ears, framed pictures of cardinals, archbishops and generals. Dominating the room was a full-length portrait of Ordonez in his suit of lights, proudly challenging the artist to capture his natural hauteur. But nothing, no gold, no painting, could diminish the presence of the man who sat opposite me.

We talked late into the night and then we talked until dawn. We talked until the car came to take me to Barajas Airport where I had waited for Gielgud that chaotic day, a lifetime ago. Welles took my hand, Paola kissed me and then Welles kissed me; we were both crying a little, which in turn made us laugh, and as I went to the car he called out Justice Shallow's line,

"Jesus! The days that we have seen!"

We would see more days together in fact after shooting *Chimes at Midnight*. Firstly, there was the dubbing of the picture, and later when I played Valentine in Shaw's *You Never Can Tell*, we opened in Brighton, and he brought Paola and Beatrice to Sussex for Christmas. When I played Bob Acres in *The Rivals* he made a beeline for the Theatre Royal in the Haymarket.

Chimes at Midnight opened to critical acclaim at Cannes, playing to packed houses in three cinemas in Paris, and breaking box-office records. In London it opened at The Academy cinema on Oxford Street and ran for three months. In New York it was savaged by Bosley Crowther the critic of the *New York Times,* and ran only ten days at The Little Carnegie cinema. Welles made light of the film's failure in America but he was badly hurt.

In time his lawyers came to an agreement with the tax authorities and he moved, as he had longed to, back to America for good. Messages arrived for me out of the blue from time to time. When I played Macbeth; when I played Hamlet; sometimes just a funny drawing on a letter from Paola. He wrote how happy he was to be back in California, with no idea that his hopes were to be dashed.

Chimes at Midnight was the last major picture he completed, though *The Immortal Story* with Jeanne Moreau, made for French television, played in selected art-houses and the quasi-documentary *F for Fake* was well-received. But the most extraordinary American talent since D. W. Griffith was not in a position to finance a major picture after 1965. He had another twenty years to live.

How could this happen to such a filmmaker? There was the familiar accusation that 'he went over budget', but going over budget is hardly unheard of in Hollywood. While Orson Welles was going cap in hand for half a million dollars to complete *The Other Side of the Wind,* those studio executives who turned a deaf ear to him were giving the nod to *Annie* and *The Best Little Whorehouse in Texas,* and for those two you can reckon on a budget of eighty million. Welles hoped the studio started by Chaplin would be more sympathetic, but United Artists was shovelling money into *Pennies from Heaven* which came in at over twenty million dollars and was a disaster. The same studio went on to produce a few more clinkers like *Buddy, Buddy* and *All the Marbles* – heard of them? – which poured another thirty million down the drain. And during the same period there was, of course, *Heaven's Gate,* which made all the other losers look like cheapies. Yes, *Chimes at Midnight* went over budget, but it was a tiny budget to begin with; in Hollywood terms no more than small change. In the end it recouped every penny and went into profit.

All of Welles's films ended in the black. Each of them was eagerly anticipated; all of them made their mark. The Studios excused the colossal waste of money on big budget disasters by pointing out that there had been a *potential* bonanza in them. Welles's projects never seemed so overtly commercial. (But then neither had *Chariots of Fire* – a story about two young British runners competing in the 1924 Olympics.)

Welles knew well how Hollywood squandered talent. In Madrid in 1965 he had been asked to contribute to the first issue of *Griffith* a new Spanish cinema magazine. Welles had met D. W. Griffith in Hollywood only once, at a Christmas cocktail party in the Thirties, but he felt deeply about Griffith's treatment at the hands of the studio moguls.

'On the assembly lines of the mammoth movie factories there was no place for him. He was an exile in his own

town, a craftsman without tools, an artist without work...We
stood under one of those pink Christmas trees they have
out there, and stared at each other... I loved and worshipped
him, but he didn't need a disciple. He needed A JOB.
I have never really hated Hollywood except for its
treatment of D. W. Griffith...'

Could Welles have imagined that the same fate would await him
when he returned to his homeland, or that he would make film people
in Hollywood uncomfortable, looming over the town which created
his legend, impossible to ignore, refusing to disappear?

In his last years he emerged less and less.

"I have become the Howard Hughes of the cinema" were the last
words he spoke to me a few years before he died. He and Paola were
now living separately, but they did not divorce, and she still loved
him. She had a home with Beatrice outside Las Vegas. Welles spent
most of his time in Los Angeles. He had taken up with Olga Palinkas,
whose dark Croatian looks were coarsely similar to Paola's. She had
ambitions as an actress and a sculptor, and to provide a home for them
Welles took a small house in Laurel Canyon where they could be
together.

One day, I passed through Los Angeles and stayed with a friend.
She told me Welles lived in the next Canyon and asked why didn't I go
and call on him. I was disinclined to turn up unannounced at his house.
"Why not go to 'Ma Maison'? He has lunch there most days. They
feed him for free. He attracts the customers."

'Ma Maison' was the 'in' restaurant that season in Los Angeles,
though it was an ugly brute of a place. It was now more than ten years
since I had seen Welles. I booked a lunch table. I left no message for
him, no warning that I would be there, afraid he no longer wanted to
see anyone from his life before Palinkas and would cancel his
reservation. Better to surprise him. He had loved me so much he would
surely be pleased to see me. On the other hand, he hated surprises.
I headed downtown. I was late. Outside the entrance to 'Ma Maison' a
kid took my keys and parked the car. Welles was coming down the
steps, a waiter on either side to hold him. His weight was immense, his
complexion was pasty. He was scowling with the effort of putting one
foot before the other. His taxi arrived. He held onto the car roof as the
driver came round and opened the door. He was panting. He wiped

his brow with a silk handkerchief. The driver and the waiters helped him into the taxi. He did not see me, and I retreated into the shadows. I found myself weeping.

On 10th October 1985 I was on my way to New York with a thriller, *Corpse* by Gerald Moon, in which I played twin brothers: a down-at-heel actor and his wealthy brother. In the opening scene, set in 1936, the actor has been shoplifting at Fortnum and Mason's – diguised as Queen Mary. The pre-Broadway tour had taken me to Michigan and I sat in a Detroit television studio waiting to be interviewed. The publicity organisers thought it would be amusing if I appeared on the news programme in my Queen Mary costume. Ready in the Green Room waiting to be called I watched a filmed tribute to Yul Brunner who had died the previous day. A girl brought coffee and said they were rejigging the main news bulletin. She thought there was a problem in the oil-fields; she had overheard them talking about wells. The cameraman lined up my shot and I asked what was the main news story.

"Orson Welles is dead."

He had been found dead that morning in Los Angeles. Olga Palinkas was not with him. He had died alone in that shabby little house in Laurel Canyon with a bathtub full of books for company.

There was no telephone for private use at the television studios so I made a call from a kiosk beside the freeway dressed as Queen Mary, and with the rush hour traffic thundering past I was just able to speak to Paola and Beatrice in Nevada.

"Everything is a mess," said Paola.

The obituaries occcupied the front pages of newspapers all round the world. It took no extraordinary clairvoyance to predict the frenzied outpouring of grief in Los Angeles where the press whipped itself into an orgy of mourning, eulogising its great lost genius; but the biggest sigh in Hollywood was the heartfelt sigh of relief.

Eleven months later Paola died in a car crash.

When the New York critics reappraised *Chimes at Midnight*, calling it "one of those wonderful thrilling things to be savoured and cherished", she and Orson had been dead seven years.

A long time has passed since that first day at Colmenar Viejo, when I stood shivering in my makeshift costume outside those painted tents. That young Prince on the screen seems so removed from me now.

I thought I was finished with *Chimes at Midnight* and then in the summer of 1998 the play was revived at Chichester and I was asked to play Henry IV. I wondered how strange it would be and whether I would be haunted by the echoes of Welles and Gielgud and of my own youth. But the voices were silent. And then, one day in the theatre when I was watching a rehearsal of the Gadshill robbery and Tam Williams as Prince Hal was running across the stage, I was back again in that wood outside Madrid and all I could hear was the great roar of Welles's laughter as he called to me:

"Run Keith, run! Go for broke!"

Three

GOODBYE MORGAN

*"If you ask me what The Spirit of Life is, or to what it is attached, I can't tell you.
I only tell you, watch for it. Myself I've found it in books. Some people find it out of
doors or in each other. Never mind. It's the same spirit, and I trust myself to know
it anywhere, and to use it rightly."*

E. M. Forster *The Longest Journey*

In November 1969, on a Sunday afternoon, I drove out of London towards Cambridge to say goodbye to E. M. Forster. Of course, I had not really allowed myself to dwell on the journey in those terms, but I had invited myself to tea with him and in my heart I knew that was why I was going. Forster was over ninety and becoming increasingly frail, but his good friends assured me he enjoyed visitors. *Where Angels Fear to Tread* had given me my first personal success and was the turning point of my career in London. We had embarked on a friendship which time and my dilatoriness had interrupted. I owed him a goodbye and myself the pleasure of seeing him again.

Northwards and eastwards out of London the road is not lovely, and it took a long time to leave the city behind. Past Islington, where striped footer scarves littered the roadway – abandoned after the previous day's match at Highbury – the borders of Wood Green, Tottenham, Enfield stray aimlessly one into the other. Street upon street of listlessly grubby front windows stare in dull surprise that a main highway should have plonked itself down here, where once had been gardens and runner-beans and hollyhocks and sweet williams, and the houses have slumped into a landscape that is begrimed, befumed, and seemingly infinite.

The weather too was wretched; that kind of dank November glumness peculiar to England. Easy to let one's mind slip away from the monotony of the road ahead, the traffic grinding past, the chill Essex mists, the oppressive drab skies, the spasms of icy rain and grease across the windscreen. Sweet to dream again of warmth and light and sunshine. Easy to think of Italy.

Some ten years before I had been to Venice for the first time and, heigh-ho, according to tradition, the city had entirely seduced my senses. I was very young and fell in love on the Riva degli Schiavoni

101

and I flung myself into the whole Italian Experience. It was an obsession. I learned Italian, all the love words first. The language came easily to me and whenever I could I returned – not just to Venice, but to Tuscany and Rome and Naples. I explored Sicily alone. Sunburned, arrogant of mien and dark of hair, nothing afforded me more pleasure than to be mistaken for the conductor of the funicular as we mounted to the walled hills of Erice, or for the rope-boy with the touring company of *Tosca* in the public gardens of Trapani where the canvas Castel Sant'Angelo rose above the flat salt fields and glowered at Africa.

So when in 1963 I went to read for the role of Gino Carella in *Where Angels Fear to Tread* I was nerveless. It was a wonderful part. I did not realise then quite how wonderful a part it was, and rehearsals were very happy. The cast was small and friendly and directed beautifully by Glen Byam Shaw. We progressed smoothly to the opening at Cambridge, and after the first night we all met E. M. Forster. I don't know what I expected the Grand Old Man of English Letters to look like, but surely not as though he should have been home pruning the roses. It was a short visit – he was after all eighty-four, and it was very late – but plainly he found the whole backstage atmosphere beguiling. The smudged greasepaint, the stacked props, the painted towers of San Gimignano/ Monteriano – all the trappings and paraphernalia of illusion amused and fascinated him. I shifted from one foot to the other and of course told him that *A Passage to India* was one of my favourite books and *A Room with a View* had sent me straight to Florence, and he smiled.

In London, a fortnight later, *Where Angels Fear to Tread* was rapturously received and homage in full measure paid to Forster. Critics reminded themselves and their readers that the great man was still alive and kicking hard, and that his writing was just as fresh and stimulating as it must have seemed to Edwardian England so many years before. The play transferred to a larger theatre, and floating along on the tide of the play's success came an inordinate amount of praise for me. I walked in a daze. My name was in lights – not very big bulbs to be sure, but to me the gleam was hypnotic. Forster himself had written to *The Times* praising me.

Approval served out so unstintingly can be an intoxicating draught and I was no temperance man. Nemesis awaited me, however, in the formidable shape of Orson Welles, who smartly arrested me along the road to tipsiness. He and his wife Paola flew from Rome especially to see the play. They were thrilled for my success and I longed to show them how much I had deserved it.

I acted my pants off for them. When they arrived in my dressing room Paola burst into tears and said through her sobs "Oh, Keith, you are so terrible!" while Welles began to laugh and gave his opinion; I was "not so much like a Tuscan dentist as a Pakistani postcard seller." They were right of course. Make-up, like the notices, had gone to my head. I scraped layers off my face and my performance and struggled back towards purity.

During that summer Morgan Forster and I became better acquainted. He wrote several, charming, shy letters to me. He loved the play, coming often to the St. Martin's Theatre, trudging up and down the steep stairs backstage. Could he go on the set? The pleasure he took in it all was touchingly childlike. How did the revolve work? Were those real tears? And the wine? Lemonade instead of Orvieto – what a hoot. Oh yes! He wanted to visit all the dressing rooms. Tea with Violet Farebrother, not so many years younger than he, imperious in taffeta and silk, who had been so splendid with the great Fred Terry in *Sweet Nell of Old Drury* so far back he could not remember when, and had she not been Terry's mistress? Weren't the Denisons good? Yes, and very kind too. And was it true that Gita Denise who sang so well as the landlady had had a triumph as *Carmen*? In *Glasgow*? Yes it was true, all of it. Someone told him I had been a boxer in the army? A soldier, merely.

The thick Leichner make-up sticks of different colours – rather fewer in my room since Welles's visit – pleased him. And my eyelashes he regarded with amazement, especially when they were peeled off and laid back in the box labelled: "Faberge Bedtime Flutter Lash. Macy's New York". Well, they were pretty nifty; and he rocked with glee when I told him how Dulcie Gray almost dropped the baby the day I had put the lashes on too quickly, before the glue was dry, and I came onstage and winked at her, playing the rest of the act with my lids stuck together like the puffy eye of a bruiser, crinkled.

But it was the baby, my toy baby son, that really tickled him. Beautifully made, neatly articulated, black bewigged and painted olive brown, he was scarily lifelike and Forster delighted in the scene in which I sang to my son while scrubbing him in a tin bucket. That scene was always a big success with the audience, though onstage there was an air of lunacy as Dulcie Gray while acting out her feelings of repugnance towards me, simultaneously, through closed lips provided the necessary baby gurgles in the general direction of the bucket.

Forster came to lunch at my flat in Westminster. He stood at the front door twinkling, a canvas satchel over his shoulder like a fisherman, clutching a strong hawthorn stick. What did he eat? "I eat everything, but not too much." He ate roast lamb and salad, cheese and apple pie, and drank red wine, coffee and a glass of brandy. After almost three hours he said: "Don't you think I ought to be going?"

When the play closed in London, it went on tour, and then I went to Spain to film *Chimes at Midnight* with Orson Welles. For the first few weeks of filming everything was so exciting, so crazy, I had no time to think of anything but getting up at dawn, hauling myself into costume and wondering where the whirligig of filming was going to take me next. From Madrid to Alicante, to Barcelona and Andorra, back to Madrid, and then back again to Andorra. There were times of idleness, sometimes whole days spent laughing with Fernando Rey and Norman Rodway, lying on our cloaks out in the clear warm autumn air. A young actor came from Barcelona on his motorbike to play Richard II who brought some grass, so we smoked that and careered over the mountain. One day the bike skidded in some goat dung. He went lickety-split over the handlebars and we were forbidden by Welles ever to get on it again; and not only that – Richard II was cut from the picture. Then one day when everyone else was working, I started a letter to Forster.

It was only a brief letter, but his response came so quickly and was so pleasing that I began to write at more length, mostly gossip, but sometimes observations about Prince Hal. Forster advised me to constantly keep in mind the Mystery of The Crown, for it is a Mystery and Hal must have found it a great one.

In another letter I addressed the question of Hal's innocence. I told Forster that I was struggling to maintain the Prince's innocence for as long as possible. He replied – very sharply – that *true* innocence may be attractive, but what about Hal when he became King? "There's not much innocence in the character of Henry V is there!"

Forster was interested in my affection for both Welles and Gielgud. Was it colouring my work? Whom did I love more – Gielgud/ Bolingbroke or Welles/Falstaff? "I don't know," I said, "I'm in a muddle." In Forster's opinion that was quite right and was not that the secret to Hal's dilemma? I must use my affection for Gielgud and Welles in my acting with them. I might easily have been given the same advice by Lee Strasberg at The Actors' Studio in New York.

When the truck lugged uphill with lunch it also brought the mail, and when the boy tipped the sack of letters on to the table I could detect the King's College crest on an envelope from Forster before the boy sorted out the pile.

We were filming on top of a high hill near Andorra, in the ruined castle of Cardona (now impeccably restored as a luxurious Parador Hotel). The castle was spectacularly beautiful, dating from the twelfth century. But there was no water, no plumbing. Lavatories were non-existent and filming went on from sun-up to dark.

There were about twenty actors, almost a hundred local extras, a sizable Spanish unit, and various gawpers who toiled up the mountain track to see the shooting. It was not discussed, though tacitly understood, that the crew had claim to the disused dungeons under the sunless north slope, and the extras to the thorn patch below the crumbling outer wall. Actors more discreetly detached themselves and made their way to their own secret comfort stations amid the still flowering gorse. It was always a jolly sight to see Gielgud, robed as the King in scarlet, tactfully disappearing behind a hedge, his crown glittering in the sun. On one occasion he returned in dismay: "I found four nuns squatting there!"

My own costume, with two pairs of tights held up by two sets of braces and two belts, under a back-buttoned tunic which I was unable to undo unaided, afforded me no such respite.

One day I felt very peculiar. Welles sent me down the mountain to the village doctor. I lay on his kitchen table. A canary sang in a cage. The doctor's wife sang as she did the laundry in the yard outside. The doctor bared my tummy, prodded and felt around, humming tunelessly. He stopped humming. He was pressing my stomach and I groaned. He looked at me over his glasses.

"Excuse me senor. But –"

"What is it?" I was frightened. "Is it serious?"

"When did you last have a shit?"

"Er –" I was very embarrassed. No one had ever asked me such a question before. "Er – about ten days ago."

He sent the taxi back up the mountain with a message that I would not be returning for some hours. He gave me a potion, some wine, and after some whispering to his wife, she gave me soup and a great deal of bread, before showing me to a small room beside the bathroom. She left me there, ostentatiously leaving the bathroom door open.

Three hours later the doctor returned.

"Is okay, senor?"

"Oh yes!" I said.

Occasionally down would come clattering one of those bricks for which Gielgud has always been so famous: "Have you ever known an American who could play Shakespeare? Oh – sorry Orson. Well I always thought you were Irish. Or something."

Then Gielgud left for New York and the rest of us went to Madrid to continue shooting. After a while a note came from Cambridge in which Morgan gently reminded me that it seemed some time since he had heard from me. I was shooting every day now, long hours. I had little time for letters. Jeanne Moreau had arrived and the inimitable Margaret Rutherford. This magically gifted actress – whose homely features masked a most moving and glowing femininity, and upon whom feyness sat as naturally as the rough Cornish cloak flying across her shoulders – stayed with us a month. When she left she invited us to a teatime party at the Palace Hotel.

Jeanne and I arrived first and found Margaret and her devoted husband, Stringer, dispensing tea and gin to the smiling elderly trio playing Lehar among the palms.

The rest of our group arrived, and we found that we had the place to ourselves. Margaret loved to dance. Shyly she asked Welles if he would partner her. He bowed, and suggested they might try a foxtrot, both were wonderfully light on their toes, laughing together as we cheered them whirling with such astonishing grace around the floor. Margaret danced with all of us, and then it was time to go. As we looked back, Margaret was waltzing happily with the cellist, Stringer on the gilt sofa shining with love.

But it was not only work that had occupied my thoughts and kept me from my letters. There was Jeanne Moreau. Of course I was in thrall to her. Who was not, or never has been? *Jules et Jim* was showing everywhere and hardly anyone had seen it less than twice. The day before she was due in Madrid I began to get nervous and edgy. I did not understand why that should be so. Looking back after all these years I still recall exactly how I felt, yet why I should have felt like that is as inexplicable to me now as it unnerved me then.

Moreau came on to the set to meet us all late at night. I, who had been so bouncy and happy-go-lucky, now hid – actually went away and hid – like a mooncalf. When they came to look for me I was tongue-tied and hesitant. The next day we had to work together – just a few shots of Doll Tearsheet trying to make love to the Prince. Well, kissing works wonders.

Jeanne led me to the Prado to see the Hieronymus Bosch. She found an old copy of Baudelaire and gave it to me, and I quickly learnt a stanza of *L'Homme et la Mer* to surprise her.

"Homme libre, toujours tu chériras la mer!
La mer est ton miroir; tu contemples ton âme
Dans le déroulement infini de sa lame,
Et ton esprit n'est pas un gouffre moins amer."

We sat in the Plaza Major after the tourists had gone, wrapped in thick coats against the cold, and students in their white ruffs and black Don Carlos cloaks and breeches played guitars, ribbons tumbling from their shoulders and their breath like steam under the lamps.

Jeanne whispered her song to me "Si tu penses à l'amour, si tu penses à la mort." We ate angulas, and chipirones in their black ink sauce. She had to go to Mexico to do a film with Brigitte Bardot, but postponed her departure till she could stay no longer. Later, Forster asked me if I still remembered the Baudelaire. I did, and do still. But what I remember best of all is Jeanne and our time together.

"Ni laide ni belle
Je veux être celle
Qui te prend par la main,
Ni jeune ni vieille
Je t'aimerai tant
Que tu seras fort,
Plus fort que la mort
Moins fort que l'amour."

Back in Britain the Socialists won the General Election by a slim majority. One of our actors, Andrew Faulds, fought a vicious battle against racism. (He lost, but only narrowly, and would be elected next year and has kept the seat ever since.) Forster was sympathetic which did not surprise me: his club was, after all, The Reform, where I had last seen him. Now I was looking forward to seeing him again very soon. It was just before Christmas and he was expecting me back in January, but the film ran into trouble and out of money and I was delayed. While new funds were raised Welles asked me not to leave for England. Apart from idling away time in Madrid I took the train to La Linea and walked across the border into Gibraltar. I found the grave of my Uncle Kenneth in the English cemetery and cleared the thistles from it. Then I took the Mons Calpe ferry to Tangier and rented a room in the Petit Socco in the casbah for eighty dirhams a week, which was less than a pound a night. There were bedbugs, and I was bitten.

I paid the Moroccan cleaner to throw away the mattress and buy a new one in the Souk while I went to the Arab baths. When I got back she had filled the room with bougainvillaea and positioned the mattress, still covered with plastic, so I could see its label "Made in Birmingham".

In the outdoor cafe beneath my room the Moroccans played dominoes until the small hours, clacking the pieces on the table tops until the rhythm coaxed me to sleep. In the day time, if it rained, I played table tennis in a Moroccan teahouse on a clifftop overlooking the Atlantic; if it was sunny we sat outside and smoked kif. It was a constant source of amusement that 'Keith', which everyone found difficult to pronounce should sound so nearly like the Moroccan word for marijuana. In the evenings I went to the Post Office and phoned Madrid. The message was always the same, "No money", so I went back to the casbah, to the cafe that overlooked the port. While musicians sat cross-legged on a tiny platform and boys in Moroccan robes danced to the music, I sipped mint tea, watching the sunset, smoked a cigarette or two and read *Martin Chuzzlewit*.

One day a boy came running after me on the Boulevard Pasteur with a telegram.

"MONEY ARRIVED COME IMMEDIATELY LOVE ORSON."

I flew back to Madrid. We finished shooting the film in April, seven months since we had started. I went to France, then to America, and one day I realised it had been three years since I had written to Forster or heard from him, and five years since I had seen him.

I learned from a mutual friend that he had often talked about me and *Where Angels Fear to Tread*. He said I should go and see him. They warned me that his memory had become very erratic and that he might have no idea who I was. But if that would not embarrass me, it would certainly not embarrass him. Most of all, since he rarely went out, visitors were his main pleasure.

My last letter from Forster had been written by his friend Professor Sebastian Sprott and signed 'Morgan' in a very shaky hand. I posted off a note saying I would be passing through Cambridge the following Sunday and would come and take tea with him. I would find the porter at the lodge. If he did not feel up to it, all he had to do was leave a message with the porter and I would understand.

The afternoon was already growing dark as I drove into Cambridge. I parked my car in the market, glancing up at the Arts Theatre where I had first met Forster. The rain had become heavier and I ran as fast as I could to King's College. The gate was crowded as people made their way towards the Chapel for Evensong. I wondered, indeed half-hoped, whether there might be a message for me. I found the porter. No message.

Sounding ridiculously pompous I announced, "I have come for tea with Mr E. M. Forster." The porter nodded briefly. Well, where were his rooms? The porter looked at me irritably. They were round the corner weren't they and don't expect him to come and show me, he didn't have time, not with Evensong starting and all these people. I had expected the announcement of E. M. Forster's name to elicit, not trumpets certainly, not even a tugged forelock, but surely something a little less dismissive?

Now the rain was coming down like stair rods and I looked with dismay at all the doorways. An undergraduate darted from an archway, his gown over his head, racing for shelter.

"Where do I find Morgan Forster?" I shouted.

"Through this doorway and up the stairs – you'll see his door," and he disappeared.

I stood before E. M. Forster's door and hesitated. Was this an idiotic gesture on my part? Would the room be full of people? I knocked and went in.

A large, long rectangular room. At this, the near end, a sofa and some battered chairs grouped around an electric fire. Behind the sofa a biggish table, and stretching down the walls on each side books in cases with glass doors. Sitting quietly at right angles to the fire, a small table in front of him, a shawl over his shoulders, and smiling up at me was Morgan.

I introduced myself. He nodded happily and invited me to sit on the sofa, a very lumpy sofa. A blanket was folded over the seat and here and there a spring was fighting its way through. I reminded him that I had written and he concurred happily. I mentioned *Where Angels Fear to Tread* but could not gauge from his smile whether it was all a blank. Curiously, I did not feel ill at ease, but I decided not to stay too long. Perhaps Forster sensed what was in my mind for he asked if I would like a glass of sherry. I shook my head and said I would not stay in case I tired him. "Oh, I like seeing people", he said at once.

A silence ensued. We smiled at each other and he nodded once or twice cheerfully.

"You've been reading Eliot?"

I touched the book in front of him.

"Yes. Do you like him?"

One Christmas, I said, I had read *Journey of the Magi* to school assembly in Wales before we broke up for the holidays.

"Will you read it for me now?"

He found the poem, carefully turning the pages, and handed me the book. I could hear the rain outside. It did not seem at all strange to be sitting there, reading to him.

'A cold coming we had of it...' and the words were certainly apposite, though there had been no camels, refractory or otherwise, on the Cambridge Road.

> 'There were times we regretted
> The summer palaces on slopes, the terraces,
> And the silken girls bringing sherbet.'

Forster's eyes never left my face as I read. Evensong would have started and the choir would be singing Magnificat.

> '... were we led all that way for
> Birth or Death? There was a Birth certainly,
> We had evidence and no doubt. I had seen birth and death
> But had thought they were different; this Birth was
> Hard and bitter agony for us, like Death, our death.'

I finished the poem, closed the book and replaced it on the table. It was dark outside and the room was cosy. I wondered if I should leave quite soon. Perhaps someone would be coming to look after him.

"The baby – " he said.

I looked at him. "The baby?"

He nodded.

"Yes. And your eye."

He moved his hand up to his own eye.

"When my eyelashes got stuck you mean?" I asked him delightedly and he laughed out loud. And for some minutes we talked about the play, the actors and the St. Martin's Theatre. Conversation drifted along the winds of memory like a sailboat, now propelled suddenly forward by a gust of recollection, now becalmed and tranquil. We talked of the theatre and how he loved it. We talked of the cinema, to which he was not partial. Too fidgety, he said.

The Birthday Honours that June had announced that the Queen had bestowed on Forster the Order of Merit – a rare honour in itself, but an extraordinary one when added to the Companion of Honour that Forster already held. I congratulated him. Yes, he was very pleased. Had he gone to Buckingham Palace to receive it? No, they had been very kind and some young man had brought it to him. Prince Charles was in residence in Cambridge at that time – it was the sort of spontaneous courtesy he would have enjoyed making.

"Did the Prince of Wales bring it to you?"

He reflected. He had forgotten. We talked about the weather. As on an ill-tuned radio it was as though the programme had suddenly slipped away.

"You've forgotten again who I am," I said.

He looked clear at me.

"Yes."

I laughed and so did he.

"It doesn't matter."

"No, it doesn't matter," he agreed.

The door opened and visitors arrived. A young couple with two small children. We all introduced ourselves. I went to collect my coat but Morgan said "No, please stay." The husband was a scientist who had been spending some time in America on a sabbatical. He chatted to Morgan. His wife and I explained to each other how we knew Morgan. The children had been quiet till now, but suddenly they began tearing round and round the room.

Their father called to them to stop but Morgan gently put his hand on the man's arm and said "It doesn't matter." The little boy had found Morgan's hawthorn walking-stick and was rattling it against the panes of glass in the bookshelves. With each crack his mother winced nervously. The little girl had found the light switch and was flicking it up and down, plunging the room alternately into darkness or light. Her mother's smile was fixed into a rictus as she explained how often Morgan went to tea at their house, and how fond he was of children. This was evidently true, for Forster alone was quite unperturbed by the anarchic atmosphere that had so surprisingly erupted.

At length, after a particularly unsettling crack of stick against glass, the mother rose determinedly. The children were calmed. Goodbyes were exchanged and I was alone with Forster. The room settled to quietness.

More than an hour had passed since my arrival and I thought he must be getting tired. He pressed me again to have a glass of something but I explained I should have a long drive back to London in filthy weather. Suddenly he said: "I don't know who those people were. Do you?" He asked it so seriously, and I explained I had never met them before. There was a pause.

"Beautiful children," he said.

He was looking into the fire. I put on my coat and searched for my car keys under the sofa blanket.

"What was that song? The song you sang to the baby?" It was a song I had learned in Ischia – an air of Donizetti's I had heard in a bar.

"I liked it when you sang that song."

I was pleased that his thoughts had come into focus now that it was time to leave. He took my hand.

"Will you write to me? I liked getting your letters."

I promised that I would. I shook his hand.

"Goodbye Morgan."

I wanted to thank him for his friendship without seeming gauche, but could find no words so I just said: thank you Morgan for letting me have such a wonderful part as Gino Carella. He still held my hand, looking straight at me. Smiling always so gently he said, "He was so good that boy and I don't know what happened to him."

I closed the door and left the warm room behind me. The air in the draughty corridor and down the wide-flagged steps leading to the open night was bitingly cold. Outside, the driving rain was turning into sleet, almost obscuring the dull slabs of light from the great windows of the Chapel. Evensong was over and I went quickly to my car. It did seem like the very dead of winter.

Four

GRACEFUL LIVING

"You don't know what it's like to be frightened. You get a beastly, bitter taste in the mouth, and your tongue goes dry and you feel sick, and all the time you're saying – This isn't happening – it can't be happening – I'll wake up. But you know you won't wake up... And you have to pretend you're not afraid, that's what's so awful."

Terence Rattigan *Flare Path*

T he world saw Terence Rattigan as an elegant, hugely successful playwright. As a boy he had been a star cricketer at Harrow and would remain passionately devoted to the sport all his life. He golfed superbly, wore beautiful clothes, drove a Rolls, dispensed largesse to his many friends, was surrounded by lovely women. But what the world saw was a mask, cunningly wrought to hide the playwright's loneliness and sense of inadequacy. Only those who knew him saw the emotional distress he often suffered. At the end of his life, dying and in agonising pain, his courteousness, his exquisite manners and his kindness were the same as they had been in his glory days at the end of the Forties when his plays occupied three adjoining theatres for almost five years.

On a sunny morning in July 1977 I was on my way to Regent's Park. I had opened at the Phoenix Theatre the night before in Tennessee Williams's play *The Red Devil Battery Sign*, which I had also directed, and I had woken to a very mixed set of notices. It was impossible to guess how long we would be able to continue, or if indeed we would be able to continue at all. I thought a brisk walk might dispel the Welsh depression into which I was rapidly hurling myself, and I set off for the Park.

I found myself passing the King Edward VII Hospital. I knew that Terence Rattigan was a patient there; I knew too that he was gravely ill. After being consigned to the wilderness for some years by the prevailing critical taste, headed by Kenneth Tynan at his most poisonous, Rattigan had managed to find a producer for his new play *Cause Célèbre*. It had opened a few days earlier at Her Majesty's Theatre and I had seen it. The play contained passages of superb writing and Glynis Johns had given a heart-wrenching performance, but what had invested the evening with a particular poignancy was the knowledge that Rattigan himself was in the theatre. Stuffed full of pain-killers, fortified by a will of steel, he had emerged from hospital and was half-slumped, half-hidden in a stage box. Bernard Levin was speaking for most of the audience when he wrote, "it would be absurd, as well as impossible, for me to persuade myself that I do not know that Terence Rattigan has for the last couple of years been staring into the eyes of the old man with the scythe." The play would have a fine success.

Preoccupied with my own opening I had not sent Rattigan a message but now, finding myself outside the hospital, I wrote a note of congratulation to leave at Reception. A friend of Rattigan's was collecting a great display of orchids. She said he was having a good day and why not slip in and see him. I found him lying on his side, immaculately dressed as always in a suit and tie. He had given an interview that morning and would give another after lunch. He had always been so proud of his looks, laughing at his own vanity, but now he seemed much older than his sixty-six years. His face was puffy with cortisone and it was quite clear that he was in constant pain, for he had to keep shifting from side to side. He apologised for his restlessness.

"I feel as though an elephant's squatting on me."

I congratulated him on his success at Her Majesty's, but he was far more interested (or at any rate made me believe he was more interested) in talking about Tennessee Williams; how lucky I was to be working with him, how he was the master poet-playwright of his age, how I must cherish my friendship with him.

When I left the Hospital all my own depression had vanished. If Ernest Hemingway's definition of courage as "grace under pressure" is right, then Rattigan was a very courageous man indeed, and not only in the face of death. "Where did we first meet?" he asked me, and I told him it was on a tennis court many years earlier...

At the Royal Academy of Dramatic Art public show in 1956, in *The Long Voyage Home* I was a Swedish sailor, given a Mickey Finn by a tart in Limehouse and shanghaied by a pair of villainous brutes in the shape of Albert Finney and Peter Bowles. I won the Bronze Medal and a contract to H. M. Tennent. Tennent's was then the all-powerful Management in London and the contract brought a salary of ten pounds a week, over twice the Equity minimum salary at that time. It also brought me a year of menial jobs, understudying and stage-managing, and a good deal of tennis.

H. M. Tennent was run by two remarkable men, one of whom was an Irishman, John Perry. In his youth Perry had been a famous Master of the Tipperary Foxhounds and a tennis player of above-average ability. In due course I was summoned to bring my racquet to the country. The tennis was taken quite seriously but there were some very eccentric players. Emlyn Williams was ambidextrous, with an aversion to running and no backhand. Whenever the ball came near him he stuck out whichever arm was appropriate and hoped for the best. Ralph Richardson's style was clearly modelled on Monsieur Hulot's. If it was Ralph's turn to serve, and he had a ball ready, he served. His opponent might be tieing a shoelace or finding a peppermint, or even gone for a pee, it made no difference; over came the ball and "fifteen love," said Ralph. One weekend I made up a doubles with Arthur Marshall against John Perry and Terence Rattigan. Perry played tennis as he must have ridden at point-to-points, socking the ball with dash and flair. Rattigan played with a sort of lazy insouciance; cricket was really his game, but he enjoyed the change of pace on a tennis court. Before the war he and Perry had won a competition in Monte Carlo, infuriating their French opponents with the merciless accuracy of their drop-shots.

"Ah, le triomphe du lob!" sighed the President as he handed them their Prize.

Arthur Marshall, in spite of his plumpness, was a man of startling agility, whizzing around the court like a bullet, rarely failing to return a shot. Determined to match the older men's expertise, I decided to dazzle them with my service game, but my eye was out and I hammered ball after ball into the net. As the score against us rose Love 15, Love 30, Love 40, and Arthur trudged wearily from one side to the other, he was finally driven to cry out, "Over the net, dear, and we can all play!"

When my parents came from Wales to visit me, they had very clear ideas what they wanted to see in London: a good Straight Play. Not farce, and they were none too keen on Shakespeare. The playwrights they enjoyed were Bernard Shaw, N. C. Hunter, J. B. Priestley, Robert Bolt, and of course Terence Rattigan. Going home to Wales for Christmas, full of praise for Samuel Beckett, it was, for example, a struggle to explain *Waiting for Godot* to my father.

"It doesn't sound much of a yarn." he grumbled.

"You're so middle-class!" I yelled at him, and in those days that was about as malevolent as you could get.

Indeed, Terence Rattigan's plays were right up my parents' middle-class street. He had nothing to say to the upper classes, recognising that the aristocracy was by and large too bird-brained to pay attention. He ignored the working classes, respecting their determination to stay away from the theatre at all costs. Essentially he wrote about the middle classes; and his audiences, being middle-class themselves, understood what he was saying.

Rattigan wrote about their angst and their dreams and he wrote with precision and delicacy. *The Browning Version, The Deep Blue Sea, Flare Path, Separate Tables* had earned him golden opinions and great wealth. When I met him that day on the tennis court his star was still at its zenith.

He had driven to the country in a spanking new Mercedes which he parked alongside John Perry's three-year-old Ford with a few derisory remarks. He was impatient to show off the car, and wanted to take everyone for a spin. There was racing at Newmarket, so with Rattigan at the wheel and the actress Joyce Carey beside him, I climbed into the back with the Irish novelist Molly Keane. Rattigan slammed his foot onto the accelerator and off we careered.

"Isn't it a grand car! Feel the power!"

Before we entered the race course, he slipped envelopes to the three of us. Each envelope contained £25.

This was the first Race Meeting I'd been to, but Molly was an old hand. She led me to the Tote Treble and showed me how to fill in the card. In the first race my horse, Tudor Prince, was the winner. In the second race I won again. The excitement before the third race almost killed me. If Scarlet Challenge won I could buy a car, get my own flat, go to America; these were opportunities almost too thrilling to contemplate! Between each race we had sunk a bottle of champagne. My head was swimming as we went to the rails to watch my fortune coming round the bend. But when Scarlet Challenge tottered past the tape he was the last horse on the field. Rattigan had lost almost a thousand pounds but he was far less depressed than I. It was only when the brand new Mercedes broke down on the way home and we had to be collected by John Perry in the derided Ford, that Rattigan's spirits were dashed. He sold the Mercedes back to the garage the next day.

The master playwright's good fortune in the theatre was about to break down too. His play *Variation on a Theme* was a disastrous failure. Suddenly he was under attack; he was smug, he was boring, he was predictable. The playwright, David Rudkin, spoke up for him, attesting that Rattigan's plays were haunting and oblique, but Rudkin's was a lonely voice. At this moment Shelagh Delaney burst onto the London scene with *A Taste of Honey,* and to rub salt in Rattigan's wound, she announced that she had gone home, after walking out of a matinee of *Variation on a Theme* in Manchester, convinced that anything she could turn out would be better than Rattigan's tosh.

A Taste of Honey was extraordinary, but after forty years it is fair to point out that Ms Delaney's published work looks slim beside the two thick volumes of Rattigan's collected plays.

Shortly after that tennis weekend my own career took off and I spent the next couple of years on Broadway in *A Man for All Seasons* and Ronald Millar's version of C. P. Snow's *The Affair.* I saw Rattigan from time to time in New York, usually with Margaret Leighton whom he idolised. I took them to Sardi's and it tickled him to remember that he had once lent me twenty-five pounds to back a horse.

Then, in 1963, I was cast as the young Italian in *Where Angels Fear to Tread.* It seemed a good idea to spend some weeks in Italy before rehearsals started.

William Walton had a fine house in Ischia. In the grounds there were three small villas which he rented out. The Oliviers were next-but-one to me; Joan Plowright was learning her lines for *St. Joan* which she was going to play at Chichester later that summer, and Olivier was resting his knee which still troubled him after his fall in *Coriolanus.* Every afternoon we all drove to a spa in Forio, where Olivier soaked himself in hot mud. There was an empty villa in the lemon grove between the Oliviers' place and mine.

Early one morning when I came back from the beach for breakfast the maid was very excited. "Il maestro è arrivato!" Parked on the rocky track was a Rolls Corniche with the Registration TR 100 and in the garden, looking out over the bay, was Terry Rattigan. There had been rumours that he might come, but there had also been rumours that he was not at all well. He gave a big grin when he saw me. He was sipping a full glass of some brown transparent liquid. "Medicine?" I asked solicitously. "Brandy," he replied. It was nine in the morning. He beckoned me into the garden, led me to a bench, making sure we were not observed, sat me down, and became very serious. He had leukaemia. The doctors had told him he had only six months left. He was telling *me,* he said, because he felt he had to tell *someone* but on no account was I to tell anyone else. As the days passed it became apparent that he had taken each of us aside with the instruction that it was a secret no one else was to know.

"Well," said Olivier "why not, if it amuses him? But it's probably cirrhosis of the liver."

There was no doubt about it, things became more lively with Rattigan's arrival. On 29th April, my thirtieth birthday, he announced a celebratory trip in a speedboat. We had hardly left the jetty before he had opened a locker and produced four huge vacuum flasks of iced vodka. By the time we arrived in Capri I was drunk, maudlin, convinced that at thirty my life was over, and in tears fell out of the boat into the Blue Grotto. A good tuck-in at Gracie Fields' restaurant cheered me up and we hurtled back to Ischia.

That evening the Waltons invited everyone to dinner. There was a spectacular sunset, the view was breathtaking, and the composer's wife, a vivacious South American, had arranged a delicious meal. At first the evening was heavy going. I was hungover and Walton wasn't feeling well. Olivier was gloomy about his knee, and Rattigan, after all, had been told he would be dead before Christmas. Conversation was spasmodic. Halfway through the meal Rattigan asked Olivier to tell his joke about the Curate and the Orange. Olivier was disinclined to oblige but Rattigan persisted. It was a simple enough joke:

> A very young Curate, afflicted with a stammer learns to his dismay that he must make an amusing after-dinner speech at the Diocesan Dinner. A friend suggests a Conundrum. "Announce that the answer is a word of two syllables and it's edible. Then they must guess the solution from your definition of the syllables: My first is an exclamation: O! My second's a kitchen utensil: Range. So my whole is: O plus range, equals Orange." The Curate rehearses the conundrum but when the moment comes he is so nervous that he blurts out: "My first is an ejaculation, my second's a bedroom utensil, you can suck my hole, and the answer's a lemon!"

Put down baldly like this it does not seem much of a joke, but by the time Olivier had finished with it the story had acquired a deaf Bishop, an Archdeacon troubled with wind, a Rural Dean with a cleft palate, a Canon with a wooden leg and of course the young stammering Curate.

Walton began to giggle as Olivier rose to his feet, and as the story unfolded and he got into his acting stride, gales of laughter spread around the table. Several times Olivier had to stop, overcome by his own hysteria and by the time he reached the end of the joke he had to shout the punch-line through the clamour.

I sat on my terrace later that night and looked back over the evening. I thought how pleased Sue Walton would have been with the success of her dinner, and what a wonderful mood William Walton had been in when we left. I thought how dazzling Olivier had been, firing happily on all cylinders, his spirits restored, and what an unforgettable birthday it had been for me. And then I realised that it was Rattigan who had worked so hard to produce all that for everyone.

Rattigan's plays were attacked for their sexual equivocation. But not since the seventeenth century has any playwright in these islands dared to confront sexual passion head on. It is a fair comment on the state of our theatre that the most succesful comedy this century has been *No Sex Please We're British.*

Rattigan asked his audiences to identify this inadequacy as something deeply sad. In almost his last play, and one of his best, he wrote "Do you know what le vice Anglais really is? Not flagellation, not pederasty. It's our refusal to admit to our emotions. We think they demean us, I suppose." The critic, Kenneth Tynan, was Rattigan's particular enemy, mainly because Rattigan embodied so many hateful characteristics that were mirrored in Tynan's own life: a resolutely comfortable middle-class background being the worst of them. Tynan's rallying cry to his supporters may have been "Il faut épater les bourgeois" but he, right down to the hem of his silk lingerie, was the true embodiment of the English bourgeoisie, and he hated it. Nevertheless, there was no critic in London who could write so superbly, and when he set out to wreak the utmost havoc with Rattigan's reputation, he succeeded. He made covert attacks on Rattigan's aberrant sexuality. This was a bit thick coming from a man like Tynan who, in an hotel suite in Spain, had once lugged in a bulging suitcase, turning scarlet when it suddenly burst open and spewed onto the carpet a school cane and some girlie spanking mags while the rest of us quickly turned towards the windows and discussed the sunset.

Charity was not an emotion in Tynan's experience but charity was Rattigan's hallmark. One critic wrote: "Rattigan chooses lost and confused people who are afraid of life and reclaims them through the sympathy of their neighbours. He makes them feel they belong to the human race."

In Ischia Rattigan had thought he had only six months left but he lived another fourteen years. He died in 1977 at his home in Bermuda, twelve weeks after he left the hospital in London where I had said goodbye to him.

A nurse brought in a bottle of champagne and one glass. "For you" he said, "I never really liked it." We talked a little about the theatre. I loved the story of his play that had been banned. He had exploded onto the London scene with *French Without Tears*, and his next play was another comedy called *Follow My Leader*. It was set in a mythical country in Europe. The *Leader* of the title was a dictator called Zadesi. Every time the dictator appeared he was to be greeted with a fascist salute and the cry "Up Zadesi!" But it was 1938 and the Lord Chamberlain was reluctant to upset the Nazi powers.

There was a call from Reception. Rattigan's next interviewer was waiting. I said goodbye. We shook hands.

"I'm dying, of course" he said cheerfully.

"You said that before, in Ischia. You told everyone. We all thought how much you were enjoying it."

A spasm of pain made him shift his position on the bed. He grinned at me.

"Why shouldn't a man enjoy his own death? After all it's the last amusement left."

Five

CATCHING THE SUDDEN SUBWAY

"These are my gloves, these gloves are gold,
and I fought a lot of hard fights to win 'em!
I broke clean from the clinches. I never hit
a low blow, the referee never told me to mix
it up! And the fixers never got to me!"

Tennessee Williams *Camino Real*

Outside the windows of Martha's restaurant in Key West the view seems to have been arranged by David Hockney. The three parallel strips of cobalt ocean, white road, azure sky, stacked in perfect symmetry one on top of the other are framed between two flawless palm trees. Restaurants in Key West tend to come and go; none is remarkable and all are at the mercy of fashion and a fluctuating tourist economy. But at Martha's the food is reliable, the service is not too eccentric and then there is that view.

Whenever I went to Key West, and that was often, I always took Tennessee to Martha's. When he brought his sister Rose to live in Key West she would come with us. We were never harassed by tourists or autograph hunters, and it was pleasant to eat by the open windows as the day slipped towards sunset and the sky darkened between the palms.

Although I spent many hours with Tennessee Williams in many cities in different countries, it was in Key West that I spent the longest times with him alone. In my mind's eye it is in Key West that I see him clearest of all. His little house in Duncan Street, sold now, has been newly restored, and on the bottom of the swimming pool he loved so much a rose has been rather vulgarly picked out in mosaic. But the garden is kempt, the picket fence gleaming white, and at night the flowering cactus bears its lovely lemon-scented blossom, just as I always remember. Sometimes when the new owners are throwing a party I can hear laughter and splashing from the swimming pool behind the fence, and I think of Tennessee leaning back in his deckchair, laughing at a Thurber cartoon in *The New Yorker*, or racing for a swim, pulling on his goggles to protect his eyes from cataracts and a bathing cap to protect his eardrums from infection. He would launch himself with a terrific splash and swim up and down, head in the water, and arms working furiously, drenching anyone standing nearby.

On Christmas Eve 1997 I cycled towards Duncan Street again. The houses were covered with festoons of coloured lights. The Cuban

121

immigrants, the gay community, and the black residents, who between them make up a majority of the population of Key West, were celebrating the Holidays with their customary exuberance. It was two in the morning, and 83 degrees but many a larger-than-life-size Santa drove his reindeer through the hibiscus, and an electric blue Virgin Mary presented a pulsating Son to the communicants stopping off on their way home from Midnight Mass for a banana split at Dairy Queen.

Duncan Street was in shadow and Tennessee's house was silent. I leaned my bicycle against a tree and drank a beer. A police car cruised by and stopped, checking me out. I put my beer behind me, never sure what the law is about drinking on the street. The nearside officer leaned out of his window.

"You okay?"

"Yes, thank you."

"Having a beer?"

"Well – "

"That's okay. Whatya doing?"

"Just having a look at Tennessee Williams's house."

"Been dead ten years."

"Fifteen. Almost."

"What?"

On the car-radio a choir was singing about chestnuts melting on an open fire.

"Merry Christmas, okay."

It was in 1983, 25th February, a bitter winter's evening when the news of his death came through. There had been a fiercely contested by-election and, in between shots of political hucksters frantically evaluating their shifting prospects in the wake of the Liberal victory in Bermondsey, the television announcer had a few seconds to give the news that Tennessee Williams had been found dead in his hotel in New York. There were no more details, and when they called me from New York they could tell me nothing except that his death had been an accident.

I was alone in Sussex. I turned off the television and the bickering politicians, pulled on a raincoat and went out into the dark. There had been a heavy sea mist. When I walked down to the shore it was impossible to see the top of the Coastguard tower. The sea itself was invisible. The dampness spread a pall of silence over everything – no sound but the dreadful rattle of the water over the shingle and the Nab foghorn howling in the Channel. So awful a sound, such a piercing cold; it was as though there had been collusion in the elements to mark the news of his death. Tennessee would have laughed. He would have said the effects were excessive. I wished I *could* hear him laugh, that wild laugh, something between a caw and a bray which erupted at startling moments if something tickled his funny bone: when he went to see Maggie Smith's *Hedda Gabbler* his delighted yelp as Hedda shot herself caused consternation in the rapt audience, being not, as Maggie observed, exactly the reaction one expected at that moment. But still I wished I could hear him laugh, and I wished that February night had never come and that he had not caught his sudden subway. By what capricious alchemy are we prevented from realising just how much we love our friends during their lives?

In the summer of 1961 I spent a great deal of time with the incomparably entrancing Margaret Leighton. She was newly divorced and I was a mess and both of us were lonely. By chance that autumn we both headed for New York. Maggie was going to star in the new Tennessee Williams play *The Night of the Iguana* and I landed the plum part of King Henry VIII in Robert Bolt's *A Man for All Seasons*.

Tennessee Williams gave a party for his cast. When I arrived, after my own rehearsals, at the building on the East Side, the entrance was dark. It was a comfortably modest building with a flagged marble hallway. Stumbling around the cavernous lobby was one of America's leading actresses, Maureen Stapleton, whose great heart was as legendary as her talent. I recognised her; I was much in awe of her. She had found the lift, shoving aside the wrought-iron doors.

"How do you work this elevator?"

It was a very small lift of the kind that both inhibits and encourages intimacy. I squeezed in beside her and closed the gates. Maureen looked me over.

"Are you in Insurance?"

In those days actors, especially from Britain, wore suits.

"No Miss Stapleton. I'm in the theatre."

"Well now you're in this goddamn elevator and it won't work. What's your accent?"

She had a large brown paper bag which clinked with a friendly sound. The noise of the party carried down the elevator shaft. Her soft body was between me and the buttons. We had a slug of vodka from the bottle.

"What floor's this party on?"

She shouted up the shaft,

"WHAT FLOOR IS TENNESSEE'S PARTY?"

Someone shouted back,

"Is that Maureen? Hey! It's Maureen!"

I pressed a button. We lurched upwards. The noise of the party drew nearer as we rocked aloft. A crowd of excited faces pressed against the gates, shouting welcomes to us, but their voices died away and their faces froze in amazement as we rose past them, up and up, till we stopped at the wrong floor. Down we came to the same laughter and cheers, and the same amazement as we sank below them to the lobby. The greeting that awaited us when we finally arrived was tumultuous.

Many such evenings lay ahead, but it is always the first that remains in sharpest focus. Faces I had paid one-and-ninepence to see on the big silver screen (with the puce stain) at the Romilly Cinema in Barry Glam, were smiling at me, plying me with wine and questions about Wales and Henry VIII. I swigged the lot down and it was all heady stuff. A baby-faced young actor, Warren Beatty, noticed the squiffy smile on my face. I was leaning against the window surveying the room.

"Are you alright?"

I nodded. He was unconvinced. He led me to the bathroom but was anxious I should not stay too long for it was the only room that could be locked and he had taken possession of it with young Natalie Wood, who just now seemed to be doing up some buttons. He yanked her outside.

Maggie Leighton found me splashing water on my face. She was at her most radiant.

"You're perfectly lovely Maggie," I started to say but never finished because I suddenly had to throw up. But, oh yes, perfectly lovely is what she was, in a grey silk dress, with rose-pink flowers clustered at her waist and throat. She held my head over the lavatory bowl and told Warren Beatty he and Natalie would have to wait. We sat on the bath as I recovered. I explained to Maggie how it was so unlike me because I had been drunk only once before, when I had thrown up on a new bedroom carpet at my brother's. Maggie comforted me by saying she had once come home after her divorce from Laurence Harvey and next day found her knickers in the oven, her shoes in the fridge, and Colman's mustard all over the walls.

"Don't laugh too much or you'll be sick again."

She took me to meet Tennessee Williams while Warren Beatty and Natalie Wood slipped back gratefully into the bathroom and locked themselves in. A queue began to form up outside with Bette Davis at the head, banging on the door.

"Stop that! And *open* this door!"

Maggie said: "This is Keith Baxter. He's Welsh."

Nothing had prepared me for the fact that Tennessee Williams was totally unlike the 'Tennessee Williams' of my imagination. I once met Dylan Thomas and he and the 'Dylan Thomas' in my head were as like as like could be. Edith Sitwell would not have disappointed you either, and if it's 'Norman Mailer' you're after then Norman Mailer will suit you fine. The man before me, however, had the gentle voice and patrician air of the chairman of a small bank in some historic Confederate State. Conservatively dressed, not very tall, he stood to shake hands, smiling shyly while Maggie talked about rehearsals. I must have been a curious sight. My face and hair and shirt were wet – and though I had combed my hair, drops were running across my forehead and down my nose. When I reached to shake his hand I realised I was still holding a cake of soap. But all he said was: "I'm Welsh too. Williams is Welsh," as he watched me slip the soap into my pocket.

Every now and then he would direct a quizzical smile at me, then look away again – down at his gleaming shoes, or up at Maggie – and dart another look at me, and laugh affectionately at Maggie when she tried to pay him a compliment.

That was the first time I saw Tennessee William, and I had no idea we would become such close friends, or that his death almost a quarter of a century later would oppress me with such a dreadful sense of loss.

In the days following his death in 1983 the English eulogies and obituaries paid due tribute to his talent while emphasising the salacious aspects of his work, and there was the obligatory trawl through the seamier incidents in his life. I listened to the newscasts, watched television, read through an avalanche of words. I recognised the playwright but I could not find my friend. Nowhere did a single commentator point out that Tennessee's passionate guiding credo – however the template of his life had been wrought – was the same as Göethe's: Mankind should always struggle towards the light. This was how he put it in his early play *Summer and Smoke* when he talked of Gothic Cathedrals: "How everything reaches up, how everything seems to be straining for something out of the reach of stone or human fingers! The immense stained windows, the great arched doors, the vaulted ceiling and all the delicate spires, all reaching up to something beyond attainment! To me that is the secret, the principle aim of existence – the everlasting struggle and aspiration for more than our human limits have placed in our reach!" The journalists, the commentators, the television pundits and opinion makers who planted their feet so firmly on the moral high ground of Pecksniffery dithered between fastidious disapproval and lip-smacking prurience, never spotting how, in Williams's world, no sides are ever taken. Only the cruel are castigated, only the self-righteous are mocked. And then again amongst the weasel words of melancholy were the innuendoes and smears. In the deluge of newsprint, the overwhelming conclusion seemed to be that to mourn his death would be to ignore the release that Death brought him from a miserable psychosis. I mourned him. I mourned him when he died and I mourn him still. I mourn the loss of a man whose style was always impeccable. A man of spirit. A brave man who possessed a defined sense of irony. Most of all I mourn him because he was a man who, quite simply, was a lot of fun to be around. The deep nostalgie de la boue, which led him on so many dark journeys, never expressed itself in locker-room talk, and he rarely indulged in gutter language, apart from an occasional expletive, and that never when a woman was present.

Towards women his manners were always unfailingly courteous. Though he knew periods of the blackest despair, he never dwelt on them in conversation with me nor indulged himself in whining and self-pity. He put all his obsessions, all his fears and passions, into his writing. They were not matters to be voiced. Apart from anything else he would have considered any discussion of such things a dissipation of potential material because his writing came first, last, and always. Not to understand that is not to understand the man at all. Those who did not know him seemed to imagine that spending time with Tennessee must have been like watching an open wound. I bear different witness.

On the day Tennessee died, the fine actor Joss Ackland, speaking of *A Streetcar Named Desire* recited the hackneyed obiter dictum: "of course, Tennessee really *was* Blanche Dubois!" and his interlocutor agreed sagely, though clearly neither of them had ever seen Tennessee's sister Rose, the walking, talking image of Blanche, and neither of them wondered whether "Of course Tolstoy really *was* Anna Karenina," or Thackeray Becky Sharp, or Chekhov each of his three sisters. The

argument that Blanche Dubois is simply a projection of the playwright
en travestie is a crude insult to the man and a diminution of his genius.
It is a specious opinion that is still propounded (most recently in a
fatuous piece in *The Spectator* on the occasion of the 1997 revival of the
play). Every real artist possesses an instinctive understanding of sexual
duality, entirely removed from sexual preference, and in those terms
– yes – Williams was his Blanche Dubois and his Maggie the Cat, just
as he was also his Big Daddy and the Gentleman Caller and Stanley
Kowalski and all the roles he drew from his artistic subconscious.

His first play, *The Glass Menagerie,* triumphed on Broadway a week
after his thirty-fourth birthday. Ahead of him loomed what he would
later call "the catastrophe of success". For forty years the press would
pursue him obdurately. He accepted this and was polite to reporters
who sought him out, but he found their questions infinitely wearisome.
He began to avoid interviews unless he thought they might help a
production being mounted.

"And then, baby, they will ask the same questions all over again
that they've been asking me for years. 'Which is your favourite play?
Who is your favourite actor? Finest actress? Why have you had no
success recently? Have you given up Speed, Quaaludes, poppers?'
Always the same questions."

The interview would grind to a halt and the cameraman would wait
until Tennessee raised a glass of wine – and certainly he did like a glass
of wine – and the shutter would click, and out from the pages of *Time*
or a Sunday Colour Supplement would peer the same boozy face that
had been photographed for years in Key West, New York, Rome or
London. He did not blame them; he knew they wanted copy. He simply
had nothing to say to them anymore.

"Every now and then word gets out, somehow, that my health is
precarious and a bunch of journalists and photographers flock down
here like vultures. Today it was *Paris Match.* They made me swim up
and down my pool endlessly for some reason, till I finally had a stitch
in my heart which still persists – otherwise I'd write longer."
He found the French to be especially troublesome.

"I am accompanied by a mysterious youngish Frenchman,
singularly lacking in physical charm, who seems to be engaged almost
constantly in writing about me in French. I studied the language six
years. I have managed to take a few peeks at the Ms and my name
keeps cropping up in very alarming contexts."

❖

After our first meeting at that party in 1961 it was to be ten years before I saw him again. Anthony Quayle and I had taken *Sleuth* to Broadway and one night my agent, Bill Barnes, said he was bringing Tennessee to the play. I looked forward to seeing Tennessee again, although I knew that the decade which had brought me much good fortune had not been kind to him. Frank Merlo, whom he had loved, had died a particularly cruel death from cancer, though still a young man. Williams's work was no longer finding favour. He had sought solace in religion, alcohol and amphetamines. He had been committed to a mental institution. But in all that time not a day had gone by in which Williams did not write.

The testament to those years is his *Memoirs*. Opinions prevailed that Williams should not have published these memoirs, or at least should have returned to them in more rational mood and edited them. But he wanted the book to stand as it was, written in pain and untouched by afterthought.

Bill Barnes brought him backstage and I took them both to Joe Allen on 46th Street. We sat at the big table in the back. Williams was, of course, as immaculately dressed as ever. He seemed slighter, and certainly older, and in spite of the expensive suit and careful tie it was clear that he had taken a beating. He spoke very quietly; made a few polite remarks about the play – which obviously he had not much cared for, but did not want to dwell on it for fear of embarrassing me – and brushed a wayward strand of hair that fell across his sunburned brow. His hands were of extraordinary beauty; small, plump, but the fingers tapered with remarkable delicacy. He caught me watching him. I must have looked very serious for he smiled and let out a chuckle.

"Don't worry, baby. I'll last through dinner if the chilli doesn't get me."

He came to *Sleuth* four times, mostly I think because he had nowhere else to go and he was lonely, and was not yet at ease around people who had known him in better times.

He had a new play opening in the Village: *Small Craft Warnings*. The first night was on a Sunday so we all trooped down to see it. After the last scene we stayed behind with the Company. It was there I first became aware of a quality in him that in my experience has been unique. Tennessee Williams was the only genius I ever met whose modesty was as genuine as his eminence. It was very moving to see him so shyly accepting the affection and admiration of the actors who surrounded him with such enthusiasm backstage in the dingy little theatre. No matter

© Copyright

© Copyright

Top; Keith Baxter's mother and father on their engagement, 1924.
Above; Keith Baxter's father.

© Copyright

Above; Family holiday, Langland Bay 1941, Father, Sister Christine,
Brother Tom, and Keith.
Top left; brother Tom and Keith Baxter aged five in 1938, Llwynderi Road, Newport.
Top right; Uncle Kenneth as Portia in the Wycliffe School production of
'The Merchant of Venice', 1911

© Copyright

© Copyright

Top; National Service, Dodwell's Ridge Camp, Hong Kong 1954.
Above; Keith Baxter (second from right) in a production of 'A Sleep of Prisoners',
St John's Cathedral, Hong Kong 1954.

© Copyright

Programme cover, signed by Orson Welles, for 'Chimes at Midnight', Gaiety Theatre, Dublin, March 1960

Orson Welles as Falstaff on the stage set of 'Chimes at Midnight', Gaiety Theatre, Dublin, March 1960.

Top; Keith Baxter as Prince Hal and Orson Welles as Falstaff on the stage set of 'Chimes at Midnight', Gaiety Theatre, Dublin, March 1960.

Above; Leonard Fenton, Henry Woolf, Thelma Ruby, Keith Baxter and Orson Welles on the stage set of 'Chimes at Midnight', Gaiety Theatre, Dublin, March 1960.

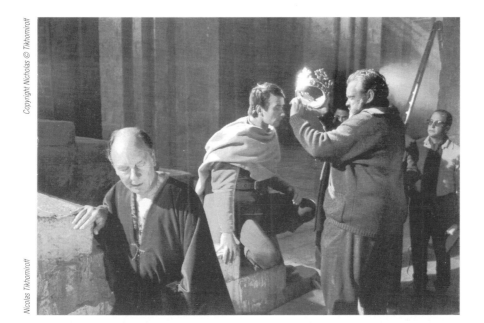

Copyright Nicholas © Tikhomiroff

Nicolas Tikhomiroff

Copyright Nicholas © Tikhomiroff

Nicolas Tikhomiroff

Top; Keith Baxter as Prince Hal in the film 'Chimes at Midnight' with John Gielgud and
Orson Welles, Cardona Castle, Spain, October 1964 - April 1965.
Above left; Keith Baxter (prompting), Orson Welles and John Gielgud as Henry IV.
Above right; Orson Welles, Prince Tasca and Keith Baxter.

© Copyright

© Copyright

Top; Orson Welles as Falstalf and Keith Baxter as Prince Hal (wearing Jane Mansfield's jerkin) in the film 'Chimes at Midnight'.
Above; Tony Beckley as Poins, Jeanne Moreau as Doll Tearsheet and Keith Baxter as Prince Hal in the film 'Chimes at Midnight'.

© Copyright

Top; Cartoon drawn for Keith Baxter by Orson Welles on a letter from
Welles and his wife Paola.
Above; Tam Williams as Prince Hal and Keith Baxter as King Henry IV in the Chichester
Festival Theatre Production of 'Chimes at Midnight' in 1998.

Copyright © The Illustrated London News Picture Library

Douglas Jeffery

Keith Baxter and Dulcie Gray in 'Where Angels Fear to Tread' by E.M. Forster, adapted by Elizabeth Hart, St Martins Theatre, June 1963.

© Mander & Mitchenson Theatre Collection

VIVIENNE

Terence Rattigan

Angela Thorne as Gloria and Keith Baxter as Valentine in 'You Never Can Tell', at
The Theatre Royal, Haymarket, January 1966.

© Copyright at The Harvard Theatre Collection, The Houghton Library

Photograph by Angus McBean

Top left; Programme cover for 'The Rivals' by Richard Brinsley Sheridan,
Top right; Ralph Richardson as Sir Anthony Absolute,
Above right; Margaret Rutherford as Mrs Malaprop and above left; Keith Baxter
as Bob Acres in 'The Rivals' at The Theatre Royal Haymarket, October 1966.

Copyright © Stephen Morton-Pritchard

Stephen Morton-Pritchard

© Copyright

Top; Keith Baxter as Vershinin with Mia Farrow (background) in Chekhov's
'The Three Sisters', Greenwich Theatre, 1973.
Above; Natasha Grenfell, Keith Baxter, Tennessee Williams and Maria St Just, Vienna 1975.

Copyright © Nobby Clark

Nobby Clark

Estelle Kohler and Keith Baxter in 'The Red Devil Battery Sign' at the Roundhouse,
London 1977.

Copyright © Nobby Clark

Nobby Clark

Tennessee Williams and Keith Baxter on the set of 'The Red Devil Battery Sign',
Phoenix Theatre, London 1977.

© Copyright

A Rhyme for Keith

Winter smoke is blue and bitter.
Women comfort you in winter.
Scent of thyme is cool and tender.
Girls are music to remember.

Testament is rock and thunder,
men are stone to labor under.

Cypress woods are wild and dark.
Boys are fox-teeth in the heart.

Tennessee
Vienna, 1975

Copyright © Keith Baxter

Top; 'A Rhyme for Keith' by Tennessee Williams given to Keith Baxter, Vienna 1975.
Below; Keith Baxter outside Tennessee Williams's house, Key West, Florida 1998.

Copyright © Margaret Fehl

Fred Fehl

Keith Baxter as King Henry VIII in 'A Man for all Seasons' by Robert Bolt,
ANTA Theatre, New York, November 1960

Copyright © John Timbers

John Timbers

© Copyright

Robert C. Ragsdale

Top; Keith Baxter as Octavius Caesar in 'Antony and Cleopatra' at Chichester 1969.
Above; Keith Baxter as Antony in 'Antony and Cleopatra', Stratford, Ontario, May 1976.

Keith Baxter as Octavius Caesar in 'Antony and Cleopatra', and Margaret Leighton as Cleopatra at the Chichester Festival Theatre, 1969.

© Copyright

Keith Baxter as Evelyn in 'Corpse' by Gerald Moon, Helen Hayes Theatre,
New York 1985.

Copyright © John Swannell.

John Swannell.

Copyright © John Swannell.

Photograph by John Swannell.

Top; Keith Baxter as Elyot Chase in 'Private Lives' by Noël Coward at the
Aldwych Theatre 1990.
Above; Aldwych Theatre programme cover for 'Private Lives' with Keith Baxter
and Joan Collins.

© Mander & Mitchenson Theatre Collection

Sasha

Noël Coward as Elyot Chase and Gertrude Lawrence as Amanda in the original production of 'Private Lives', Phoenix Theatre 1931.

© Copyright

Bert Andrews

Keith Baxter, Truman Capote (centre) and Anthony Quayle after the first night of 'Sleuth', New York, November 1970.

© Copyright

Bert Andrews

Keith Baxter (left and right) with Anthony Quayle (centre)
in 'Sleuth' by Anthony Shaffer, The Music Box Theatre, New York, November 1970.
(composite photograph)

© Copyright

Bert Andrews

Keith Baxter and Anthony Quayle in 'Sleuth', New York 1970.

Copyright © Gianni Bozzacchi

Gianni Bozzacchi

Keith Baxter as David and Elizabeth Taylor as Barbara in the film 'Ash Wednesday' 1973.

how many awards he won, and they were many, nor how many honours he achieved, and they were great, I never saw him so content as he was when encircled by a company of players who had just performed his work. But a stranger passing by such a gathering would never guess that the diffident man, in the unostentatious suit, was the centre of everyone's attention and the focus of their affection.

What he saw in me then I do not know. I was much younger than he, and youth did please him, but he was no Aschenbach and I was no Tadzio. At the time I thought that perhaps it was the fact that Anthony Quayle and I were the stars of *Sleuth*, the biggest hit on Broadway – and Tennessee needed to reach out and touch and be brushed again by that sort of success. We both knew – he how much better than I! – how ephemeral and tawdry that sort of glamour is. But it is a drug, and that was the drug he lacked then. Once you've tasted its highs the withdrawal pains are fierce. He seemed so vulnerable, so in need of protection: and that is always a fine feeling – that you're strong enough to shield your friend from hurts.

All rubbish, of course. He was stronger than anyone I ever knew, and I think I recognised that in my heart even then. Certainly he was lonely, terribly lonely, no denying that, but he was at ease in my company and I in his.

He was in two minds about the English school of acting. He admired English actresses. He had been well served by the best of them: Jessica Tandy, Vivien Leigh and Margaret Leighton, classically trained, all expert in high comedy so that even their most emotional work never lapsed into maudlin vulgarity. He himself had a well-developed sense of the ridiculous. Even when his affairs were at their worst he never failed to see the funny side of things. His characters are equally blessed with humour: Big Daddy, Alma Winemiller, Stanley Kowalski, Maggie the Cat, Kilroy and Lady Torrance – all of them leavened with a wry awareness of their own predicaments. We were having a meal at Sardi's; I was eating scallops, when I asked him what he thought of English actors. He thought their style tended towards bombast. A scallop was lodged in my windpipe. He thumped my back.

"Not the Welsh," he said hastily.

"The Welsh have cojones, as all the dark races do."

Tennessee was on his way to La Guardia airport for a flight to New Orleans. We walked towards the exit and the hat-check girl took some time to find his case. While we waited Tennessee said that he had been writing hard.

"My new play has a good part for you."

A taxi arrived. He left for the airport, and a few days later I played my last performance in *Sleuth* and headed for a holiday in Jamaica.

One Friday afternoon in Islington, towards the end of September 1975, I was stepping out of my front door when the telephone rang. It was Bill Barnes, in London at the Berkeley Hotel with Tennessee. I was due in Hampshire for dinner and if I did not get across the Thames before rush hour I would never be there in time. Barnes was insistent. They were going back to New York next day. They had been in Vienna. A theatre was about to mount a production of Tennessee's *The Red Devil Battery Sign.*

"It's the part he wrote for you."

Tennessee came on the line.

"Hello baby. Are you coming over?"

I drove to the Berkeley. Of course I wanted to see Tennessee. But I also knew that the play had collapsed in Boston the previous year on its way to Broadway and that the producer, the notorious David Merrick, had been buttonholed by an incredulous journalist: "You're not closing the play for good, Mr Merrick?"

Merrick had replied, "No, I'm closing it for bad."

How could I get out of accepting the play without hurting Tennessee's feelings and impairing our friendship?

At the hotel Barnes was in cracking form, Tennessee more subdued. No fool he, I sensed he recognised my embarrassment. We made small talk, I apologised for having to rush away, the traffic would be awful. They put a script into my hands, we said goodbye.

I walked down the corridor to the elevator. Then I remembered I had left my cigarettes on the sofa. I went back. As I raised my hand to rap on the door I heard Tennessee's voice.

"Oh God, Billy, I love Keith. What if he doesn't like it?"

I slunk away noiselessly and drove towards the Solent. All that night and the following day the script in its green folder lay on the windowsill of my room, daring me to open it. Late on Saturday I started to read, and I knew that whatever its faults and whatever its past history might have been, or whatever its future might promise, it was something that I had to do.

Its theme was sexual passion, an emotion that overwhelms each and everyone of us, even if very briefly, at some time in our lives. It shapes and alters us irrevocably, and for many people the motor goes fiercely chugging on into old age (Verdi, Augustus John, Catherine the Great). We know this to be true, so why is it that no major native playwright in Britain since Oscar Wilde has dared to tackle so elemental a force with such overt vigour. It was the theme that underpinned all Elizabethan drama, every one of Shakespeare's tragedies and comedies, it dominated Jacobean and Restoration theatre, and what have our twentieth-century playwrights offered in its place? The ellipticism of Pinter, the icy intellect of David Hare, the angst of Rattigan, the mocking brilliance of Ayckbourn, the smothering verbosity of the Great Neuter himself, Bernard Shaw. Stoppard gets very near to the heart of the matter, but then Stoppard's origins lie in Middle Europe. This deficiency leaves a yawning chasm in our contemporary dramatic literature and, faute de mieux, the English-speaking theatre has looked across the Atlantic to American drama, to Clifford Odets, to William Inge, and to the twin giants Eugene O'Neill and Tennessee Williams.

The Red Devil Battery Sign is an indictment of the capitalist structure of the United States, and of the concomitant misery and corruption it so easily engenders. This of course is hardly an original theme and, by itself, would be mere polemics. Transfiguring the argument is Williams's fierce imagination at its most ferocious and ardent, expressed in beautiful dialogue that rings with a savage eloquence. I could not understand why the play I held in my hands had been such a total failure in Boston. I had heard Tennessee had been unhappy with the production, but it seemed impossible to credit that such an extraordinary piece of writing had been dismissed so roundly. (Much later I learned that Tennessee, who never accepted failure on the road as terminal, had taken the text apart and the version I was reading was over two-thirds new). I called Tennessee in New York to accept the part, hoping that my enthusiasm would make amends for the way I had pussyfooted around at the Berkeley the previous day. I doubt I deceived him. Outside my window swimmers were calling to each other and I could see the Isle of Wight ferries slipping between the sailboats. It was lunchtime in New York and Tennessee was in the restaurant of the Elysée Hotel, where he always stayed. He sounded very happy but there were electronic whistles on the line and his voice kept disappearing. He said he would be back soon. The last thing I heard was when he shouted "You've got to meet Maria!"

Maria Britneva was born in Leningrad. The daughter of a doctor executed during a purge, Maria had been brought as a baby for safety to England. Of good family, she and her mother and grandmother lived in reduced circumstances in London where they relied on the charity of her relations. Mrs Britneva made a little money by translating Chekhov and Maria struggled to make a career in the theatre. It was not easy for her. The West End was dominated by the plays of Maugham, Coward and the young Rattigan, and Maria was too 'foreign' to fit easily into that genre; nor was she ideally suited for Shakespeare. But she persevered and in 1948 she was playing a small part with John Gielgud in his production of *Crime and Punishment* presented by H. M. Tennent and adapted by Rodney Ackland. Gielgud was amused by her and was kind to her. She was delighted to be invited to a glittering party at his house. The Oliviers were there and Noël Coward, and sitting on a sofa minding his own business and looking underfed was a shy young man wearing mismatched socks. Taking pity on him, and hearing his American accent, the girl assumed he must be an understudy for the London production of *The Glass Menagerie* which Gielgud was about to direct. She also thought he was attractive. The party swirled noisily around them, the stars all chattered to each other. She moved towards the young man on the sofa and something she said made him laugh. Though short of funds, she invited him to lunch, which took some nerve. John Perry, one of the directors of H. M. Tennent, told me that lunch with Maria in those days meant cold pilchards out of a jagged tin, but lack of funds would never prevent her from creating fiesta, and nerve she would always have in abundance. All the same, she was taken aback when the young man who readily fell in with her plans confessed to being Tennessee Williams.

How could he have known then that, after his beloved sister Rose, no woman would ever mean so much to him as Maria? What did he see in her that so beguiled him? He enjoyed women's company and she was petite and pretty enough in her way, though nothing to compare to Vivien Leigh across the room, who was such a dazzler. Maybe it was the girl's marvellously expressive eyes that intrigued him, and the laughter that was never far away. Certainly the man whose restless spirit so often wrestled with dark forces would have been captivated by the girl's lightness of heart, the keenness of her wit, the accuracy of her beady observations; "I never trusted Paul Bigelow. His jaw was twisted permanently south-east." Maria's vitality was irresistible and it would be to this energy that Williams would turn for nourishment again and again in the years that lay ahead.

I met Maria in October 1975 at lunch with Tennessee at the Berkeley Hotel, the day after he arrived back in London. Through almost thirty years their friendship had traced an extraordinary trajectory. At first the girl had been very much the petitioner for his affections. Unhappy with her life, she had turned to Williams for advice and help. His own career was at its peak and he was tender with her, amused by her, avuncular, treating her as a favourite pet. He gave her wise counsel, holidays and treats.

In the middle period of their friendship their lives had undergone a sea change. While Tennessee was fighting to sustain commercial success and was tortured by the death of his lover, Maria had been occupied by marriage to Peter St. Just. She was now a peeress; The Right Honourable Lady St. Just, with two beautiful daughters.

By 1975 it was Maria who had become the giver of comfort, the unflinchingly loyal friend. She would never fail him.

She had fallen in love with him in 1948 and she never really fell out of it. She was not a sentimentalist and she was not given to self-delusion, but one evening, after dinner with Tennessee and too much wine, Maria and I lurched back to her home in Belgravia when she grabbed my sleeve.

"You know, Keith, Tennessee is not really queer."

I pushed her into a hedge in Wilton Crescent.

After Tennessee died, she showed me her diary for 1949. Tennessee had invited her to Rome for a holiday. When she arrived she met Tennessee's lover, Frank Merlo. Williams had never been dishonest with her; it was she who had allowed herself to be emotionally misled. In Rome, faced with his homosexuality, she had had to come to terms with it. Alone in her room she wrote:

> 'I remember the exact feeling I have for Tenn and that I hold him
> in my heart's core – and guess I always will if such a word exists
> as always. I don't think that I've ever been as tired of anything as
> I am of my face and myself. I want to wake up new like a daffodil.'

Her loyalty to Tennessee's sister would be unwavering. Tennessee had installed Rose in Stony Lodge, a comfortable nursing home some miles from New York. Whenever Maria was in Manhattan, whether Tennessee was in the city or not, she went to see Rose. Tennessee paid for other friends to visit his sister but Maria made her own way. When Tennessee died his Will named Maria as his literary executrix, an act that aroused much fury and venom in New York amongst people who could not stomach the idea that Maria now controlled the plays. She turned out to be a prudent steward of his work. She demanded only the best for her friend and by and large she got it: major productions of

Orpheus Descending, Sweet Bird of Youth, Cat on a Hot Tin Roof, A Streetcar Named Desire, The Rose Tattoo. She secured players like Lauren Bacall, Vanessa Redgrave, and Maggie Smith. The plays were presented in London at the National Theatre and in the West End, directed by Peter Hall and Richard Eyre. Eyre would write her a note which she cherished in which he said he understood how wise Tennessee had been to put his work into Maria's hands. But what Maria understood was that it was not so much the work as Rose whom Tennessee had put into her hands, and Maria's stewardship was to last only while Rose lived.

I liked Maria from the moment I met her at the Berkeley. We were in cahoots from the start, and when Tennessee said he thought he would like to sleep off his jetlag, Maria asked me what I was going to do for the afternoon. I told her I was going to Hyde Park, pointing to two Golden Retrievers sitting in the back of my car. She grabbed my arm. She gasped:

"It's an omen!"

Her car was parked almost next to mine. Sitting in the back were her two dogs. Golden Retrievers. It was a bond.

Tennessee wanted Maria to play my wife in the play and sought my approval. While we walked the four dogs I asked Maria what she thought. She wanted to do it very badly. I gave my approval and never regretted it, though I did ask Gielgud what he thought. Properly cast she could be splendid.

"But nothing English."

And if she were to be a Mexican peasant?

"Oh she can do that!"

We flew to Vienna to rehearse *The Red Devil Battery Sign* at the English-speaking theatre in Josefstrasse. We stayed in a pension run by Frau Bulow who had been an opera singer in Budapest. She was given to snatches of *Der Rosenkavalier* which she sang in great swooping gasps while hoovering, catching the cord of the machine round her ankles as she curtseyed low whenever Tennessee came in sight. "Herr Villums," she would murmur as she sank to the ground.

She was equally awed by Maria's title and when Lord St. Just came for the weekend the excitement almost overwhelmed her. Frau Bulow's husband had a gammy leg and a ragged baritone voice with which he accompanied his wife while she dusted and he polished the silver.

The play required three musicians, mariachis, and on my floor there were two Bolivian guitarists and our Mexican composer. There was also a Lithuanian aerialist and a Czechoslovakian who was travelling with a small circus and did something with animals. He was a taciturn man who spoke no English so we communicated with a series of friendly grimaces and grunts. One morning Tennessee and I were waiting for Maria in the breakfast room. The Czechoslovakian entered. He grinned and gave a sort of half-bow, and we grinned back. He joined us at our table. We rashly attempted a conversation. The pimply Fraulein dispensing coffee must have explained that we worked in the theatre. The change in the man's lugubrious countenance was astonishing. Tennessee and I and the Mexican composer and the Bolivian guitarists were all gripped, shaken and hugged in an outburst of Czech bonhomie. He conveyed to us that he himself was a fellow artist, though he worked in a circus. With the steel coffee pots and chunky cups and saucers he tried to demonstrate the tricks his wild animals performed. He had a tiger, a lioness and a puma. He showed us their pictures in a scruffed programme he carried with him. With immense brio, in a torrent of impenetrable Czech, he began to create a pyramid on the table. The finale of his act involved all his animals in an elaborate set piece, in which the beasts leaped over each other and posed on iron stands. Growing increasingly guttural as his excitement mounted, the tangle of cups, coffee pots and milk jugs were balanced higher and higher under his stubby fingers. Inevitably there came the crash. The Fraulein sobbed; she would have to make good the breakages from her earnings. Tennessee and I soothed her and filled her purse full of pfennigs while the man from the Czechoslovakian circus sadly swept up the ruins of his entertainment.

(Some years later, when I was acting at Chichester, Tennessee came into my dressing room. He picked up a piece of thick white china with half a handle which I kept on my dressing table as a souvenir. I wondered if he had remembered.

"That, Tennessee, is a Czechoslovakian puma."

"Yes, baby," he said, replacing it carefully on the table, "with uncanny acrobatic skills.")

On Christmas Day Maria and I walked through the Fair below the Rathaus, where gypsies set up their stalls in the snow and sold spiced wine, fruit, jewelled birds and delicate glass ornaments for the Christmas trees. We were a week away from the opening of the play. We ate Christmas dinner with Tennessee and his American lover, Robert Carrol, in an exquisite room in the famous Hotel Sacher. They walked with us through the snow to our taxi. It had been a good evening, as good as it could have possibly been, for Tennessee's nerves were beginning to fray.

We all knew that the major European critics would descend on Vienna to review the play. Maria had been with Tennessee through the disaster in Boston. During dinner at the Sacher she never flagged in her efforts to keep his spirits high. Standing ankle-deep in the snow she kissed him and made him laugh, and he waved goodbye to us with a loud "Buon Natale!" and Robert reminded him we were in Vienna, not Rome.

We all slept late at the Pension Bulow after the opening night. There was no rush to scour the notices since none of us could speak German. I was woken by the Fraulein calling me to the telephone at eleven. It was the Director of the theatre, Franz Schafranek. Every critic was unqualified in his praise. During the course of the production I had taken over more and more of the direction at Tennessee's instigation and with Schafranek's generous approval. Now Schafranek wanted to read the reviews to me but he was laughing too much. Then he would discover a paragraph that had escaped him and would read it in a babble of German. So nothing made sense to me.

"It is one thousand per cent rave!" he shouted down the line.

As the notices came in from all over Austria, from Berlin and all over West Germany, from Paris, Switzerland, and Italy, it was clear that Schafranek had spoken nothing less than the truth. Theatre is taken seriously in Europe and the critics are given more space for their reviews. The notices were long, most of them a full half-page, and some longer than that. The play was hailed as Williams's master work: one critic called it his *Faust*, another his *Gotterdammerung*. Amidst this extraordinary avalanche of praise I asked Schafranek if there was not one negative review, a sentence, a few words that might contradict the general euphoria. But no, it was as he said. I saw the translations, a Niagara of enthusiasm. Tennessee walked around in a daze. It was many years since a new play of his had been received with such acclaim and the sensation must have been sweet for him after the collapse in Boston. There were gala performances to audiences in black tie and white tie. We played to the President. We played to the Chancellor. We played to the Diplomatic Corps. We played to youngsters in jeans and dirndl. American students came in their numbers and returned more than once. For them, haunted by the trauma of Vietnam, it was a profoundly emotional experience. A voice had spoken for these young men and women, and for their aspirations and dismay. That the voice belonged to a man over three times their own age amazed and captured their imagination all at once.

With the success of the play in Vienna I first noticed this birth of a new appreciation of Williams by young people. He had always been respected of course, but in the way that one respects writers whose work you have to study for exams. Now, in the mid-seventies, young people all over the world began to recognise in Williams's writing the voice of an authentic revolutionary who spoke in poetry to their hearts. He did nothing to cultivate this acclaim; he was no guru. He was not partial to people sitting at his feet, literally or figuratively. He wrote straight out as he saw it all, no special pleadings, just what he felt. Youngsters suddenly found a voice that rang as freshly in their ears as the voices they had heard alongside them at the barricades in Paris, in the streets of Belfast, on the campus of Kent State; except that this was not a voice that was concerned with dialectics. This voice spoke with a savagery illumined by compassion for the predicament of the whole human ethos.

Tennessee, of course, merely thought that he had written a play.

That the play's reputation had been redeemed was all that mattered. He was touchingly grateful:

"YOU ARE AN INVALUABLE PROPERTY! – Did you know that's what artists are called in the States? Properties!"

He was thrilled by Maria's performance. Covered in brown make-up, dressed in black, she resembled one of those black beetles that lurk on the Mayan ruins at Chichen Itza waiting to bite the barefoot sightseer. Tennessee gave me a book of pictures for the opening night with a poem inscribed inside.

Inevitably we all began to make plans for the future of the play beyond Vienna. Bill Barnes thought he could set up a production in Los Angeles but Tennessee was apprehensive. He was convinced that "all of California is Reagan country: the media is aggressively conservative." Failure in Los Angeles would be a deathblow to any plans for New York, and utimately New York was where it would have to be judged. Bill assured Tennessee that the Californian date would be only a warm-up.

> "But 'entre nous' Billy has sometimes assured me that ravens are blue and that buzzards are nightingales craning their necks to better observe the view. It is not conscious dissimulation but what I call the 'Mary Pickford Syndrome' in our national consciousness. Most of us would believe that the IRA bombings were holiday firecrackers if Richard Nixon said so on the putting green of San Clemente while Pat smiled at the birdie until it moulted."

Williams wanted the play done in London first. For the moment as far as I was concerned the question was academic. As soon as the play finished in Vienna I was flying to Stratford, Ontario to play Antony to Maggie Smith's Cleopatra. Tennessee wrote that he would wait for me.

"Wherever and however, I can imagine no one but you playing the part."

He had left Vienna shortly after the play's opening. He had an eye infection and wanted to have it treated in America. The day after he left, I went to meet some friends arriving at the airport. They brought with them the English papers. Margaret Leighton had died.

So much had happened since Margaret had first taken me to meet Tennessee at that party on the East Side all those years ago. She had been a happy part of my life and always such a good friend to me – a blithe spirit if ever there was one. I felt very desolate and strange at this curious ending of a circle, and the Viennese winter did little to ease the sadness. It was a very expensive city and we were not earning large salaries. Schafranek's wife was a very talented American actress and she arranged free seats for us at the opera, which was a tremendous perk. Maria and I set off to see *Lohengrin*.

"I don't want to go by tram. We'll take a taxi. Let's pool all our living-allowances and you pay everything and we'll see what we have left."

We took a taxi to the Sacher. We had a cocktail. We saw the opera. We had a modest dinner afterwards and a taxi home.

"Wonderful!" said Maria, contentedly. "We must do this again. How much is left?"

I emptied my pockets and started counting.

"Twelve schilling and five pfennigs."

And there was the sickening anti-semitism.

My good friend the American humourist Burt Shevelove, co-author of *A Funny Thing Happened on the Way to the Forum,* flew to Vienna to see the play. On Sunday we went to Grinzing for lunch. The taxi refused to take five of us. Burt went ahead with Maria while the rest of us took the tram. As we arrived at the terminus we saw Burt waiting. He was trembling with anger. He pushed me into the public lavatory. The walls were covered with swastikas and anti-Jewish graffiti, illustrated by crudely daubed obscenities. A few nights later one of the theatre's patrons gave a party after the play. Over coffee the Anschluss was mentioned. A Viennese woman in her fifties turned to Burt.

"You're a Jew."

We had no idea, she told us, how awful it was for the ordinary people of Vienna when the Germans had marched in.

"Believe me Burt! The people were crying!"

Burt looked at her. His face was stone.

"They were crying" he growled, "because there weren't enough uniforms to go round."

Not surprisingly, I was glad when the run of the play ended and it was time to head for Ontario. Tennessee kept me informed of all his plans. He was having treatment for his eyes and had cancelled a trip to Australia.

"The kangaroos must dig me from a distance."

I wrote that I would be flying to Canada via New York and he replied immediately.

"If I miss you in New York, I'll see you in Canada – unless I go blind or catch the sudden subway."

He did not go blind, and that subway stop lay seven years in the future.

Stratford Ontario is a charming little town but after a while we all felt very cut off and began to miss our friends at home. I arrived at the end of February in a blinding snowstorm. We rehearsed hard until the season opened at the end of April, but then our days were free and one began to long for visitors from the outside world. John Gielgud and Ralph Richardson were in Toronto, on their way to Broadway with Pinter's *No Man's Land*. I invited Gielgud to come to dinner in Stratford. There were many friends of his in the Stratford Company: Hume Cronyn and Jessica Tandy, Maggie Smith and her husband Beverley Cross. We gathered round the front door when we heard Gielgud's car arrive. We were all tanned. 1976 had been a cloudless summer, though not as hot as in England, where the freak heat had left not a blade of green. Beverley opened the door and Gielgud burst in.

"Beverley! You're so brown! You're as brown as a lawn!"

Gielgud had spoken to Maria before he left London and knew that she and Tennessee were on their way to visit me. He had a message for me.

"You're going to do Tennessee's play in London."

The Red Devil Battery Sign opened in London on 8th June 1977 at the Roundhouse, Chalk Farm – what Tennessee referred to as 'that old engine shed.' I was in South Africa shooting a film during pre-production planning, and after a fifteen-hour flight arrived in London at ten in the morning ready to go to the first day's rehearsal. Maria was at Heathrow to meet me. The director had quit after a series of disagreements with the American producer. The designer had quit as well.

A church hall in Pimlico had been hired for rehearsals. We drove straight there. The producer Gene Persson was waiting. He appeared remarkably unfussed by the turn of events. He had decided to take over the direction of the play himself, but after a few minutes it was clear that he was quite incapable of doing so. We read the play and pushed some chairs around, doing our best to make some sense, but it was all a nonsense.

"What shall we do?" he asked.

"Pray." I said. "There's a church very handy."

I took Estelle Kohler, the South African actress who had been engaged to play opposite me, to the pub and tried to raise her spirits by a pretence of lightheartedness which she must have known was bogus. She was generous enough to be amused but I knew she was as heartsick as I was. Then, too, the American actor who had been cast as my son-in-law was having trouble with his part. He was young and nervous and had recently been ill. He was not ready for the tumult of rehearsals and the crisis made him even more unsettled. He needed sympathetic handling. Instead, the producer decided to sack him in the bluntest way. I insisted that I should be allowed to handle it. It was a horrible thing to do but I took the boy to lunch and told him that everyone gets sacked some time or other – why, when I had been sacked from the film of *Cleopatra* I didn't speak for twelve hours – which was very odd for a chatterbox like me. He did his best to laugh but it had been a body blow and he was struggling with tears.*

Tennessee flew into London on our second day, he took the measure of things and was appalled. He wanted to know who would replace the young actor. We had a group of half a dozen boys cast as hoodlums. I asked one of them to read with me. He had real ability, an untroubled spirit and a terrific sense of humour. He was cast immediately. His name was Pierce Brosnan.

I drove home. The doorbell rang. Maria had driven Tennessee to my house in Islington. He was asking me to direct the play, and if I did not agree the project would have to be abandoned. We sat in the kitchen drinking tea. Tennessee pointed out that there was no time to find another director whose credentials he could trust, and in Vienna the staging of the play had been handed over to me with success. Bill Barnes called

*Ten years later he found a successful career as a television producer in Los Angeles.

from New York to say that if the production foundered, the play's reputation would be unsalvageable. I needed very little persuading. The idea was irresistible. I telephoned the very young costume designer, Bob Ringwood,* and asked him if he could do a set for me overnight, I took Tennessee and Maria to a little Italian restaurant in Camden Passage where the three of us got plastered.

At seven-thirty the next morning we had a production meeting. John Hersey, the greatest lighting designer in London arrived first. Ringwood brought a model of the set. It was very simple but brilliantly flexible and wonderful to light. Things were looking up. The only cloud on the horizon was the constant suspicion that Gene Persson, the producer, was short of cash.

"*The Red Devil Battery Sign* is a dark, haunting, and coherent play, as strong as anything he has written." said Bernard Levin in *The Sunday Times* after we opened at the Roundhouse. There were raspberries of course, and some abuse, but most of the serious critics were enthusiastic and Tennessee returned to New York in good spirits.

There were plans to move the production to Shaftesbury Avenue. By now I was sure that Gene Persson had no funds at his disposal. In spite of the good notices there was no advertising and there were few posters. But if a producer can sustain a new play through 21 performances in the West End (or on Broadway) he has a statutory claim to 40 per cent of any monies the author might make on a movie deal. The Roundhouse did not count as a West End theatre. Naturally Persson would want to shift the play, and keep it running, somehow, for three weeks.

Tennessee flew into London. His agent in London was also my agent. The two of us went to see Tennessee at the Ritz. Tennessee was in bed. The curtains were still drawn, though it was almost noon. Persson had taken him out to dinner the night before. They had sat opposite Maria and me in Joe Allen, drinking brandy. It was not a drink that agreed with Tennessee and now, this morning, his head was fuddled.

"Open the curtains, baby," said Tennessee.

I drew the curtains. The sun poured in from Piccadilly and Tennessee gave a groan.

The agent had prepared a paper, which he brought with him. It put down in detail the minimum amount needed to accomplish the transfer from the Roundhouse. I begged Tennessee to join me in demanding that the producer should open his books. It was imperative that the move be properly funded and Gene Persson must prove that he had the money to do it. Otherwise it would be better to close after the

* Ringwood is now an award-winning designer in Hollywood: the costumes for *Batman* are amongst his credits.

141

scheduled run at the Roundhouse. The play's reputation had been vindicated by the superb notices in Vienna and at the Roundhouse, where the young audiences had been wildly enthusiastic. We could withdraw honourably, having successfully completed an announced season. We could seek a new producer in America who would set up a production in New York. If Tennessee sanctioned a transfer to the Phoenix Theatre, and the production collapsed through unpaid bills and lack of advertising, it would be the play that would be blamed, and its reputation might never be redeemed.

Gene Persson arrived. He refused to open his books to me. He said, rightly, that he was not obliged to do so, and I couldn't wait around to argue. I had a matinee at the Roundhouse and shook Tennessee's hand. He grasped my hand in a desperate appeal.

"I trust Gene. Don't you?"

There was no answer to that one. I wanted Tennessee to have his success, and could see why it was so important for him to believe that Gene Persson would give it to him. I made my way to the Roundhouse for the matinee and later my agent said he had been unable to make Persson reveal the financial set-up.

"Only Tennessee could order that and he just sighed and shifted in bed and said we must all trust each other."

The play closed after eighteen performances in the West End. The actors' cheques had been written on rubber and signed on a trampoline. Equity forced them to be honoured. Gene Persson left the country. I paid the mariachis and Tennessee paid the other debts. He returned to America, utterly floored by the collapse of the play. I had been able to call him with some cheering news. The playwright, Frank Marcus, critic in *The Sunday Telegraph*, had written:

> "Here is a major poetic visionary who makes all but a handful of our native dramatists look puny by comparison. His imagination bursts the seams of theatre."

It was late on Sunday morning in Islington and the Sunday papers were strewn over my bed. In Key West Tennessee was making his morning coffee. I read him the Marcus review. He did not interrupt me and when I had finished there was a long silence. I was jiggling the receiver, wondering if we had been cut off.

"Tennessee – ?"

"I'm here, baby. Shall I write to Mr Marcus? Or would he consider that presumptuous?"

I hope he did write and was not too shy to let Marcus know how touched he had been.

One day, *The Red Devil Battery Sign* will be staged in Tennessee Williams's own land. I should like to be part of it, but whether I am or not I am certain that, in time, it will be recognised as a major work, the way he thought of it himself, and as critics in Europe thought too. Under my dressing room door on opening night he slipped a note:

> "Dearest Keith, Maria says to write you another poem. I think the play is a poem and the poem is yours. Love always, Tennessee."

At Christmas in 1977 he sent me a picture-postcard of his house in Key West. "Here's where I go for my 'Rest and Seclusion' with lovely swimming, bridge, poker. Won 18 cents last night." And the next year I was mooning around in New York waiting to start rehearsals for Christopher Isherwood's *A Meeting by the River* when Tennessee called and said "come south." The heat was stifling in Manhattan – over ninety degrees and unpleasantly humid – and a friend happened to be driving to Florida to deliver a new automobile to his parents. It took us three hours to get out of the city to New Jersey. It was the Friday afternoon of Labour Day Weekend and the Holland Tunnel was clogged with cars overheating and breaking down. Had we not been caught in a one-way system we would have returned to New York, but we drove through the night, speeding through Pennsylvania and the Virginias, stopping for a few hours at a motel in North Carolina, then racing through the searing heat towards the Atlantic. We pulled up by a deserted beach in Georgia. The sand was pink in the late afternoon sunshine, the Atlantic warm and comforting, and the Big Macs and French fries tasted dandy. At one in the morning we crossed the state line into Florida, filling up at Jacksonville and I took over the driving as Jeff fell asleep. There was no rush now and the highway was deserted, save for the occasional monster truck zooming out of the darkness. A local station was playing old jazz. It was exhilarating, driving like that, tooling down US1, with Tommy Dorsey on the radio, *I'm Getting Sentimental over You*, the Atlantic glowing on my left, and the palm trees throwing strange shadows in the moonlight across the bonnet of the cadillac. We pulled into Fort Lauderdale at dawn and lay all morning on the beach.

Key West is only one hundred and fifty miles from Fort Lauderdale but it takes five hours to drive there. You skirt Miami and then the Expressway peters out. Sometimes the road narrows and you go many miles without an overtaking lane, and you drive across the Keys, the small necklace of islands linked only by this road, until you arrive at the last Key of all: Key West. Towards the end of your drive there is the Seven-Mile Bridge skimming over the clear green-blue water, and if you could stop you might see strange and beautiful shapes gliding beneath your feet; giant rays, or marlin and shoals of wild-coloured fish glittering just below the surface. That first time I drove to Key West a sudden and violent tropical storm attacked us as we started across the bridge. Waves sharply whipped the placid surface of the water into a maelstrom, and a wind of Biblical fury threw splashes of salt water against our faces. The sky across the Gulf of Mexico had turned black and we barely had time to close the car-windows before the tempest broke in force. The rain beat against the windscreen too fast, too heavy for the wipers to clear it. The way ahead was almost lost to us. The turbulent ocean seemed perilously near and greedy. We dared not stop for fear any car behind might blindly drive right into us. Then, as suddenly as it had come, the wind dropped and the storm was over. Ahead of us the setting sun burned through the clouds and the sky was ablaze with colour, and over the firmament a rainbow of most arrogant brightness arced in triumph. It was, you might allow, a dramatic enough way to arrive anywhere.

It led me to expect something that would be – what? I didn't know exactly – savage certainly. Beetling cliffs probably, thick jungle, and gimcrack houses perched amongst luscious shrubs along grassy paths. Instead I found Toytown and tuberose. Burger Kings and Holiday Inns.

Key West is an ugly bit of a place blessed only by its seductively sensual climate and the gingerbread old conch houses dotted around the carefully tasteful geometry of its flat streets. Once it must have had great charm in a raffish down-at-heel sort of way with its rough and ready eating places and romantically sleazy bars down by the water. But that was before the hurricane of '38 blew the railway out to sea: before the Navy came and built its yards there, and before President Truman came to stay when they built a better road and an airstrip. Then the artists came, fake and real ones alike, and their followers came too; then Gay Liberation came with sophistication and hysteria shrieking along behind. Then Castro took over in Havana and the Cubans came, the Haitians, the cocaine smugglers, the discos – and suddenly the whole shebang bubbled over into a frenzy of ultra-chic, illicit drugs, reckless sex. Key West is not like Bognor.

There are no decent beaches, but any sailboat will take you out to the coral reef where the swimming is superb and the sea has never been cold. Best of all is to cycle at dusk around the back streets of the town; through the old cemetery with the pastel-coloured monuments and ancient inscriptions fading below the stone angels, past the dead woman's reproach to her family, "I told you I was sick;" along streets no wider than a lane, where mothers croon lullabies to their babies on the porches of tumbledown wooden houses, and softly call a greeting to you in Spanish; down through Mallory Square where the old man holds the iguana on his shoulders for tourists to photograph as the red sun sets obediently behind the masts of a ketch or two; along past the old wooden pier where young men parade each afternoon, glaring fiercely and longingly at each other; and home to Duncan Street, cycling effortlessly through the strange-sounding streets; Leon where the frangipani overwhelms the senses with its sweetness and Von Phister where the night-flowering cactus blooms and the air smells of lemons.

Tennessee dug out two old bikes from the back of his garage. Once we were cycling to lunch, down Duval Street, when a Chevrolet pulled up beside us at a light. Tennessee, immaculate as always in a crisp shirt, summer trousers and panama hat, cycled forward as the light turned to green. A young couple were in the car, a child between them on the front seat.

"Oh God!" said the woman to her husband, "it's Tennessee Williams! Slow down honey! Excuse me."

Leaning out of the car, "Are you Tennessee Williams?"

Tennessee mumbled an assent but never stopped pedalling.

"Honey will ya slow down for CHRISSAKE! Gimme some paper!"

She found some paper and as the car crawled along beside us she thrust an arm through the window.

"Gimme your autograph will ya Tennessee?"

Tennessee gave a bleak, brief smile and cycled steadfastly forward.

"I think," he said, "the moment is inopportune."

When I arrived at Duncan Street that first evening, Williams was swimming in his pool and could not hear my calling. I could hear *him* alright, splashing like a grampus behind the fence. The white picket gate was open and I made my way past the white gazebo, with the fading names painted under the eaves: Paul Bowles, Maria Britneva, Jane Bowles, Frank Merlo. The front door of the house was unlatched and swung open when I knocked. It led into a comfortably untidy sitting room. Books everywhere. A huge Bible (the King James version) on a lectern. Friendly sofas. A photograph of Lynn Redgrave, with David Hare and me laughing in a New York elevator. Doors opened onto a spacious brick patio surrounded by hibiscus and bougainvillaea. Beyond the patio and up a few steps was the pool, and in the pool swimming determinedly was Tennessee. I did not disturb him for he seemed set on a routine number of lengths, but eventually he slowed, caught sight of my shoes, pulled off his goggles and beamed up at me.

We went to dinner at Martha's Restaurant by the airport. We ate conch chowder and yellowtail, and when we returned to the house we sat out by the pool and listened to a scratchy record of Lotte Lenya singing Kurt Weill. We watched the moon rise over the palms and Tennessee found a crumpled cigarette under his deckchair.

"Shall we smoke a joint?" But it turned out to be a Camel and I coughed myself to sleep.

He was an easy host for he expected nothing of his guests and mercifully planned nothing for them either. I swam a lot and raided his bookshelves. It was in Tennessee's garden that I finally conquered *War and Peace.* After lunch he set up his easel by the pool and, making a tremendous mess, covered the canvas with bright splashes of oil paint. Portraits: he painted his friends or used a model. Often he worked from his imagination. I cooked steak-and-kidney pudding for dinner which we ate with grits and yams. We played poker with Texas Kate and her sons. We watched *I Claudius* on television, Tennessee marvelling at Siân Phillips's Livia. Siân and I had been friends for years. Jokingly I said she used to push me in my pram.

"For goodness' sake stop!" wrote Siân, "Tennessee thinks I'm old enough to be your mother!"

There was an evening when we sat happily silent in a garden overlooking the ocean. Somewhere behind us a party was in full swing and guests were plaiting little light bulbs in their hair. A shape appeared in the darkness, twinkling. Tennessee sipped his white wine dreamily.

"It's a catamaran. Or Cuba. Or our hostess."

She bore down on us coquettishly:

"Sitting in the dark, feeling sorry for yourselves! Oh, you theatre people, you want too much!"

Tennessee banged a fist onto the table.

"Ask for all! Be prepared to get nothing!"

It was a line from his play, *Summer and Smoke,* but it confounded Mrs Moldawer.

❖

The following Spring rehearsals started in New York for *A Meeting by the River*. Christopher Isherwood's book had been turned into a play by Isherwood and his lover, Don Bachardy. It was strongly cast: my twin brother was Simon Ward and our mother was the legendary Siobhan McKenna. Everyone, the actors, the producers, the director, Christopher and Don, had high hopes for it. But the chemistry was wrong and rehearsals were marred by appalling bickering. The writers believed that the book was being betrayed by the actors and the production. The director and the actors were infuriated by the authors' inability to understand the different dynamic between a novel and a piece of theatre. We opened out of town and then came to Broadway, previewing at the Palace Theatre on Times Square. The atmosphere backstage was electric with acrimony. Isherwood was bristling with petulance, and though the actors did their best to keep their spirits up it was hard to face an author who was so hostile, especially a writer whom we had all admired so extravagantly.

Maria arrived from London for Tennessee's birthday. When he met her at Kennedy Airport and asked her what she wanted to do, she insisted on coming straight to find me. They arrived at the Palace as the curtain was about to fall. The preview, like the previews before it and the previews that were to come, had not gone well. The chatter around Broadway was not good. Eagerness to be the first with the news is not, as foibles go, a particularly unusual one, but it is surely only in America that so common a trait should find such passionate expression, and bad news seems to inspire a frisson that is almost orgasmic.

Ever since the dubious ecstasy of Paul Revere's ride 'The British Are Coming! The British Are Coming!' (after all, 'The British Are *Not* Coming' would never have merited an exclamation mark), Americans have had a penchant for savouring disaster.

As it was in 1775, so it was in 1979. The previews of *A Meeting by the River* were jam-packed with audiences who sat in baleful excitement, tight-lipped with complacency. Imagine the surprise as I stepped forward for my bow to be greeted with a sustained salvo of "Bravo! Bravo!" from the rear of the stalls. Siobhan gripped my hand and whispered, "There you are then!" – magnificent in her optimism as in everything else. "'Twill be a triumph!"

In my dressing room after the show, she beamed at Tennessee and Maria. "Did you hear the reception Keith got! Wasn't that grand!" and

Maria had the tact to bury her nose in the flowers. She looked about the mirrored room. "This is very posh," she said. My dresser, George, polishing glasses, said tartly that it had been Judy Garland's last dressing room and Tennessee sat up:

"Oh God, baby, is that an omen?"

A Meeting by the River closed after its opening night. On my way into the theatre an autograph hunter at the stage door had said to me brightly,

"Hi, Mr Baxter! I hear it's a calamity!"

The first-night party after the show turned into a wake as the news filtered through that the television reviews had been bad. We dropped Tennessee at his hotel and I took Maria and her daughter Katya for a goodnight drink at Sardi's. It was late and the restaurant was almost empty. Vincent Sardi tried to hide *The New York Times* from me as I passed, but I said I was a big boy and took it from him. It was a lethal notice from Richard Eder and with *The Times* critic against us there was no chance of survival. I walked home, knowing there would be no second performance and that I would never see Isherwood again.

A little before eight the next morning Ned Sherrin telephoned to say the other papers were both bad, though "*You*'ve done alright." I did not feel alright. I was very low. Opposite the bed in the rented flat was a bookcase and, facing me, was the spine of Isherwood's *The Berlin Stories*. I had been staying in the apartment for four weeks and had never noticed it before. It was a long time since I had changed trains with Mr Norris and sipped a prairie oyster with Sally Bowles. I took the book to the kitchen. The coffee had percolated and was ignored as I read through the book without stopping. No matter how wretched an experience *A Meeting by the River* had been, nor how disappointed I had been by Isherwood's prissiness, no one could ever take from him the esteem those stories had brought him or diminish their brilliance.

Later in the day Tennessee telephoned. He said Key West was a very good place for licking one's wounds, and he asked me to bring the London script of *The Red Devil Battery Sign* with me which he wanted to cut and work on. The main task was to lose twenty minutes, and this meant one whole scene must be excised and others reshaped. I had made detailed notes to offer Tennessee, some of which he implemented and some he discarded. When one scene had gone, the information had to be worked in elsewhere. I had even written deliberately banal dialogue, to indicate what I thought the scene should tell the audience. I gave him this material on my first evening before dinner and he placed it on his desk. Next morning those suggestions he accepted had been incorporated seamlessly into the text. He had even used lines I had written, but by the addition or deletion of a word and a slight rearrangement of the phrasing and rhythm, he had turned my dross into unmistakable gold. It was instruction from a master and I could hardly help comparing how this titan of playwrights was so flexible, and how the inexperienced Isherwood had proved so obdurate.

Tennessee wanted to paint me. I was very flattered. Some time earlier, in Los Angeles Don Bachardy had drawn me in a footer shirt, and in his picture I looked like a Redskins quarterback. In Tennessee's picture I did not look like a footballer. He painted me sitting by the pool wearing a swimsuit, reading Dickens. He was working on the picture when I flew north to Washington to play in Maugham's *Home and Beauty* at the Kennedy Centre.

My friend, Jean Marsh, was the first to see the picture. She was doing a play in Miami. She went to Key West for the weekend and rang to say my portrait was in the window of The Gingerbread Gallery. She told me I had orange hair, with a butterfly sitting on it. I was stark naked and there was a card: 'Keith Baxter: $4000'.

"And what's that in your hand?"

"*Our Mutual Friend.*"

"Is that what you call it?"

Tennessee's house in Duncan Street was full of animals. An English bulldog of the gentlest disposition arrived one Christmas. I opened the door and the little puppy, wriggling with goodwill, lumbered over the step and collapsed at Tennessee's feet. He was named Cornelius after Tennessee's father. There was a marmalade cat with a squiffy eye called Topaz, and Juanita the parrot. She had been badly treated by a Polish visitor who had been staying in Tennessee's house. He would poke the bird with a broom to get it out of the cage. I took the broom handle away and coaxed Juanita outside. Within a few days it was apparent that Juanita had taken a fancy to me. She would dance on the perch and hop from one side to another at the sound of my voice, and would sit on my bare shoulders and never bite or scratch me with her formidable talons. She had a few words of Spanish, several foul phrases in English, a repertoire of whistles and screeches. But above all was much given to laughter. She could laugh genteely, like a dowager with uncertain teeth, or ribaldly like a fishwife, though her favourite was a great peal of maniacal guffawing. It was as good as putting a penny in The Laughing Sailor.

If we were alone, which we often were, and Tennessee did not want to go downtown after dinner, we sat by the pool with a bottle of wine, reading to each other. He was fond of Kipling, Pinter, Ezra Pound and Hart Crane; especially Hart Crane. He would pluck a book out at random. Once he found Pinter's *The Caretaker* and started on the second act, interrupting the reading to comment admiringly on Pinter's use of language. I was slightly stoned and it was weird sitting beneath the stars in the scented garden, listening to a speech about Sidcup read in a southern accent which would elongate the most ordinary words beyond their measure.

"Tennessee. How many vowels are there between the d and g of 'dog'?"

"As many as I can squeeze in, baby."

He read slowly and only his own work well, but he was enthusiastic. I was staying with him in January 1980. He knew I had just played Hamlet in Canada. He searched for his Shakespeare, found his favourite scenes and read all the other parts, getting quite carried away by Claudius at prayer, and weeping so copiously at the Queen's description of Ophelia's drowning that we had to open another bottle of Californian red to buck ourselves up, then shouting so loudly as Laertes in the grave that Juanita fell off her perch squawking in fright.

Every night before he went to bed he prepared the coffee machine in the kitchen. When he woke, at whatever hour – maybe three or four in the morning – he got up and pushed himself groggily to the kitchen, made coffee, and took it to his studio beside the pool. He would work himself awake, then work until he was exhausted. There were always several projects to hand; an incomplete poem, or a short story, or the latest play called *Masks Outrageous and Obscure*. Often, if I had been downtown by myself, when I came home around dawn I would hear the typewriter and know that Tennessee was working. It was a lonely sound. I leant my bicycle under the trees, stood silently for a moment in case Tennessee had heard me and would like to talk, and then I would make fresh coffee by the pool as the sky lightened before he went back to bed.

Usually he did not hear me. The typing never stopped and the irregular tap tap tap of the keys would sound across the garden as I went up to my room.

Those were golden days with him, and there were good times in England too – in Wiltshire with Maria who could banish all dark phantoms and make him cry with laughter. At the Lyric Theatre in London where we saw Ralph Richardson in William Douglas-Home's *The Kingfisher*, and when Ralph was poured a cup of tea onstage, Tennessee could not be convinced that the teapot did not hold neat whisky. (Ralph for his part told me he was sure that Tennessee himself was afflicted by 'the great malt that wounds' so the score was even.)

At my house in Islington when he stayed with me and fished out the manuscript of my play about Edith Cavell, he sat on the stairs and declaimed one of Lloyd George's speeches to my dogs. I don't know which was odder, the sound of a Lloyd George from the deep south, or the sight of a Golden Retriever squatting on the landing, carrying an empty hypodermic in its mouth: "Vitamins" said Tennessee.

And then there were the times with Rose.

The 'rose' motif is embroidered through the writing of Tennessee Williams just as his devotion to Rose, his sister, illumined the pattern of his life. One of his plays is titled *The Rose Tattoo* and the main action of *The Red Devil Battery Sign* takes place in The Yellow Rose Hotel. There are numerous other 'rose' references in his works. The two clearest portraits of his sister are in his earliest success, *The Glass Menagerie,* and in his later triumph, *A Streetcar Named Desire. The Glass Menagerie* is a chiaroscuro portrait of the playwright's early years in St. Louis. Tennessee named the stage family 'Wingfield', and the son bears the name 'Tom', Tennessee's own name at home. So the initials T. W. stand for both the playwright and his stage alter ego. The two women in the play are impressionist versions of Williams's mother and sister; the mother so garrulous and touching, the sister, 'Laura' – whose nickname in the play is 'Blue Roses' – so oddly withdrawn and shy. The meticulous writing of 'Laura' reveals Tennessee's own attachment to Rose. It is an accurate portrait of his sister in her teens, painted with his heart's blood.

Preoccupied with his own life, Tennessee had managed to thrust into the back of his mind his sister's increasing strangeness. At fifteen he passed her on the stairs at home one day and hissed at her: "I hate the sight of your ugly old face!" She crouched into a corner of the landing. He always said this was the worst thing he ever did and when, years afterwards, he went through his 1936 diary and found:

> "Rose is on one of her neurotic sprees – fancies herself an invalid
> – talks in a silly dying-off way – trails around the house in
> negligees. Disgusting," he wrote alongside the entry, "God forgive
> me for this."

As small children they were inseparable. It was to Rose he turned with all his dreams and doubts. The girl's own dreams and sexual passions alarmed her mother and Rose was institutionalised and subordinated to a variety of severe treatments. At the end of *A Streetcar Named Desire,* when Blanche Dubois is committed to a state institution, we see an accurate portrait of Rose at the same age. In 1943 her mother authorised a pre-frontal lobotomy, a situation he referred to in *Suddenly Last Summer.* Williams's feeling towards his mother had always been ambivalent and the operation did nothing to improve matters. He was obsessed with feelings of guilt, had he been less self-absorbed might he not have prevented the surgery?

His devotion to his sister grew steadily stronger as she withdrew into a world of increasing silence. The greatest satisfaction that success brought him was the knowledge that Rose would always be properly cared for. Her home became the private nursing home within easy reach of Manhattan where he could pay her frequent visits.

In 1979 Tennessee brought Rose south to Key West. A house was up for sale in nearby Von Phister Street and Tennessee asked me to inspect it with him. It seemed ideal; large enough for Rose and a cousin to look after her. He sent for Rose. A furious cable arrived from Maria St. Just. Had Tennessee gone mad? Why was he taking Rose away from an environment where she was surrounded by faces that had become familiar, and where she was happy?

Two years later Tennessee realised that Maria had been right and took Rose back north. The experiment had really been a selfish desire to have her near him in Key West, to see much more of each other, and he hoped she might like the sunshine and the change. For a while she did.

Rose Williams must have been a girl of dynamic character and compelling looks. The first thing I noticed when she strode into the garden at Duncan Street was how beautifully dressed she was. Her clothes may have been bought for her, but her style was entirely her own. The white hair was cut short, almost mannishly so, but the severity it gave to her appearance was offset by the extraordinary eyes and the curved generous mouth. She wore a coral crêpe-de-chine dress and a broad-brimmed hat, pulled firmly down and slanted in a bold rake across her brow; white straw with a pale green bandana. Difficult to describe her walk; 'lope' is nearest to it. There was nothing hesitant about her. She moved with authority and took possession of her space like an actress or the headmistress of an exclusive girls' school. Only her eyes lacked sureness.

When introduced to strangers, she offered her hand politely but without interest, and her conversation was usually limited to 'no' or 'yes' when asked a question. Sometimes she said 'yes' when you expected 'no' and vice versa. The unpredictability of her answers lent a stimulating precariousness to social occasions. One relentless Key West hostess, assiduously cultivating Tennessee, brought Rose a stupendously vulgar floral arrangement. Rose stared at the garish tropical blooms and turned her back on them.

"Rose! I chose them specially for you! They're such darling colours – don't you love them?"

"I do *not*!" said Rose with aplomb.

At dinner generally her silences were long. In company she had eyes usually only for Tennessee. Occasionally if someone else was talking she would fix the speaker with a steady gaze – and then, if you turned and caught her watching you, she would smile immediately and her face would be transformed. Gone the implacable regard, the puzzlement behind the eyes. When she did have something to say, her speech pattern was southern, formal and blunt. As Tennessee got into my car to go home she called: "Tom! Don't get intoxicated!"

Once, as we arrived at Texas Kate's house in Elizabeth Street and I held the gate open for Rose, she passed through and stopped, extending a gracious hand, saying, "Good evening! So very good to be here. Such a fragrant evening. My! You're looking fine!"

It might have been lines from *A Streetcar Named Desire* spoken by Blanche Dubois. Tennessee and I pressed after her, eager to see who had elicited such volubility. In the flower bed stood a startled boxer dog, frozen in amazement as Rose, with a cheery wave disappeared around the corner.

A few weeks before Tennessee died he came to England from New York. I spent the evening with him at Maria's. I had not seen him for ten months. He was in low spirits, and though I had heard this was not unusual now, it was unusual in my experience of him, especially when he was with Maria. The previous year he had stayed in my house and my cleaner found a scrap of paper under the bed. He must have scribbled it during the night. I brought it with me to Maria's. He read it and shook his head,

"I can write such rubbish."

I asked when he was returning to Key West and he looked miserable.

"Key West has become so corrupt."

Key West has more than its fair share of riff-raff, and there were many who preyed on him. He was generous to friends who had fallen on hard times. Sometimes I took a hundred-dollar bill and tucked it under the loose brick of a run-down flat on Southard Street where Conrad Veidt's daughter could collect it. But he had always seemed able to detach himself at will. For the first time in all the years I had known him he was weary of the place. All his pets had disappeared: strayed or stolen. Juanita had been strangled. His papers had been plundered. I asked him what he would do. He gave a bleak smile.

"I'm on the run," he said.

It was a favourite expression of his. Several of his letters are signed "10 on the run". Maria wanted to take him to Wiltshire for the spring. As always his face lit up when she embraced him, but he had it firmly in his mind to go to Italy: Rome first, then perhaps Taormina, where he had known great happiness years ago. Then he would go back to New York.

Afterwards we wondered if this trip had been a way of saying goodbye to places and people that he had loved. I telephoned him at the Berkeley the day he left England, encouraging him to go to Wiltshire with Maria. But he had finished his packing and was impatient to be off.

On 4th July in 1980 I had taken Tennessee and Rose to dinner. It had been a cloudless Key West day with a pleasant breeze, and the heat was bearable. Rose was in gala mood. As we drove down Flagler in the open car she laughed as the wind snatched at her hat.

"I went to Flo Fields today!" she suddenly announced. I thought she had been shopping and asked if Flo Fields was a department store.

"Flo Fields is my daughter!"

Tennessee gave a delighted chuckle.

"Really, Rose?"

"Oh yes, Tom!" she beamed, "she's producing!"

"I shall be a great-uncle," chortled Tennessee, nudging me.

"Every day some extraordinary revelation."

We drove for a few seconds in silence.

"Unless of course – " he paused, "unless she's producing a play? That would put an entirely different complexion on the matter."

He gave a great whoop of laughter. Rose laughed with him. The sun was still high, and as we turned onto the coast road and the limitless ocean stretched before us, Rose burst into song. *Million-Dollar Baby* she sang and Tennessee joined in. They knew all the words, though neither she nor her brother had the least idea how to hold a tune. Off-pitch, off-key, sharp and flat they merrily bawled out the song. Then Rose sang *Onward Christian Soldiers.* Next, we all sang *Tipperary, Paper Moon, O Come All Ye Faithful* and *Dixie.* We drove past Martha's Restaurant almost as far as Stock island, then back again, still singing, to the restaurant.

Much later, when they were having coffee, Tennessee turned to Rose. She had fallen silent during dinner. Tennessee held her hand. They were a handsome pair, both so suntanned and elegant. Anyone passing the table would never guess the shadows that had affected both their lives.

"What would you like to do now, Rose?"

Sometimes, when we had finished eating, if Rose did not want to go home, we went for a drive or to an ice-cream parlour.

"Do you want to go home?"

She shook her head. She looked at her brother and a smile spread slowly across her face. She said something I could not understand, something like "I want to go on the J. S." I looked at Tennessee. He never let go of her hand. He told me that the J. S. was the paddle-steamer on the Mississippi where he and Rose went dancing as adolescents fifty years ago. I paid the bill and we went outside and sat on the wall by the ocean and waited for the car to be brought.

The immensity of the Florida night enfolded us. The wind had dropped and in the town they were letting off their Independence Day fireworks. Coloured lights exploded over the palm trees.

"Are we going on the J. S.?" asked Rose again.

Her brother put his arm around her.

"It doesn't sail tonight, Rose" he said.

"Perhaps tomorrow, Tom?"

"Perhaps tomorrow."

The circumstances of Tennessee Williams's death were immediately interpreted by the media as suspicious. There were hints of suicide. Dakin Williams, whom Tennessee always held in a kind of affectionate contempt, announced an hysterical theory that his brother had been murdered. The facts were, alas, all too banal. He had choked on the plastic cap of a bottle of pills. Anyone who wants to take a pill, and who has had something to drink, and holds a glass of wine in one hand and the pill-bottle in the other, might easily think of taking the cap off with his teeth. Tennessee had done so, and the cap had slipped into his throat and choked him.

He always wanted to be buried at sea. He told all his friends so. "As near as possible to the point where the poet Hart Crane had died." But Dakin Williams took him to St. Louis and he was buried there.

Eighteen months after his funeral I was in St.Louis. My plane landed a little before noon and I went to the hotel and changed. Tennessee had always dressed so carefully, I owed it to him to be neat. I bought some flowers in the hotel and took a taxi to the cemetery. It was called Calvary. The sun was high and the humidity was intense. At the office by the gates I was given a map. I started walking. I took off my jacket and walked beneath the trees to find shade. I arrived a point where the paths crossed and I could make no sense of the little map. A boy was mowing around the graves. He was a handsome lad in overalls, a small red cross picked out on his cap. He asked if he could help me. I told him the number of the plot I could not find.

"You must be going to visit with Mr Williams."

I thought how Tennessee would be pleased, not just by the comeliness of the boy, but by his southern manners and the courteous way he showed me the right path.

The grave was marked by a cross. A tall slab loomed over it. His brother had buried him in a city he detested, from which he had made his escape as quickly as possible, and in the dark shadow of his mother, for whom his feelings had always been ambivalent.

The scrap of paper on which he had scribbled during the night in Islington is in front of me as I write this. He had said, that last time I saw him, "I can write such rubbish", but I do not think so.

"The clock ticks. It reminds me not to fear the prison of present Time. It will pass. I shall have escaped."

Escape was an important theme to him. "10 on the run" was his signature. He understood very well the lyric of Noël Coward's *Sail Away*:

"When the storm clouds are rising
In a clear blue sky,
Sail away, sail away."

"He's as peripatetic as a flea," said Maria. Now he is free. His work remains to remind us that the human spirit is indomitable, that we must struggle upwards towards the light, and that life – even at its worst – is always funny.

Six

MARCH HARE

"You are old" said the youth; "one would hardly suppose
That your eye was as steady as ever;
Yet you balanced an eel on top of your nose –
What made you so awfully clever?"

Lewis Carroll *Through The Looking-Glass*

While filming in Spain a letter found me in the mountains: would I play Valentine in a production of Shaw's *You Never Can Tell* to open at the Theatre Royal in the Haymarket with Ralph Richardson. An exciting offer; a terrific part in a grand play in the loveliest theatre in London with a great actor. I accepted at once. But my agent was annoyed. He was already negotiating a deal with Twentieth Century-Fox in which I would go to Australia to play a vicious young boxer discovered in Alice Springs by Sean Connery. I had also been approached in Madrid by the veteran director, King Vidor, who was setting up a movie about Christopher Columbus and wanted me for the lead. But my sights were trained on the Haymarket and Sir Ralph.

Ralph Richardson's technique, his persona, his diction, were of a particularity that defied criticism. He had a singular way of phrasing a line, pronouncing the words with a quirkiness of emphasis that could be simply breathtaking or absolutely mad. Thus his performances could be very odd indeed. But young actors would rather trample barefoot through fifty miles of broken glass to see him at his oddest than cross the road to see another actor's sanity.

In Graham Greene's *The Complaisant Lover* Ralph played a dentist. During the play the dentist discovers he is being cuckholded. He suspects his wife's lover is Clive Root. The dentist questions his wife. Yes, she admits, she has a lover. The dentist asks: "And is Root he?" When he came to the line, Ralph twisted on one foot, holding the other in the air behind him for several seconds while he asked: "And is Root – (pause) – he-he-he?"

Working with him at the Haymarket promised more excitement than I would find in Alice Springs.

But when I returned to England there was a hitch. Richardson had been filming *Doctor Zhivago*, and Tom Courtenay had taken his eye. I was to go to meet Richardson and be vetted by him. I was furious. I wanted to chuck the whole thing and dig out my boxing-gloves and head for Heathrow, but the producer told me not to be a fool and I duly reported to Richardson's house in Hampstead. I had been told to present myself at four in the afternoon and was advised to be precise. I caught the Tube to Hampstead and took a pleasant walk up to Jack Straw's Castle. Richardson's house lay beyond, in a small close a few yards down the hill. It was ten minutes to four. I sat on a wall and had a cigarette, keeping an eye on the minute hand of my watch. At exactly four o'clock I touched the doorbell. Before my finger left the button the door sprung open. It was Richardson. Had he been pressed with an eye to a peephole? He gave a great gasp of surprise, something that sounded like, "Ah! Ha ha ha! Heigh!" and staggered backwards, clutching the doorjamb for support as though I was some genie that had exploded out of the empty milk bottle in the drive. He shut the door firmly and turned and looked at me. There was a short pause. Lost for words I mumbled that I hoped he had been expecting me? It was a pretty silly thing to say since he had made the appointment himself only that very morning. Yes, he was expecting me. He said so. Or, at least: "Oo, oo, oo. Ah!"

I must not make him sound as though he were a buffoon. He was a highly intelligent man with little gift for chitchat and he was intensely shy. These inhibitions resulted in an inability to sustain the kind of social conventions other people found so easy. At such times he resorted to these curious exhalations. He led me upstairs, heigh-heighing all the way. He took me to his den, as vast as Shotover's, and he began to talk in disjointed phrases. He showed me the workings of a clock, his pet ferret, a hat he had bought in Northumbria, and he asked if I would like some gin or a spin on his motorcycle? He never uttered one word about *You Never Can Tell* or the Haymarket.

We went downstairs where his wife, Meriel Forbes, was waiting for us. Famously beautiful, she was very kind and took us into a drawing room where tea was laid. The chauffeur arrived and Sir Ralph asked if I needed a lift downtown. He ushered me into the front seat. The chauffeur sat in the rear. Sir Ralph seized the wheel and we shot off like a bullet.

Next day I was told the part of Valentine was mine.

You Never Can Tell was directed by Glen Byam Shaw, a name remembered now only by those actors who worked with him and cherish his memory as a perfectionist. He was a gentle man, a director of the most perfect taste and style. No playwright was ever better served by his director.

We live in an age of deconstructionism in the theatre, where directors often take a work and pull it apart in order to attract attention only to their own inventiveness – and to hell with the author's intentions. This was not Byam Shaw's way. He loved actors – he had been an actor himself – he encouraged them to give their imaginations free rein. But in the end his loyalty lay to the playwright, the playwright, the playwright.

The second Act of *You Never Can Tell* is set in an hotel in Torquay. Valentine runs up from the beach onto the terrace. I suggested I could have been playing cricket on the sands, and it might be a good idea if I ran on barefoot, tie off, shirt open, jacket and boots over my arm, carrying a cricket bat. I could re-dress as I talked to Harry Andrews. Harry loved the idea. He told me which moments would be effective for me to pull on my socks and boots. Richardson watched a rehearsal and showed me where I could get a laugh by mis-tieing my bootlaces. After two weeks Glen took me to one side. He quietly asked me to drop the whole thing. It was a very funny scene but *I* was getting the laughs, not Shaw, and the dialogue was more original than my business. The audience would look at my bare chest and not listen to the dialogue.

"It's a pretty chest, but they don't need to see it."

I sulked for about a day, but he was right. He had understood – even before I did – that I had invented the whole business just so I *could* show off my chest, with the rippling new pectorals I had worked so hard at the gym to achieve. I was using the play to serve my narcissism and I deserved the reproof I got.

On the other hand, it was Glen Byam Shaw who inspired Richardson to achieve a piece of absolute magic. In the second Act a three course lunch is served for seven actors. The lunch breaks up in confusion, leaving an irate Harry Andrews slumped in a fury at the head of the table. He is talked out of his mood by the old waiter. During this short scene, Richardson cleared the whole table, dishes, cruet, glasses, napkins, salad bowls, water jugs, decanters: all went onto one enormous tray. It was beautifully worked, with carefully rehearsed 'misplacements' of crockery that had to be adjusted on the tray later, so that the business would always seem spontaneous. This spontaneity was nothing of the kind of course; it had been prepared as diligently as D-Day. Each spot for every knife, fork, spoon and dish was marked out on a map on the tray until Richardson could do without it. Each 'misplacement' and its 'correction', and the necessary reshuffle of the china, which infallibly made the audience hoot with laughter, convinced the actor had got himself into a mess with the props, all was rehearsed punctiliously, so that at the end, when he folded the table-cloth, placed it on the top of the stacked tray, and said: "You never can tell sir; you never can tell", a salvo of applause accompanied Richardson as he shuffled to his exit.

Watching him rehearse this elaborate piece of business so meticulously, under the encouraging eye of Byam Shaw, was a delight for the company. Indeed the satisfaction and pleasure it clearly gave to Richardson, as fascinated by its intricacy as he was by the workings of a clock, was extremely moving. At one rehearsal, sitting next to Celia Bannerman, the lovely young actress playing Dolly, I noticed she was in tears.

We opened in Brighton on Boxing Day. The cheers were deafening. I saw Richardson walking along the front the next morning looking a bit glum. The producers wanted him to wear a wig. His decrepit old waiter had long Victorian sideburns but they wanted him to have also a head of snowy hair. A wig was ordered from London but it would take a day to arrive. What was he to do until it came? That night Richardson took his six spare sideburns and marched them in three glued rows across his bald pate. He looked alarmingly sinister, serving the soup like a poisoner and losing every laugh.

At the Haymarket the production was greeted with the universal acclaim we had anticipated. The whole of London seemed to echo the *Sunday Times's* view: 'Sir Ralph At His Peak.' It was exciting to be in a company with him, watching his fiercely concentrated technique and dazzling idiosyncratic style at such close quarters. He came down early to the stage to feel the sense of the audience. The Haymarket curtain has a tiny spyhole sewn into it and Ralph would scan the audience through it. If he spotted a couple of empty seats he would murmur: "Mr and Mrs Wood are in front."

His dedication to symmetry and his fascination for props was unfeigned. When something technical was set, it must remain set for the duration of the run. At the opening of the second Act, Ralph had a short scene which preceded mine; he had merely to enter, carrying a tray with tea and biscuits, make a Shavian quip and exit. One evening as I arrived backstage I saw Ralph staring at his tray in horror.

"Celia Bannerman has eaten a biscuit!"

I pointed out that there were nine more on the plate.

"But the pattern! The pattern! It's gone!"

You Never Can Tell was followed by *The Rivals*, again directed by Glen Byam Shaw. Ralph scored another triumph with a definitive Sir

Anthony Absolute. The critics vied in their praise for him in culinary terms; one described him as "a juicy chump chop," and another as "a rich plum pudding."

He had wanted me to play the tortured lover Faulkland, but Faulkland's introspection seemed to me merely the reverse side of Valentine's exuberance, and I was sick of playing romantic parts. Instead, I asked to play Bob Acres and, at length, he agreed. He watched me covertly during rehearsals, but like a hawk. I asked to make my first entrance carrying a dead hare as a surprise for Jack Absolute. There was some problem dealing with the hare after my exit. I was going to take it off with me when a voice called to Byam Shaw from the stalls:

"No, no, Glenny – leave the rabbit!"

Richardson had a scene following mine and he desperately wanted to use such an interesting prop. He tried sitting on it, he tried chucking it on the fire in mistake for a log. Nothing worked; he had to abandon the idea. It rankled. Years later, whenever we met he would ask:

"Where's the rabbit?"

Rehearsals were enormous fun and Acres is a lovely part. In my second scene, when Acres is about to break into smart Bath society and has been to the hairdresser to have his hair combed, to the tailor to have his wardrobe changed, and to a dancing-master to cure his clod hopping, I introduced a neat little dance timed to the dialogue. It was gauche as well as charming. A flautist was on stage. We had practised in private. Mindful of Byam Shaw's disapproval when I had taken off my shirt in *You Never Can Tell*, I was nervous when it was time to show him my invention as we went through the scene. Approval came at once. He thought the dance was original and touching and was supported by the text. Out of the corner of my eye I saw Richardson making his way through the stalls towards Byam Shaw. The two of them nodded happily and we broke for the day. Richardson was waiting at the stage door for his car. He congratulated me on the little dance: it was inspired. I could not claim the credit; I was a rotten dancer. The sequence was adapted from a moment in *Petroushka* and I had been helped.

"Someone in the Company?" asked Ralph.

"Nureyev."

Nureyev came to the opening night, escorting an attractive girl, Joan Thring, whose husband, Frank Thring was Australia's best-known actor. On their way from my dressing room they passed Richardson on the stairs. It may have been Joan Thring's beauty or Nureyev's bright green suit, or his celebrity, that attracted Richardson's attention, but he called into my room next evening. Nureyev's name was not in Richardson's vocabulary and he stumbled over the pronunciation. I told him that my cleaning-lady had the same problem. Nureyev stayed in my apartment in Millbank while he was between homes, and the bathroom was always covered with the intimate underwear that dancers use – dance belts, g-strings, tights – which old Annie, eighty-years-old, had never seen before. She telephoned me in shock.

"He's done another wash."

"Who, Annie?"

"You know who. The jumping man."

Rudolph came several times to the play and we would sometimes bump into Richardson as we went downstairs to the stage door. Nureyev bowed gravely to Richardson, who equally gravely bowed back, adding a friendly "Heigh heigh," and proposing a toast next evening to "The Jumping Man" when I went to his dressing room in the interval.

Margaret Rutherford was Mrs Malaprop. She gave an unforgettable performance, not shirking the pantomime-dame aspects of the character, but mining the role for all its romance. She could bring the house down, but never for one second did she lose her own innate femininity. I thought how heart-breaking it was that this gentle woman, blessed with such an inner core of goodness, should have been saddled with a physical appearance that induced such laughter. She knew she looked funny, and she knew that, as an actor, she could use it. Early in the rehearsals of a scene with Richardson, at the beginning of the play, the director said he had no idea what to do. They were both acting superbly but it was not amusing, and twenty minutes of the play had passed without a big laugh and it was, after all, a comedy.

"Shall I eat a piece of toast?" said Margaret.

She knew that as she munched the toast all her chins would waggle, the audience would laugh and that would be good for the production. But she never saw herself as a gorgon. She never saw herself as a grotesque. In her soul she was a girlish, loving, romantic woman and it was those qualities that lent such unique pathos to her work.

Unless the weather was really impossible, Margaret and her husband, Stringer Davies, would walk from Marylebone station to the Haymarket. They would arrive early in mid-afternoon, in time for Margaret to have a good sleep before the performance. But the walk would have agitated her and she would have a pill to relax. When it was time to wake for a cup of tea before putting on her make-up she was still sleepy, so another pill was produced to stimulate her. But this sometimes proved too distracting and she would take a pill to calm her. By the time she came into the wings for her entrance she was often in a state of real confusion.

It was difficult for Richardson. His first scene was with Mrs Malaprop, during which she had long speeches containing some of the most famous malapropisms, and he had little to do but listen as Margaret struggled to get through. Backstage, the stage manager stood in the wings ready to prompt; Margaret's understudy was at a crack in the set; Stringer was below the window with the script in hand. As I ran down for my first entrance I passed Richardson on the stairs going back to his room. He looked at me bleakly.

"Oh cocky! It's nightmare tunnel!"

There were times when Margaret seemed to have total control of the text onstage, but the terrible irony was that these were the very times when she was most distressed and tearful offstage. She knew that there was something happening to her brain. There was a history of insanity in her family and she was terrified that she was succumbing to it. She had been told her only hope was a course of electric shocks and she hated it, but subordinated herself to the treatment. She would then return to the Haymarket calm, relaxed, tranquil. But with all the text scrambled in her head. After a while it was whispered that she was about to give notice. Richardson was in despair. Though her failing memory unnerved him, he liked working with her, and he knew, too, that they made a formidable pair at the box office. Vivien Leigh came to the play. She had admired Margaret Rutherford and was praising her performance in my room when Richardson burst in. We should all go down to Margaret's room and beg her to stay. We went downstairs. Margaret was sitting at her table with Stringer beside her. She was clutching her head between her hands. Ralph spoke gently; Vivien with the greatest tact and affection. The tears started to flow down Margaret's face: "I can't" she wept, "Oh please! I can't."

She was replaced by Isabel Jeans. Isabel had superb delivery and was an Edwardian; girls were 'gels'. She had been a great beauty. One critic praised her performance, adding in his final words that she looked "like a piece of Dresden that has just been dropped." I found her in her dressing room with a pair of scissors, snipping off the offending words. She had a risque sense of humour and enjoyed being out with a man. As we sat in Joe Allen the conversation turned to love. She found it difficult to use the word 'sex'.

"Do you like '*it*'?"

I confessed that I certainly did. She shook her head.

"I never liked 'it'. I liked everything else, the 'venez souper avec moi', the jolis cadeaux, the tête-à-têtes. But I didn't like '*it*'!"

And she could be alarmingly reactionary. She did not understand the Miners' strikes. Coming from South Wales, I was appalled. The miners' working conditions and their wages were a disgrace.

"But why do they need more money? They have no position to keep up, they have no servants and they never go anywhere."

The Rivals is a happy play for actors and we were a very happy team. I would bump into Richardson sometimes coming out of his room, adjusting his lace cuffs, patting his feathered tricorne as he headed for the stairs.

"Is it safe to go down, d'you think cocky?" as if the audience were manning machine-guns. All the parts in *The Rivals* are good, none of them are exhausting, and they are placed with very agreeable gaps, leaving plenty of time to visit other dressing rooms. Ralph would say:

"I'm going to Dr Gordon, will you join me?"

Draping his burgundy velvet coat over a chair, in his britches and waistcoat, wigless, pipe in mouth and parrot on shoulder, like an upmarket Long John Silver, he neatly side-stepped over Jose's droppings on the Aubusson carpet and passed the gin.

"Are you fond of Dr Gordon?"

In New York in 1970, Anthony Quayle and I were at the Music Box in Anthony Shaffer's *Sleuth*. Next door at the Morosco were Richardson and Gielgud in David Storey's *Home*. In the New Year, Shaffer and I gave a party in his rambling apartment. We covered the walls of one room in tinfoil and set up a discotheque with coloured lights, a smoke machine and a fan. It was a big party; we invited everyone we knew and everyone came. A pianist played in the sitting room and Ethel Merman sang and there was a lot of noise. When the din was at its loudest, Ralph's wife said: "Where's Ralphie?"

It was very late and she thought they ought to go. I tried to find him. I had last seen him through a haze of confetti in the discotheque where Andy Warhol and his gang had established themselves. I had had a slow waltz with Candy Darling, born a boy, Jimmy Slattery on a farm in Iowa, now recreated in the image of Garbo, while Ralph was deep in animated conversation with another of Warhol's 'superstars' Jackie (I'm-not-a-boy-I'm-not-a-girl-I'm-just-Jackie) Curtis, who gyrated on the spot, with one hand on Richardson's shoulder while Warhol took polaroid snaps and Elaine Stritch lazily cast handfuls of confetti towards the fan. But now Richardson had gone. I wandered through the apartment. Merman was singing *They Say that Falling in Love Is Wonderful* to a group round the piano. John Gielgud saw me.

"Are you looking for Ralph? He's in the dining room behind the curtains."

I walked through the crowded room towards the window. A pair of shoes, sprinkled with confetti, protruded below the folds of the curtain. Ralph sat alone, wrapped in the curtain, looking across the reservoir to the lights of Manhattan.

"It's time to go, Ralph."

"Where's the rabbit?" he replied.

Seven

PRIVATE LIVES AND LAUGHTER

"How far have you grown away my dear love? How lonely are you in your little box so high above the arena? Don't you ever feel you want to come down in the cheap seats again, nearer to the blood and the sand and the warm smells, nearer to Life and Death?"

Noël Coward *Design for Living*

I met Noël Coward properly for the first time on my first night in America, but I had seen him before of course. As a very little boy in South Wales I had queued with my family at a British restaurant during the War, exchanging our penny vouchers for thin soup and over-cooked cod, and then queued another half-hour outside the Odeon cinema in the rain to get into *In Which We Serve,* which everyone thought was Coward's masterpiece. No one – least of all Coward – would have described the character he played in the film as comic, but what I clearly remember is the affectionate murmur of laughter from the audience the moment he appeared on the screen.

Ten years later, at the Royal Academy of Dramatic Art, Roy Kinnear and I were student ushers when the Queen Mother came to lay the foundation stone for the new Vanbrugh Theatre. The bomb site through which we hurtled from classes in Gower Street to the annexe in Malet Street had been cleared, and a nice piece of drugget set down, surrounded by a sea of gilt chairs. Roy Kinnear was seating Sybil Thorndike when Noël Coward appeared. He was portlier than I had expected, very sun-tanned, and he wore his slightly-too-small top hat at a jaunty angle. Roy handed him a programme and Coward thanked him, kissed Dame Sybil, winked saucily at John Gielgud and whispered something which reduced Gielgud to a giggling fit while the Dame chuckled helplessly into her gloves. There was a glimpse of blue bonnet as the Queen Mother arrived. Dame Sybil poked Coward with her umbrella,

"Now boys, we must pull ourselves together!"

Roy joined me, tears of laughter coursing down his face. I asked him what Coward had said.

"I've no idea! – but isn't he *funny!*"

So the first impressions I had of Coward were that wherever he was there would always be laughter.

Some ten years later, in September 1961, I was at Waterloo station saying goodbye to Margaret Leighton who was leaving for America. An attendant brought a telegram to the boat train. It was from Noël Coward in New York:

"WHEN SHALL YOU ARRIVE TO REHEARSE YOUR AMUSING LITTLE FROLIC AND SEE MY MASTERPIECE STOP HURRY HURRY STOP"

The 'amusing little frolic' for which Maggie was engaged was a new play by Tennessee Williams, *The Night of the Iguana*, and Coward's 'masterpiece' was his musical *Sail Away*.

Only a few days after Maggie had sailed, I landed the part of Henry VIII in the American production of *A Man for All Seasons*. In the evening of the 1st October I arrived in New York. I came into the city on the airport bus and the first sight of the Manhattan skyline before the bus dipped into the Midtown Tunnel was as overwhelming as I had expected. A message from Maggie at the hotel told me she had finished rehearsals and I was to come at once and meet her at some little German restaurant on West 44th Street. When I arrived she was with Noël Coward. He passed me a glass of wine and the menu.

"Have some knockwurst, it's very good for jetlag but lay off the sauerkraut – it'll give you wind."

He looked around and lowered his voice.

"The food's good but the place is entirely staffed with Nazis. I whistle *Rule Britannia* and undertip."

The excitement of arriving in America, of being in New York, of seeing Maggie again, of meeting Noël Coward, all this was making me light-headed. It was very late when we started to walk back to my hotel. We stopped at the kerb as the traffic streamed past. Above us soared a gigantic advertisement for cigarettes. On it a garish likeness of Babe Ruth puffed out smoke rings the size of lorry wheels.

"Have you telephoned home?" asked Maggie. "You must let them know you're safe and sound."

It would be eight in the morning in Barry. Coward stepped into a telephone booth.

"This is Noël Coward. I want to make a telephone call to South Wales and charge it to my account."

I gave him the number. There was a short pause.

"This is Noël Coward. Here is your son."

He handed me the receiver. Echoing down the line was my mother's voice.

"Where are you?"

"Where am I?" I asked Coward.

"You're standing underneath the Camel advertisement in Times Square."

I shouted it to my mother down the fuzzy connection, and I heard her call to Mrs Crisp who lived across the road.

"He's in Times Square with Noël Coward, standing underneath a camel!"

I saw Coward from time to time with Maggie that fall, while his show was on Broadway. Then he came to *Where Angels Fear to Tread* in London. After that I lost touch with him until 19th March 1966, when he turned up with Lilli Palmer in my dressing room at the Haymarket after a matinee of *You Never Can Tell*.

Coward was thrilled by Byam Shaw's production, by Ralph Richardson, by all of us. He raised his finger and pronounced the production flawless and perfect. It had a special appeal for him, for as a young writer he had sent off his first play to Shaw who had smartly returned it, advising Coward to keep away from any more of his work.

"Quite right," said Coward. "Unconsciously I had pinched the whole idea from *You Never Can Tell*."

I was shocked by Coward's appearance. He was alarmingly thin, and under the perennial tan his skin looked drawn and grey. He had been laid low by a bug in the Seychelles, and he had delayed the London production of his three new plays under the collective title, *Suite in Three Keys*, but his spirits were ebullient and he was determined to get well and open in April at the Queen's Theatre. The plays were a sell-out. After years of being consigned with Rattigan to the critical trash-can he relished the triumph, but it was the last time London would see him on stage.

The three plays were given on two successive evenings: a full-length comedy, followed the next night by two one-act pieces – a serious play and a farce. Of the three works, it was the short serious play *Shadows of the Evening* that I found the most remarkable and it moved me deeply. It was the least successful, the least sleek, the least adroit in construction – but imprinted with Coward's unmistakable trademark: dialogue cut to the bone, often teetering dangerously on the edge of sentimentality, but always stepping sure-footedly back from the abyss. He played a man who knew he was terminally ill. In 1931 in *Private Lives* Coward had written about death, counselling flippancy: "Death's very laughable. Such a cunning little mystery. All done with mirrors!" But those were the words of a young man.

Now the playwright was so much older, often exhausted, in discomfort and in pain. Nevertheless, he stared Death down onstage as lightheartedly as he stared it down in life. In the last moments of *Shadows of the Evening*, having organised a trip across Lake Geneva for an evening's gambling in France, he revealed to his companions that he was perfectly aware of the situation which so distressed them, but wanted no long faces.

"Come my dear ones," he said.

It was the authentic voice of Coward himself as he stretched out his hands to his friends,

"Don't forget your passports. I have mine. It is still valid for quite a while."

I saw a great deal of Noël while he was at the Queen's and I was at the Haymarket. My flat in Millbank was small, but it overlooked the Thames and it was the first home of my own in London. I loved it, and began to give supper parties. Simple food, but there was plenty of plonk, and every Thursday night the little flat almost burst at the seams. Thursday nights are best for actors. There is never a matinee next day, so the parties never finished before the river began to reflect the dawn light.

Coward came most weeks and was the best company in the world, funny and full of curiosity about the new young people I invited; he was especially taken by Angela Thorne. I always asked friends of his own generation – Gielgud, Emlyn Williams, Vivien Leigh – so that he would not feel trapped. But he was always wonderful with young actors, sensitive and kind, putting them immediately at ease, seeming to give the lie to the legend that he could be a martinet if provoked. Angela asked him if it was true that he had sacked a well-known young film star in the first days of rehearsals for *Hay Fever*, which was playing to capacity at the National Theatre. It was perfectly true, said Coward. He had asked all the actors to learn their lines beforehand.

"She hadn't, so I sacked her. She rang me up. She said 'You're a pig.' I may be a pig I told her, but at least I know my oinks."

Coward would play no engagement longer than three months. At the end of July he returned home to Switzerland, and then on to Jamaica in pain. In November he was rushed to Chicago for a medical examination. He had a stone on the kidney.

"There was nothing to be done," he said, "but grit the dentures and rise above it."

The operation was a success. Soon he was on the move again, and in the spring of 1967 was back in London. By now we were doing *The*

Rivals at the Haymarket and Noël came to a matinee and we had tea at
the Cavendish afterwards. He had enjoyed his afternoon, but not as much
as *You Never Can Tell.* He had not cared for Margaret Rutherford's Mrs
Malaprop, but this obviously stemmed from an old sore. He had never
forgotten, or really forgiven, that she had refused the part of Madam
Arcati, the dotty spiritualist in *Blithe Spirit* in 1941. She had gone to his
house and he had read the new play in front of a little group who laughed
diligently in all the right places, and when Coward had finished he put
down the manuscript and looked contentedly at Margaret, expecting
congratulations and commitment. She turned him down. He telephoned
his friend, the producer Hugh (Binkie) Beaumont in a rage. How could
the woman be so stupid? It was the best part she would ever get, and he,
Noël Coward, had written it especially for her! The waitress at the
Cavendish set the tea tray down before us, just in time to hear Coward
conclude his account: "Fortunately she realised she'd been a cunt."

Binkie Beaumont was the producer of *The Rivals.* I asked him for
his version of the Madam Arcati brouhaha. Coward's story was
accurate. He had indeed telephoned, gibbering with fury. Binkie calmed
Noël down and advised him to lie low; then he telephoned Margaret
Rutherford. She was in great distress. She knew the role had been
written for her and she knew that Coward thought Madam Arcati was
an hilarious creation.

"But she isn't funny. I *know* women like that."

Beaumont soothed her. He begged her to accept the role and to
act it exactly as she saw the character. He promised there would
be no pressure from Coward to make her play for laughs. Then he
telephoned Coward.

"Let her play it the way she wants. It will be the way *you* want."

And so it was. The play came to life with Madam Arcati's first
entrance. The audience began to laugh, and they laughed louder and
louder as the evening proceeded, but the laughter was underpinned
throughout by the sublime innocence of Rutherford's performance.

Margaret Rutherford and Noël Coward were poles apart. As an
actress and as a woman Margaret had no instinctive sense of humour,
while Noël saw the ridiculous side of everything. His slant on life was
a puzzlement to her, and she was equally beyond his comprehension.

Few men could have had more friends than Coward. He was good
at friendship. He worked at it hard. In Paris, New York, or London his
days were filled with lunch parties, cocktail parties, dinner parties,
supper parties. Then there were plays, movies, musicals and exhibitions

to be fitted in. Everyone wanted to see him and he never disappointed them. He adored them. No wonder that when he withdrew to his homes in Switzerland or Jamaica he often slumped with fatigue.

Not all of Coward's friends were superstars. Two of his dearest were the Spanier sisters. Ginette and Didine Spanier were Englishwomen of French parentage. It was an affectionate tease that they kept up their heavily-accented English with weekly visits to Berlitz. Born in Paris, as children they moved with their parents to Golders Green ("Halfway to Manchester," Coward said). In the Thirties Ginette found a job working as a salesgirl in the gift department of Fortnum & Mason, serving Wallis Simpson and the Prince of Wales, and a very young Binkie Beaumont. Then in 1939, with spectacular mistiming she returned to the Paris she had always loved, married to a doctor, and stepped into a five-year nightmare. At the outset of War her husband, Paul-Emile Seidmann, went to the front with a small hospital unit. Ginette followed him, taking a room in a boarding house nearby. France was in chaos, the roads packed with lines of refugees as the Luftwaffe bombed its way forward. The French armies collapsed before the German advance, and then came the treaty of collaboration. From that moment, Ginette said, all her love of France was killed and she burned with an intense loyalty for England. In 1986, in my house in Sussex, a young English priest who had lived in Paris and become an ardent francophile heard Ginette's accent and rushed towards her, beaming,

"Ah madame! Vous êtes francaise!"

"Non," said Ginette crisply, "je suis britannique."

Her husband's unit was ordered to return to Paris and disband. Ginette rode beside Paul-Emile in a convoy of French field ambulances with a German escort. She would never erase from her mind the memory of re-entering the occupied capital. It was a tranquil summer morning, she recalled, one of those days when Paris looks its incomparable best. The convoy swept into the deserted Place de la Concorde, pink and gold in the sun. Then she saw that every building was festooned with swastikas, huge banners hanging still in the warm summer heat.

"As if the whole of Paris was covered by spiders."

What sickened her most were not the full-blown official flags, but the effusion of swastikas at every window, some tiny and home-made, badly smudged black crosses on a red-crayoned background. She realised Parisians, ordinary people, had been preparing these flags for weeks, hoarding them, waiting to greet the Nazis as they marched in.

Never having paid much attention to the fact that she was Jewish, it was now brought home to her in horrific fashion. As the ordinances against the Jews were published, Ginette and her husband moved to Vichy France, to Nice where Dr Seidmann saw patients in a small hotel room and Ginette hawked a suitcase of toiletries, including sanitary towels, around the shops. Soon Paul-Emile received an official letter forbidding him as a Jew to practice medicine or sign a prescription. Then they started rounding up the Jews in the south. The Seidmanns fled to the mountains where they were sheltered by French people as hostile to the Vichy government as they were. For the rest of the War the Seidmanns were on the run until, cycling through the German lines in September 1944, they saw an empty carton of Lucky Strikes and realised they had reached the American army.

Ginette Spanier's family had received no word of her for five years. They feared the worst, but now she was fêted and cosseted. By a tremendous stroke of luck she found herself directrice of the fashion house of Balmain. Installed in a beautiful apartment near the Etoile, Ginette established an informal salon in Paris. She was not a proper hostess. "She doesn't even serve nuts!" complained her sister, Didine. Nevertheless the first thing anyone did in Paris, once the bags were dumped, was to call Elysée 1516 and make a beeline to 70 Avenue Marceau where you might find Danny Kaye, Lena Horne or the Oliviers, and anyone else passing through. She sent me a telegram.

"PLEASE TAKE THE 1700HRS FLIGHT TO
ORLY FRIDAY TICKET AT THE AIR
FRANCE DESK I HAVE INVITED SOME
FRIENDS FOR YOU LOVE GINETTE"

The apartment was packed. Her friends were already there; Maurice Chevalier, Marlene Dietrich, Claudette Colbert and Noël Coward. John Schlesinger's movie, *Midnight Cowboy* had been released and Colbert and Dietrich were in fierce dispute, with Coward egging them on while pretending to be neutral. Colbert thought the picture brilliant; Dietrich thought it "wubbish". As their argument grew more heated I withdrew to another room to get a drink. The doors were flung open and Colbert burst in.

"If that damn Kraut doesn't shut up I'll choke her with an aubergine!"

Coward kept a small apartment in New York, a pied-à-terre when he visited the city en route for Jamaica. When he was not in residence he let it to friends. Hearing that I was bound for Broadway with *Sleuth* Ginette called Noël and it was arranged that I should use the apartment for the run. When people learned whose flat I had taken, they imagined I was surrounded by white-on-white Syrie Maugham décor and glittering chrome. But the furniture was unpretentious and comfortable. There were many books, a card-table with sharpened pencils, and scratch-pad, one framed photograph of Elaine Stritch, a piano, and some charming pictures of Jamaica that Coward had painted over the years. The tenant before me had been the director, John Dexter, and when I finally left I passed it on to Eileen Atkins.

I wrote to Coward thanking him and telling him how happy I was. A strangely cryptic cable arrived at the Music Box Theatre:

"DONT WE ALL STOP LOVE NOEL"

I puzzled over it for days until I remembered telling him that the bed tended to squeak in moments of high passion. Then he came to New York for ten days and I moved out to an apartment over 'Sarge's Deli' on Third Avenue with cockroaches the size of crocodiles. I met Noël for a meal at Sardi's after my matinee. He was sitting in a booth with Toby Rowland, an American friend of ours. It was the Seventies when everyone was singing about going to San Francisco and wearing flowers in their hair. My shirt came from a London store called 'Your Mother Wouldn't Like It', kind of see-through, covered with daisies. Toby said:

"You look like a lovely bouquet!"

"But not," said Noël, "freshly plucked."

When I left *Sleuth* after seventeen months on Broadway I was invited to spend Easter with Coward and I flew to Jamaica.

"We're rather crowded," said his great friend, Graham Payn, on the telephone. "We've got the Bonnings."

I drove across the island to Blue Harbour. The 'Bonnings' turned out to be the conductor Richard Bonynge and his wife, Joan Sutherland.

Blue Harbour was a ravishingly pretty house built on a wooded hill. Everywhere there was the sense of the sea and tantalising glimpses of it. The entrance from the road led to the top floor of the house. Downstairs was the dining room and a sitting room with wide verandahs. Then the stairs reached the garden. A winding path led through the trees past two guest houses (the lowest one, very near the sea, was christened 'Cape Wrath' by Terence Rattigan). Finally, there was the huge pool on the edge of the Caribbean, surrounded by palms. The whole place, indeed Noël Coward's whole life, was run by Cole Lesley ('Coley') and Graham Payn. These two extraordinary men, so wise and kind, and such fun, were indispensable to Coward. They were organised and sensible about the day-to-day details of things, making sure everything ran like clockwork, but they were equally painstaking with the smallest niceties. When I arrived the first thing Coley did was to give me a gin and some postcards and stamps, showing me to stick the stamps on first because "they're such big buggers." Graham Payn's good looks, pleasing voice and infectious charm should have guaranteed him a very successful career in the theatre, but his advancement had been inhibited by the knowledge of his association with Coward. He never complained and no one, not even Coward himself, ever sang *Matelot*, the song Coward wrote for Graham in *Sigh No More*, with more delicacy and charm.

Coward no longer stayed in Blue Harbour when he was in Jamaica. He had built a little studio house for himself called 'Firefly' on top of a nearby hill. When I had finished my drink Graham took me straight up to see him. It was a very bumpy track and I was hurled from one side of the car to the other. Some boys were playing cricket in a field. Graham hooted the horn in greeting.

"Aren't they sweet! Look at them waving – they're shouting, 'Love to Master'!"

To me their cry sounded more like "Black Power Now!" and their waves seemed rather clenched.

We whirled on up the track, hitting a particularly wrenching corner.

"Don't worry! The Queen Mother came up in the Rolls and said it was the greatest fun!"

We arrived at the crest.

The view was breathtaking. The little house was on two storeys, and the room in which Coward spent all his time had shutters that let fully down so that the whole wall was open to the sky and to the view. A blue pool looked very tempting. It had been scooped out of the top of the hill. It would be like swimming in the sky.

As we parked the car, Graham turned to me: "Try and persuade him to swim. The doctors say he must exercise but he's as obstinate as a mule." Noël was sitting at a card-table, working on a crossword. He wore a simple cotton dressing-gown.

"Dear Keith."

He beamed at me. My clothes were a constant source of amusement to him. I was in faded jeans and a ripped shirt.

"You've come as something, but I'm not sure what."

It was bakingly hot.

"Let's have a swim," I said.

He rose unsteadily, grumbling good-humouredly.

"Not if it's blowing a hurricane. I don't want to be buffeted about."

He took my arm and we moved slowly to the door, encouraged by Graham. We emerged into the Caribbean noon. The air was like a furnace. One small leaf stirred on a distant hibiscus and Noël pointed to it.

"Wuthering Heights!" he shouted, collapsing into a chair and refusing to budge.

He lived alone at 'Firefly'; it was his refuge from the stream of visitors whom he sometimes found exhausting. He ate every meal by himself. He was devotedly cared for by Miguel, a Jamaican whose wife lived in the village. He read voraciously. Occasionally he toyed with his paints, but not often now. The piano in the unused sitting room needed tuning. He would have no telephone, not even an extension to the main house down the hill. It was a time of much political unrest in Jamaica, there had been riots in Kingston, a gruesome murder in Montego Bay. The previous night the electricity supply had been cut. I thought of the boys playing cricket in the field, and as we drove back down for lunch at Blue Harbour I asked Graham if he was not worried for Coward, so isolated in his eyrie.

"Of course! We all worry. But it's what he wants and he's absolutely adamant. It's the way he wants to live. He's afraid of nothing."

And indeed it was exactly as Graham said. A year later Miguel discovered him collapsed on the floor before dawn, but Coward forbade him to wake Graham and Coley at such an early hour. Shortly afterwards he died and was buried in the garden of 'Firefly'.

Every day I went up to see Coward before lunch. Sometimes I was alone with him. We sat in the shade by the pool if there was no wind, while he pumped me for news from Broadway and gossip about mutual friends in England. Something might remind him of a song. Cigarette in one hand and a gin in the other he sat bolt upright in his chair and took me back to a pre-First World War world I never knew. He never sang his own stuff, just snatches of music-hall numbers and ballads from forgotten operettas; *They Call Me Countess Mitzy But I Can't Imagine Why!* The song had a fiendishly complicated lyric which he enunciated with perfect precision.

Occasionally he could be coaxed into the pool. He swam naked, jumping into the deep end, one hand holding his nose and the other covering his privates like a schoolboy.

It was in the pool one day that he said:

"You'd make a very good Leo."

Obviously I did not respond with sufficient enthusiasm, for I have never found *Design for Living* all that interesting.

"It's a very funny play," he said sharply. "Or *Quadrille*. You could play that. That's also very funny."

I swam a few lengths. He called across the water,

"Isn't there any play of mine Your Graciousness might consider?"

He was grinning his Chinese smile. I shouted back,

"What about *Private Lives*? That's a very funny play."

He wagged a reproving finger.

"It's a very *serious* play."

Twenty years after that afternoon by the pool at 'Firefly' I did get to play Elyot in *Private Lives* with Joan Collins at the Aldwych Theatre in London. The production was an enormous success. Joan looked absolutely ravishing, but in truth we were both far too old for that pair of scatterbrained amoralists.

In Jamaica, in picturesque surroundings, in the tropical climate he loved, Coward fashioned his life into a pattern that clearly gave him the utmost content, encircled by the companions he cherished. Outside, the world was turning. Prurient appetites were demanding to be fed and Coward's sexuality was held up for investigation. He was accused of dishonesty in his work, of having been sexually duplicitous, but as his biographer Clive Fisher pointed out,

"We easily forget now that England used to to be much more puritanical and repressive, that otherwise law-abiding men risked blackmail, prosecution, ostracism and imprisonment with every illicit embrace." *

In fact Coward never felt the slightest qualm about his homosexuality, but he manoeuvred his professional life along paths that were hedged with discretion. Women found Coward sexually exciting, and he was wise enough to see how enormously it increased his audiences, but there was nothing ambivalent about his private life, nor any masquerade amongst his friends and associates. He had, in any case, always offered clues to the discerning. In his apartment in New York an album of photographs taken of Coward over the years contained one remarkable black and white picture, taken in his prime, presenting a paradox. Though the patina of stage make-up is clearly evident, the face white, the bowed lip-line sharply painted, the eyes shaded by lashes thick with mascara, the lineaments are resolutely masculine, the jawline firmly chiselled. In the eyes, directed so implacably into the camera is a look at once laconic and provocative. It is a look that challenges: "I am not what I may seem; but neither are you."

* 'Noël Coward' by Clive Fisher

Was Coward happy? Yes, assuredly. If there was ever a regret it was perhaps best expressed in a remark he once made as we sat by the pool.

"I have never quickened the sexual pulse in any man I desired."

The fierce sun did nothing to dissipate the momentary chill. He puffed at his (forbidden) cigarette and smiled.

"However I have risen above it."

Rising above it was a practice he had perfected. Professional reverses, monetary embarrassments, vituperation in the press, he had schooled himself to rise above them all. He was lucky in his friends and their loyalty was unstinting. In Paris, in a small restaurant, Marlene Dietrich told me a story about him in the Forties. He was staying with her in Hollywood. She was leaving the next day by train for New York. While she busied herself with her packing, Noël sat in a wing-backed armchair with a deck of cards playing patience. The front door burst open and a frantic Cary Grant rushed in.

"They've just arrested Bugsy Siegel for racketeering! We must all say we've never met him!"

Coward murmured that he did not think that would be possible since they had all spent several very merry evenings at Siegel's house enjoying his lavish hospitality. But Grant was distraught.

Dietrich was fascinated. Here was the man Noël *adored* – whose sexual magnetism he had celebrated in one of his songs *Mad about the Boy*, disintegrating before his eyes. But he never stopped playing patience, Dietrich said, laying one card upon another with complete calm. Yet, when he flicked a look at Grant, there was nothing but contempt in his eyes as he sat ramrod stiff in his armchair.

"You see," said Dietrich "there was in Noël a moral integrity that was made of steel."

When it was time for lunch I drove back to the others at Blue Harbour. In the afternoon we lazed around the swimming pool. Joan Sutherland sat in a swing, sewing coloured patches onto my jeans, singing snatches of the *Jewel Song* from *Faust*. In the evenings the whole troupe of us rattled up to 'Firefly' before dinner. We would stay there as the sun set and the velvet sky grew dark. Miguel served drinks that were always astonishing for they were unpredictably mixed. You might get a glass of plain tonic water or a knockout belt of unlaced gin. We stayed until Coward tired.

One evening he kept us late. It was the last evening of our holiday. I was returning to England, the Bonynges were off to the Met in New

York for Donizetti's *The Daughter of the Regiment*. Noël was particularly animated, and sang a comic ditty of Albert Chevalier's which he remembered from his boyhood. He also sang Gilbert and Sullivan with Sutherland while the rest of us lala'd the accompaniment. Then, holding his hand, Joan sang *I'll See You Again*. Afterwards Coward said: "Goodnight my darlings" and we went back down the hill.

He was in London later that summer of 1972 and I saw him with Graham and Coley. But in the spring of the following year he died at his beloved 'Firefly', and it is there that I think of him sitting contentedly against the dark tropical sky, surrounded by friends, as the words of the loveliest of his songs floated into the night with their message of enduring affection. There may have been tears in his eyes, but his lips were curved in the smile that always promised laughter.

Eight

OGNI GIORNO, OGNI NOTTE

"Because I know that time is always time
And place is always and only place
And what is actual is actual only for one time
And only for one place
I rejoice that things are as they are..."

T. S. Eliot *Ash Wednesday*

It is St. Mark who tells us about the man jogging along the coast road in Judaea. When the man ran up to the disciples and asked how to inherit eternal life, he was told to give away his possessions and, says St. Mark, the man "went away grieved." St. Mark's bones are reputed to lie in Venice, and it was in a restaurant in Venice twenty-five years ago that I unwittingly obeyed St. Mark's instruction and, though I cursed my foolishness, I found to my surprise that in the end it brought me peace of mind.

The best way to arrive in Venice is still by train. You slither the last kilometre across the lagoon towards the city called La Serenissima, though there is nothing serene outside the smeared and greasy carriage windows, nor as you arrive at San Lucia Station, shooed out by a yawning porter. Nothing remarkable at all until you are through the station and emerge onto the steps and there at your feet is the Grand Canal and you stand for a moment, enslaved again.

If you take the vaporetto down the Canal, passing under the Rialto Bridge, and get off at San Toma, an alley leads you towards the walls of the great Frari Church and you can visit the School of S. Rocco and stand in awe before the Tintoretto Crucifixion. But if you are not in the mood for sightseeing you may decide instead to have a meal at the best little trattoria in the city.

It was Tom Ferris who discovered it in 1972. We had been to the Accademia and lunched at a restaurant by the bridge where the food was overpriced and indigestible. He stared at the glutinous mass on his plate. "I don't understand it! Here I am in Italy and the food stinks."

Ferris is American of Italian-Irish parents.

"Why can't we find the sort of Italian place we have in Brooklyn? A family restaurant with Momma in the kitchen, Poppa behind the bar, the kids waiting table and the food's home-made and *great*!"

We set off on a search.

I was drawn to a restaurant, tucked away behind Santa Maria della Fava. A small side canal ran alongside, and a woman was sunning herself at the door.

"What's the name of this place?"

She grinned at us, revealing a glittering gold tooth, and slipping a hand inside her tight black blouse hiked up her splendid breasts.

"Ristorante Maria! I am Maria!"

She jerked a cooking spoon towards the church, "like the Madonna!"

We followed her through the bar. She flicked a dismissive hand towards a man wiping glasses "Mio marito", and her husband gave a nod. She ushered us into a large airy room with windows overlooking the canal. A pretty little girl, ripely pubescent, unmistakably Maria's daughter, brought us menus. "Good," said Ferris, "a family restaurant at last!" The meal was delicious and if we hadn't lingered over the wine things might have turned out differently, but when I raised my glass to propose a toast to a Quest well ended I saw Tom had turned ashen. A yard away, on the steps of the kitchen, a very large rat sat leisurely cleaning its whiskers. As we scraped back our chairs the rat gave us a disdainful glance and sauntered back over the pots and pans for a second helping of the excellent carbonara sauce.

"It's just Venice" I shrugged, but Americans are fussy about that sort of thing.

The very next day we found the Trattoria Max. It was late in the afternoon, the sort of airless day you get in Venice when your clothes stick to you and the heat is trapped in pockets in the alleyways. A seat in the shade with a bottle of Soave is all you long for. The Trattoria door was open, the bar looked cool. Sergio, who welcomed us, was a rugby aficionado who knew all about Wales; his wife Onorina took us to a table in the garden; her brother, Max (after whom the restaurant was named), opened the wine and his wife Ada came to show us the fresh fish; their teenage son Fiorenze brought us bread and cutlery; Giulia-Marina, eighty-years-old, was in the matriarchal kitchen cutting up squid; her husband Augusto, ninety, the head of the family, surveyed us magisterially from a chair beneath a fig tree. It started to rain, and the other diners fled inside, but we were sheltered by a large umbrella and ate rabbit cooked in oregano with polenta, lingering until the restaurant closed. We never bothered to eat anywhere else.

In March, the following year, I returned to Venice, on my way to make a film with Elizabeth Taylor. A driver was waiting for me at Venice

Airport to take me up to the location. But first I went for lunch and grappas with the family at the Trattoria Max and after my goodbyes I fell asleep in the warm car the studio had sent for me. What my thoughts were as I slumbered I cannot now remember but I certainly could never have dreamed that in a few months' time the little trattoria was to be the scene of one of my most embarrassing performances, and the prologue to that scene began as we headed up through thick snow towards Cortina d'Ampezzo.

❖

It was dusk when the car left me in the courtyard of the Miramonte Hotel with my luggage. Fairy lights picking out the Victorian gazebo twinkled merrily. Liveried footmen helped guests as they stepped from the ski-lift in the grounds. An elderly man lit torches in the snow; Count Esterhazy's child was twelve tonight and the torches ringed a giant snowman in his honour. Behind the hotel a mountain loomed, its mass visible only against the background of the early evening stars. In the far distance the sun which had left this valley an hour ago caught the jagged peaks of the Dolomites and burned them red. The lobby of the hotel rang with greetings in a cacophony of languages; pageboys wandered through with messages on salvers; furs were dropped across gilt armchairs; porters pushed trolleys of battered luggage; dogs barked. It was very glamorous, like a scene from a movie – which is exactly what it would be.

You will not find *Ash Wednesday* on anyone's 'Best Film' list, but it was fun to make, mainly because it starred Elizabeth Taylor. Minor background roles were filled by a rum assortment of faces. Hanging around the lobby were a Prinz or two, several Principessas, contessas galore, a Marquis from Paris, another from Spain, an Austrian Baron and two Hungarian Counts. A few had actually paid for their rooms. The rest were hired to give an authentic air of class to the picture. It was a casting director's idea to search out titled emigrés in Rome, long in lineage but short of cash, who would like a paid holiday en grand luxe, in return for appearing as extras in a film. Meals and pocket money would be provided, but please bring jewels. Accordingly bony foreheads, hooked noses, watery eyes and weak chins straight from the Almanach de Gotha decorated the hotel and waited for action.

Some of the actors had already arrived. The dazzlingly handsome Helmut Berger, named by *Vogue* as 'The Most Beautiful Man In The World', had swept up the day before in the Rolls Royce Visconti had given him. Delighted with the frisson his arrival had caused in the lobby as his Louis Vuiton bags were unloaded, he was waiting to welcome me with a bottle of Dom Perignon and a joint. We had never met, but he was marvellously friendly though could not help making a little grimace of distaste as my assorted bundles were carried past. "It's very important to have good luggage," he murmured. His spirits were ever so slightly dampened when the Burtons arrived. It was not the elegance of Elizabeth Taylor and Richard Burton as they stepped from their Mercedes that ruffled him, it was the convoy of trucks that followed them. "Trucks!" said Helmut, "Their luggage needed *trucks*!"

The first day's shooting is always tense and I was in the first shot of the first day, filming in the little piazza facing the church. There are always plenty of sightseers when you are shooting in the street and the word was out that Elizabeth Taylor was to appear. The crowd was immense.

The scene was set up. I was playing a photographer taking sexy fashion pictures of a pretty model; as the villagers emerged from Mass, the girl would drop her fur coat, and I would 'shoot' her in skimpy panties, surrounded by the outraged faces of the 'churchgoers'. Extras were inside the church, practising their outraged faces on each other. When "Action!" was called, out they came, the girl dropped her coat and we got the shot. Then Elizabeth arrived for the next set-up. The crowd roared. Suddenly there was the flurry of a white surplice by the camera. A priest was summoning the director and the producer for a crisis meeting with the Monsignor who was in a rage. When the church had given permission for the filming, no one had explained the unseemliness involved. Dominick Dunne, the executive producer from Hollywood, said he was very sorry and Paramount Pictures, whom he represented, would be very sorry too. What could be done to make amends? Elizabeth retreated to her caravan behind the church, taking me with her.

No one has ever usurped Elizabeth Taylor's diadem as the supreme screen goddess and superstar, and no one ever will now, for the game is over and all the rules have changed. Even compared with the other legendary actresses of the cinema she holds a unique position. Dilys Powell, writing in *The Sunday Times*, admitted as much while she pondered over Elizabeth's performance as Cleopatra, which Miss Powell had thought unsatisfactory. She reflected in her review that, unlike every other women star, Bette Davis, Joan Crawford, Greta Garbo, Katherine Hepburn – Elizabeth Taylor lacked one quality the others shared: a streak of masculinity. And of course Miss Powell was right; where femininity is concerned Elizabeth Taylor is unequalled. She has outlived and eclipsed the careers of all her rivals: Lana Turner, Rita Hayworth, Ava Gardner, Marilyn Monroe. And unlike them she has won two Academy Awards. Is it any wonder that in Cortina d'Ampezzo the hills were alive with the sound of camera shutters? I was prepared to be dazzled by her extraordinary beauty, though nothing could ever truly prepare one for such loveliness. But I was not prepared for her kindness, her sense of fun, her genuine warmth and modesty. Nor, I am ashamed to say, had I been prepared for her talent. In Britain, alas, theatre people often disparage American movie stars like Taylor, dismissing them as dim-witted dummies on whom, by some extraordinary fluke, fortune has incomprehensibly smiled, remembering only the rubbish in which they have appeared. It was true that Elizabeth Taylor had appeared in a fair amount of rubbish, but then so have most actors.

Any actor playing a scene with Elizabeth Taylor finds that when the cameras turn she has a sudden spontaneity and freshness that is as startling as it is stimulating. What is more unusual is her generosity as a player. Painstaking, she will rehearse as often as *you* wish – and sometimes, for your own good, will stop rehearsing. She will patiently help you, leading you towards a more interesting slant on a scene. She is also capable of pushing you, physically and forcefully, into a camera angle that is more flattering for you. I have worked with other famous screen beauties and in their orchards, I assure you, you will not find Elizabeth Taylor's kind of altruism blossoming on trees.

We sat drinking vodka and orange juice in her caravan while the producer and the Monsignor sorted things out. The caravan's previous inhabitant had been Sophia Loren. There were many tassels, much gold thread and the colour scheme was a particularly virulent shade of fuschia. After a few vodkas, however, the decor did not seem so bad.

We were alone, except for a secretary busy squeezing oranges and opening Stolichnaya. An hour went by. And a second. We talked about Wales. We talked about New York. We talked about her children. Her daughters were with her on location; Maria, whom she and Burton had adopted, and thirteen-year-old Liza Todd, whose father had died when she was an infant.

Liza doted on Richard Burton, who was like a father to her, and Richard, in turn, adored her. Liza could even speak a little Welsh. We discussed diets. We talked about the tap-water, did I think it had a peculiar texture? And the food? Had my digestion been affected? Hers was playing tricks.

There was a rap on the door and Dominick Dunne ushered in a beaming Monsignor. A thousand dollars had solved the matter. The Monsignor wanted to pay his respects. He also wanted Elizabeth's autograph. He bowed low, trying not to ogle the walnut-sized diamond on her finger.

"You two have been having a good chat," said Dominick.

"We've been discussing bowel movements," smiled Elizabeth as she signed a photograph.

There were to be many crises for Dominick Dunne to deal with during the shooting of *Ash Wednesday*. It would turn out to be the last major picture he worked on before he gave up Hollywood and turned, first to journalism, and then to immense success as a novelist. An enchanting man, in appearance always so dapper, his face is cast in a gloomy mould that masks a wayward and anarchic sense of humour. Bullied by messages from Paramount in Los Angeles, he would go to his room early, hang a DO NOT DISTURB sign on his door, and instruct the hotel switchboard to refuse all calls. But when I went past his room I could tap gently three times and hiss through the keyhole "Dominick, it's Keith," and he would open the door cautiously and usher me in to sip champagne while he unburdened his Hollywood angst. The film was already over budget. Elizabeth had the contractual right to work fairly short days. As a result, we were seriously behind schedule. Paramount regularly sent vast bouquets and telegrams to Elizabeth, gushing over the daily rushes as they arrived in Los Angeles. Meanwhile, Dominick was bombarded with phone calls: "Get that cow on the set on time!"

One of the few brief pleasures in Dominick Dunne's life during the filming was the arrival of his daughter Dominique. A sparky, intelligent girl of thirteen, I spent a good deal of time with her. We went to Venice together and the family at Trattoria Max fussed over her. She returned to school in Los Angeles before my birthday, but her father brought some presents onto the set. "And that's from Dominique," he said, setting down a package. It was the 29th April and Dominique had stolen the steel marker from Table 29 in the hotel dining room and folded it in tissue paper. It stands on my desk – in front of me now as I write these words – but the little girl who had wrapped it so carefully, whose whacky sense of humour made me laugh so much, is dead. Growing into an accomplished young actress in Hollywood, she was pursued by an older boy whose rages frightened her. When she refused to see him any more he strangled her, taking five long minutes to do so. At his trial the Los Angeles judge wore designer sunglasses and jeans. The killer escaped a homicide charge and served eighteen short months.

For most of the filming of *Ash Wednesday* Elizabeth was healthy and full of vigour, but there were times when she was unwell. All through her life, ever since a childhood fall from her horse in *National Velvet*, she suffered recurring pain. In 1960 she almost died, and her throat still bears the scars of the operation that saved her life in London. Sometimes she had to wear a neck-brace during her waits between scenes. She asked for no sympathy and scorned it if it was offered. But far greater pain for her was knowing that Richard Burton was profoundly unhappy. She was determinedly cheerful, on set and off, but it was obvious to everyone that she was fighting like a tigress to save her marriage. When Richard's unhappiness made him cruel, sometimes very cruel, she ignored it. She was without pride. She loved him unreservedly, and any future without him appeared to her an abyss.

Anyone who is an actor could understand the special sort of hell Richard was going through. Although he was an undisputed 'star', he was nevertheless not working. Sitting around, not being part of the project tests the temper of any man. When the man is possessed of a fierce masculine pride while his wife is being courted and pampered, that temper is liable to explode, and Richard's fuse was short. No one regarded Richard with anything less than respect. It was how he regarded himself that counted. He thought *Ash Wednesday* was junk. He disliked the director. He did not speak Italian, and had nothing to say to the crew who were in awe of him and kept a wary distance. He liked and admired Henry Fonda, but Henry was with us only a short time before leaving for his next film.

Then there was Helmut Berger. Richard had nothing in common with Helmut, whose character he hardly understood, and what he did understand unnerved him. To make matters worse, Liza had become infatuated with Helmut. Helmut must have seemed a glittering character to Liza; fun-loving and outrageous. He took her to discotheques, and she followed him around devotedly. Richard, irrationally jealous, sought my sympathy. I tried to assure him he had nothing to fear, that nothing could be more innocent. Helmut was very protective of Liza, and Liza was simply having a lot of fun. But one morning we were filming in a restaurant high above the slopes. Fonda, Berger and I shared a caravan and the three of us were lying on our bunks waiting to be called onto the set. Henry was sketching the view. I was reading. Helmut, eating chocolates and sipping champagne, was playing Gilbert O'Sullivan's *Alone Again, Naturally* on his portable record player. The door flew open. An assistant ordered Helmut into a car that would take him by a back route to a room where he was to stay hidden. "Now! You must leave *now!*" Burton's chauffeur had phoned from the Miramonte: Richard had a gun, and was on his way up to find Helmut. Helmut was bundled into the car. Fonda shook his head in dismay and was called onto the set for his scene. I was alone when Richard arrived. There was no gun. The two of us went for coffee and he calmed down.

With no one to talk to except the little girls until Elizabeth finished the day's work, Richard was left to his own devices; drifting around the hotel waiting for *The Times* to arrive, or dashing down to Venice to buy books. He devoured books. He was also a marvellous raconteur, but anecdotes about Welsh funerals and English actors meant little in Cortina. Once, at a dinner for the cast, he told a story about John Gielgud with whom he had worked for a year as a youngster in *The Lady's Not for Burning*. Gielgud never stopped giving notes and changing ideas all through the run. During the final matinee in New York, Gielgud asked everyone to stay on stage at the interval. The actors surrounded him belligerently.

"Good God, we finish today! What have we done wrong?"

"No, no, I was just wondering," said Gielgud, "that woman in Row G. Is it Veronica Lake in a lavender blouse?"

Richard told the story well, doing a wicked imitation of Gielgud. Knowing how notorious Gielgud is for checking out the audience during a performance, I laughed happily. But the story fell on stony ground. The German actor next to me was puzzled.

"What is this 'love under blows' please?"

"*Lavender blouse,*" I whispered. "It's a kind of shirt."

A storm cloud passed over Richard's face and he lapsed into a brooding silence.

On days when Henry Fonda did his scenes with Elizabeth, I had time on my hands and I spent those days with Richard. I am very grateful for them. He treated me like a younger brother. Ten years older, he was born in South Wales only thirty miles from my own birthplace. He went to school in Port Talbot where my father was later to be Dockmaster. Richard was the twelfth of thirteen children, the son of a drunkard. His mother died when he was two and he was brought up by his sister in Taibach. There had been few childhood friends. He had been pushed out at fifteen to earn his living in the local Co-op, but it was better, he said, than following his father down the mines.

We ambled through the pine forest, ducking under snow-laden branches towards a copper brazier where a footman served wine spiced with cinnamon. Watching the snow falling there was something inconsolably sad about him, as if he had never lost the sense of loneliness expressed in his boyhood diary with such wrenching simplicity.

"I am sure that wherever I go I will not be wanted."

Sturdily built, at forty-eight he still had the body of a rugby half-back, long and solid in the trunk but with short legs. "Like a pit-pony," he said. As a boy he had been troubled with boils, and his skin had been pitted with acne. His face was lined and drawn but retained its beauty, and his blue eyes, though often darkened with melancholy, were wide and fine. He had made his début at a time when the London stage was dominated by actors of flamboyant lyricism – Redgrave, Gielgud, Olivier – and Burton's stillness and simplicity attracted immediate attention. His voice, beautifully modulated, his physical presence so controlled, created an impression of sensitivity combined with a startling virility. He was a wonderful actor. Most particularly he was a wonderful reactor, and on film he was generous and attentive. He understood the art of listening. In three scenes in films with actors whom he admired extravagantly – with Edith Evans in *Look Back in Anger*, with Alec Guinness in Graham Greene's *The Comedians*, with Maggie Smith in *The VIPs* – it is Burton's unstinting concentration, never taking his eyes off his fellow players, that generously leaves them free to shine so gloriously.

I had worked with many of Richard's closest friends and they were my friends too; John Gielgud, Paul Scofield, Anthony Quayle and Emlyn Williams. Richard loved talking about the theatre. Though he often professed to scorn it, his heart was always there and he ached for the camaraderie it had offered him. He knew I had played Prince Hal but he never discussed it. He obviously regarded Hal as his own territory, for it was as Hal that he had had his first tremendous triumph. He was more fascinated by Macbeth, which I had done at Birmingham just before coming to Cortina. "The greatly flawed hero," he said over and over again, staring into his mulled wine. "The greatly flawed hero." I urged him to play it. He would have been superb. But the prize he was pursuing was *King Lear*.

In the eleven years that remained to Richard there would be many plans to stage a production around him, but somehow or other the plans always foundered. "Shall I write you a poem?" he said suddenly.

"Give me a theme. What would you prefer – a rondeau or a triolet?"

He reached in his pocket for a pen and scribbled away on the back of an envelope. "Fonda can paint," he said. Henry was a skilled water-colourist, "but I paint with poetry." He wrote in silence then crumpled the paper into a ball. "It won't come today." He held out his steel beaker for more wine and swallowed it quickly. He tried very hard to control his drinking, but it was as surely in his blood as it had been in his father's.

Richard usually kept away from the filming but one day he made a joyous contribution. An exterior scene was being shot at dusk and Richard came to collect Elizabeth. An assistant arrived with yet another hostile cable from Paramount. "How can I cope with this mania?" sighed the director. Out of shot was a small building with an illuminated sign; the Friedrich Abeles Radio Telefono plant. Richard suggested that the camera-angle be slightly adjusted to include the factory sign and an extra close-up sent in the rushes to unnerve Los Angeles. In green neon above Elizabeth Taylor's head as she spoke her lines pulsed the initials: 'F.A.R.T.'

There were many, many parties during the filming. One evening the hotel served turkey. Richard thought American turkey was superior, and how in November he always looked forward to Thanksgiving. Accordingly, although it was the third week of May, a few days later, Elizabeth gave a surprise 'Thanksgiving' dinner. The Miramonte Hotel should have closed by now. The guests had gone and all the aristocratic extras had returned to Rome. Only a skeleton staff remained. Fourteen of us ate turkey and sweet potatoes in a room that could seat two hundred. We ate in a candelabra-lit white damask island, but neither the blinds that shrouded the windows nor the great curtained swags of yellow satin could dim the glare of the hot sun outside. "Happy Thanksgiving darling," said Elizabeth.

Henry left and that was a good party. Then Helmut hired an Alpine Band in lederhosen and feathered hats, playing jolly stompen-mit-der-foot-und-clappen-mit-der-hand type music and that was another rowdy farewell night.

By the time it was my turn to leave, filming had moved to Treviso where we were billeted in an eighteenth-century palazzo, eleven kilometres from Venice. I often drove in to have supper with Max and his family. I decided to give my final party in their restaurant. Gore Vidal was in Venice with Paul Newman and Joanne Woodward and they wanted to come to the party too, but seeing the chaos we provoked as soon as we stepped outside Harry's Bar I knew there was no way we could all walk through the alleyways with Elizabeth Taylor and Richard Burton without causing pandemonium. Instead, we went to Torcello where the Cipriani taverna would stay open for us after the tourists had left. The island is some distance from Venice and the route twists and turns through the lonely marshes. I hired a boat. There were musicians softly playing mandolins. We sailed out in the evening as the sunset flooded the water gold. The actress Monique van Vooren, blonde and glamorous, was weeping. Her arms were round a young Norwegian sailor whom she had met that morning. I asked how old he was. The two of them answered simultaneously.

"Twenty-seven," said Monique.

"Nineteen," said the boy.

He was returning to Oslo next day, to his ship. I thought that was the reason for Monique's tears.

"No, darling."

She sniffled, waving her glass towards the sunset.

"It's so stinking gorgeous."

Torcello was an important trading centre when Venice was just an untidy muddle of wetlands. A tall rectangular campanile points against the sky, "The warning finger of God" said Richard. Gore held court in a stone throne which Attila the Hun had left behind him on a visit. The Newmans went into the Basilica. Elizabeth was sitting on a low wall watching Richard chatting to the musicians. I found wine for her. She looked lost and vulnerable. I asked her if she would not like to see the Church. She shook her head.

"There's a mosaic of The Last Judgement."

"I think it might depress me."

Two days later it was time for me to go home. Richard came to say goodbye. He was feeling low. He sipped a glass of port. His hands were trembling. He was not quite sober. "I've been reading Wordsworth, but I have no Intimations of Immortality." The news had come through that both Noël Coward and Hugh (Binkie) Beaumont had just died. I had started my career under contract to Beaumont. Richard had done the same twenty years before, and we both adored Coward. The Burtons visited him every Christmas in Switzerland.

I was packing my clothes. Richard sat on my bed watching. I slung a jacket into my bag. "That's no way to treat a coat!" He retrieved it, deftly folded it and packed it neatly away. His face suddenly lit up with a grin of irresistible sweetness. "My party trick from the Co-op. I worked in Men's Outfitting. I was Richie Jenkins then."

When Richard died, eleven summers after those days in Italy, the columnists exploded with weasel words deploring his failure to fulfil expectations, but these were expectations other people had demanded of him. He had done what he had wanted with his life; achieving fame and riches and he had experienced passion. Above all he had escaped from the mines, the Co-op, and from a life of stultifying mediocrity that the young Richie Jenkins must have feared would be his inevitable destiny.

In the September following shooting, I was summoned to Rome to dub some dialogue for the picture. Richard and Elizabeth had sent me a spectacular present, worth several thousand dollars, a long chain of alternating links of gold and gunmetal, supporting a heavy gunmetal cross bound in gold wire. It was made by Bulgari. I have never worn jewellery but this was something extraordinary. I cradled it lovingly in my hands amazed by its beauty. It was the most beautiful thing I had ever been given and if I had known then that one day I would treat it with such wantoness I would never have believed it. The chain was so long that I wound it round my neck and knotted it so that the cross hung at my collar bone. It was heavy, not entirely comfortable, but it certainly looked good nestling under a black tie at a dinner party. Against my suntan with an open shirt it looked even better. I was proud to wear it and wanted Elizabeth to see it.

In the three months since filming had finished, Elizabeth's life had gone into freefall. She and Richard had separated. Now she was back in Rome where they had filmed *Cleopatra*, where it had all started so wildly. Everywhere she turned in Rome she was beset by reminders of their love. She gave me the fondest welcome and was delighted with her cross.

"Does it make me look like a young Roman Prince?"

"Maybe a hustler on the Via Veneto," she said as I fingered the gold. "A *very* successful hustler of course."

She did not care to leave the hotel much, and no wonder. Once we went to a restaurant that was an old favourite of hers, I Tre Scalini in the Piazza Navona. The table was not booked in her name and we arrived quietly and anonymously, but before the meal was over faces were pressed against the window and the excitement grew outside. When we emerged the Piazza was jammed with paparazzi. Traffic was at a standstill. After that Elizabeth preferred to eat in her suite.

One night dinner was interrupted by a call from London. Elizabeth was gone for a long time and when she returned there were tears in her eyes. The call had been to tell her that her old friend Laurence Harvey was dying. It was going to be his forty-sixth birthday the following Sunday and there was to be a surprise party for him, though he probably would not be able to leave his bed. Elizabeth promised to be there. It would be hard to avoid the press who besieged her everywhere, but she would book a seat under an assumed name on a scheduled flight to London. But then where could she go? She had always stayed with Richard at the Dorchester. That would be impossible. Any hotel would be impossible. She turned to me.

"When I come to London, will you put me up?"

My dubbing in Rome was finished by Friday afternoon. I went straight to the station and caught the midnight train to Venice, arriving at dawn. I walked to my little pensione in San Polo, passing the Trattoria Max on the way but it was so early that everything was shuttered. I threw my bag into my room, grabbed a swimsuit and headed for the Lido, Elizabeth's cross nestled comfortably against my neck. I was used to its weight by now. By noon it was cloudy on the beach and a breeze whipped up the sand. I made my way to the pier to find a boat back to San Marco. An unmistakeable screech came from one of the little tables by the ticket office.

"Keith! How are *you*?"

Truman Capote was having a drink while he too waited for the ferry. With him was his new friend from New York, John O'Shea. Truman was in good spirits. He ogled my cross and I told him it was a present from Elizabeth. Truman was wearing a large white hat. A puff of wind sent it careening into the road. He scampered after it.

"My dear, isn't this weather inclement!"

The boat arrived and we all embarked. Truman and John were off to Harry's Bar for lunch and invited me to join them. It was spitting with rain. After a brief stop in San Marco for a quick cocktail to cheer ourselves up, and a second one just to make sure, we headed for Harry's with a pretty American girl from New Mexico whom we had somehow collected on the way. It was almost two in the afternoon. Harry's Bar was packed and lunch was protracted. It was past four when we staggered to the door. I walked with them to the Gritti Palace, almost asleep on my feet after the overnight train journey, the morning swim, the vodka martinis, the risotto and the wine. They watched me step gingerly into the traghetto across the Grand Canal and as the boatman pushed out from the steps Truman yelled:

"What are you doing tonight? Come to Peggy's. It's a party! Drinks here first. At six! It's casual!"

I meant to have only a quick nap at the pensione but I overslept. When I turned up at the Gritti, Truman had left for the party.

The palazzo housing the Guggenheim collection faces the Gritti Palace across the Grand Canal. Lights were on in the palazzo as I rather ostentatiously hailed a gondolier from the hotel. I stepped into the boat. "Palazzo Guggenheim!" The gondolier flung his arms wide in protestation. All manner of grievances were encompassed in the gesture, most particularly the shortness of the journey and the miserably small recompense he would receive. Grumbling he navigated the gondola out into the middle of the Canal. He kept up a steady whine; the size of his family, the shrewishness of his wife, the dilapidation of his home, the enormity of his taxes, the rapacity of his landlord. His beady eyes were fixed on the gold cross round my neck. I covered it with my hand, feeling by now that it was a kind of talisman that would always keep me safe. He deposited me on the slippery marble steps before the great iron gates of the palazzo, grabbing his money and watching me as he turned his boat around. He must have known that the gates were locked and never opened. I could see people in the main salon but they paid not a bit of attention as I waved and called with the water lapping at my shoes. A servant drew the curtains, looking at me with contempt. A few yards away, out in the Grand Canal, the gondolier was watching in triumph. Gone was all dismay from his face. I was at his mercy. He knew no craft would stop there, not a vaporetto, not a traghetto, not a water-taxi. No other gondolier would pick me up; I had summoned him originally, I was *his* fare. We haggled till we came to an agreement. It was robbery but he was all solicitude now.

"Mi dispiace, signore. Che sfortuna!"

A nest of pillows was created for me and, singing his heart out, he headed upstream round a side canal to a back entrance. Gently he helped me out and told me how hopeful he was that life would always treat me kindly.

The salon of the Palazzo Guggenheim was full of people, some of whom were asleep on sofas, glasses still clutched in their hands, others recumbent on the floor. The girl from New Mexico was snoring gently in a chair. A servant, disdainfully picking his way over the bodies, asked me what I'd like to drink. There was vodka, gin, whisky, wine. I asked for a vodka martini with ice and made my way across the room to Truman who was chatting to Mrs Guggenheim in a corner.

She greeted me with an absent-minded handshake and a very friendly smile. She was not a handsome woman but there was an amiable eccentricity about her that was very appealing. She was dressed in a sort of long-flowing muu-muu. Its colours were rich and dark, but when she gestured, the material fell in soft folds and the gold thread stitched through it caught the candlelight, its iridescence shimmering for a second, creating a momentary effect that was altogether opulent. Her hair had been done – probably that very morning – but as the day had progressed it had been teased out of its shape, plucked at by her fingers which were tugging at it now as she showed me her precious Jackson Pollocks. On her feet, peeping out from below her dress, were well-scuffed old carpet slippers with big moth-eaten pompoms. They gave her appearance a beguiling dottiness. There was nothing feather-brained about her conversation however, especially when she talked about Pollock or the other canvasses she pulled out from a cupboard.

"Are you hungry? We're dining at Harry's. Will you join us? There are some things over there meanwhile."

She waved vaguely towards a table. The servant returned with my drink. In a brimming glass that was more tankard than tumbler, slopped a massive measure of vodka. A tiny ice cube was melting mournfully on the surface.

"Isn't there any more ice?"

He looked at me as if I were mad. In a palazzoful of serious drinkers only a wimp wanted ice. My head was spinning again and I thought I should eat. I moved hopefully towards whatever 'things' Peggy Guggenheim was offering, which turned out to be three untouched plates of hard-boiled eggs cut in half and dabbed with tomato ketchup. I ate six eggs rapidly. No other guest touched them, they were far too busy knocking back the hard stuff. But if the buffet was frugal there was no shortage of liquor; bottles covered every inch of every surface of every table. They stood like soldiers; reinforcements to the rear, and dead men rolling into wastebins down below.

It must have been two hours before Mrs Guggenheim came and found me snoozing by the window.

"Let's eat!"

A light rain was falling. Mrs Guggenheim found umbrellas for us and slipped a raincoat over her shoulders. Truman wanted to take a gondola. The millionairess said he was out of his mind, they were far too expensive. She was right about that, I knew. She strode off, splashing through the puddles in her carpet slippers and we tagged untidily behind towards the Vaporetto. I would like to remember the conversation that night at Harry's Bar, but I was concentrating hard on never attempting a word of more than two syllables. I remember laughter and I remember Truman putting on his spectacles to examine my cross more closely.

"It must have cost thousands!"

I don't remember saying goodnight to any of them.

The rain had stopped and I was sitting on a little bridge outside my pensione when I realised that I had been a whole day in Venice and had not visited my friends at the Trattoria. It was not too late surely, not even midnight. When I walked round there were people still eating in the garden.

Onorina was the first to see me as I swaggered in. I asked for coffee and a grappa and she led me to a table.

"How is everyone, all the family?"

She turned back to me. Tears flowed down her face. Her brother Max, for whom the restaurant was named, had died three weeks earlier. He had had a heart attack without any warning. I could think of nothing to say. She brought me coffee and it grew cold on the table as the rest of the family came to speak to me – the dead man's widow, Ada, with their son Fiorenze, and Augusto, the old man, in black from head to toe for his son. I had seen them three months ago and the old man had been so proud of his boy. I have a son he had said, and his son had a son, therefore he was reconciled to death which, at ninety is how it should be. He had sat at the same table, strong and upright. I had teased him. He could not really be reconciled to Death.

"Certamente!" He had gripped my wrist. "La morte sarà la mia amica."

But Death had not come as his friend. Death had arrived as a marauder, plundering the old man's treasure.

He sat beside me heavily. No strength was in his grip now as he held my hand, no sparkle in his watery eyes. In three months he had shrunk, shrivelled inside his mourning clothes. When he tried to smile in friendship, he could manage no more than the rictus of despair.

None of this touched my heart so deeply as the dreadful stoicism of the dead man's mother. In those days my Italian was fluent, but any words I attempted shamed me in their banality. Giulia-Marina was wiser than I. She listened to me intently, patted me on the hand, ordered her daughter to make me more coffee and told me to drink it before it got cold. She touched my throat.

"Bellissima."

It was a present I explained. From Elizabeth Taylor. She smiled and nodded.

"Bellissima."

I unknotted the chain and handed it to her. Slowly she let it slip through her fingers until only the cross nestled in her hand. She gathered up the links and held them to the light, the gold shining against her black dress.

"Bellissima."

She handed it back to me.

"Take it," I said. "It's yours."

"No."

She pushed it towards me. I closed my hand over hers.

"Please" I said. "It's for your son."

"For my son?"

Her family assembled around us. I was the only stranger left now. They took the cross from Giulia-Marina and handed it to me.

"I don't want it. It belongs to Giulia-Marina."

In the middle of the night I woke with a terrible headache. Somewhere in my bag I knew there was a crumpled packet of Alka-Seltzer. I dissolved two tablets in some mineral water and sat on the edge of my bed nursing my aching head.

As I looked dully round the room, noting the clothes discarded all over the floor, I began to recollect the events of the previous day: the meeting with Truman at the Lido, the lunch at Harry's, the party at Mrs Guggenheim's palazzo, the arrival at the Trattoria, the conversation with Giulia-Marina.

And then I remembered I had given her the cross.

I fell back on the pillows with a groan. My head throbbed violently but worse, far worse, was the shame that ate away inside me. I had given away something that I cherished, a unique present from someone who had shown me great kindness. And I had given it away, not honestly, not out of true openhandedness, but as a gesture, brushed with theatricality, induced by drink to promote a fake image of bounteousness. There is no seltzer to ease the nausea of self-disgust. I loathed myself for recognising it, but I wanted Elizabeth's present back. She would be in London tomorrow. If she asked me why I wasn't wearing it, what would I say?

It was eleven when the sun woke me and I checked out of the pensione. It was very warm. I made my way through the crowds of tourists. I had three hours before heading back to England. I went to Harry's Bar to wait.

Freddy Young, then drama critic of the *Financial Times*, was sitting on a stool. The English actor Maurice Denham with whom I had acted in a television production of *Saint Joan* was next to him. I joined them. The doors swung open and in came Truman and John O'Shea, as breezy as ever. I introduced everyone and we moved to a table.

"Why Keith," said Truman, "you're looking a bit hangdog."

I said nothing, but as I took off my jacket Truman asked why I wasn't wearing Elizabeth's cross. I told my tale. It caused much merriment. John ordered some champagne.

"You must go and ask for it."

I was to go at once, he said. I was to say that of course they would have realised how drunk I had been, and please could I have my cross.

"Take a bunch of flowers" said Maurice.

"A *large* bunch" giggled Freddy.

"What makes you think," spluttered Truman, "that the old woman still has it?"

"Yes!" said O'Shea, "she was banging on the jeweller's door this morning asking for a price!"

"This morning?" shrieked Truman. "She woke him up last night!"

I left them and took the boat to the airport and was in Islington in time for dinner. Elizabeth arrived in the small hours of the morning. She had flown incognito as planned and went unnoticed to Larry Harvey's party. Seeing him so ill had upset her deeply. She was very emotional when she arrived at my house and stayed for a few moments catching her breath while I held her. I showed her to her room but she did not want to sleep. She sat on the floor by the fire. She wanted to talk about Richard, only about him. She looked childlike and forlorn, sitting by the fire. I had two golden retrievers then. They curled up beside her and she stroked them as she talked. It was a little before five in the morning when she went upstairs. I had intended to tell her about her cross but decided against it. As she disappeared into her room I asked her what she'd like for breakfast.

"Bangers!"

At eight I went round to the butcher's. I called on my cleaning woman and asked her to come early and cook some breakfast. When we returned home there was no sign of movement upstairs so Paquita made some coffee while I read the morning paper and waited for Elizabeth. There was a loud rat-a-tat on the front door. When I had moved into the house it had needed a new roof and several new floors. The builder who had done it for me was a local man, whose conversation was always conducted at full volume, liberally sprinkled with friendly abuse. He was a true Cockney living in the City Road. If he was in the area he always called by for a cup of tea. I opened the front door and he burst in, grinning. I asked him not to make quite such a clatter. There was someone sleeping upstairs.

"It's ten in the morning! Who is it?"

I said it was Elizabeth Taylor. He doubled up with laughter.

"Go on! Elizabeth-bleeding-Taylor! My arse!"

At that very moment Elizabeth appeared at the top of the stairs. I would have given a great deal to have had a camera trained on Don Doncaster's face as his words died in a gurgle. Elizabeth came down smiling. She had found a bathrobe which was far too big for her. It made her look childlike, adorable, more vulnerable than ever. She was scrubbed clean, without make-up, smelling of soap. Tucking her feet beneath her, she sat on the bench between Don and Paquita and ate a huge breakfast. A driver came to take her to the airport. She told him to sit down and join us. She missed three flights back to Rome. Finally when the driver said if they didn't leave at once they would miss the last plane of the day. Elizabeth passed him the telephone book.

"Hire one then."

As she kissed me goodbye she told me how pleased she was I had liked the cross which Richard had chosen for me.

The next years of my life were spent in America. Occasionally friends would announce they were having a week or so in Venice and I'd give them an itinerary: Torcello, San Rocco, Harry's Bar. And I always told them to eat at the Trattoria Max. Afterwards I questioned them. Had they seen my cross, was anyone wearing it? But no one had ever seen it. So it was as Truman had foreseen; the old woman had sold it and it served me right. I was a fool and it was still the best Trattoria in Venice.

Then last year I took the vaporetto from the railway station down the Grand Canal to San Toma, walked up the little alley towards the Frari and found the Trattoria again. The family were all there except the old man, Augusto, whom death had finally claimed. Fiorenze was a man now, engaged – his fidanzata was arranging the flowers. Onorina his aunt welcomed me with much laughter, and Ada his mother brought wine. Why had I never written? Why had I not told them I was coming?

Three friends were with me. I had told them the story of the Trattoria and Elizabeth's cross, just as I have written it down here.

"Look!" said one. "There's the old lady."

Giulia-Marina came towards us. She was older of course and she walked with a cane, but her back was straight and she was beaming. Around her neck was the cross.

She said she wore it every day and every night.

"Ogni giorno, ogni notte. Per il mio figlio."

For her son. She asked if I wanted it back and I laughed.

"Oh no. You keep it."

St. Mark got it right I thought as the bells pealed and the pigeons wheeled above our heads as we walked happily through the Piazza that bears his name outside the Cathedral that holds his bones.

INDEX